T0342468

THE ART OF VIDEOGAMES

New Directions in Aesthetics

Series editors: Dominic McIver Lopes, University of British Columbia, and Berys Gaut, University of St Andrews

Blackwell's New Directions in Aesthetics series highlights ambitious single- and multiple-author books that confront the most intriguing and pressing problems in aesthetics and the philosophy of art today. Each book is written in a way that advances understanding of the subject at hand and is accessible to upper-undergraduate and graduate students.

1. *Interpretation and Construction: Art, Speech, and the Law* by Robert Stecker
2. *Art as Performance* by David Davies
3. *The Performance of Reading: An Essay in the Philosophy of Literature* by Peter Kivy
4. *The Art of Theater* by James R. Hamilton
5. *Cultural Appropriation and the Arts* by James O. Young
6. *Photography and Philosophy: Essays on the Pencil of Nature* ed. Scott Walden
7. *Art and Ethical Criticism* ed. Garry L. Hagberg
8. *Mirrors to One Another: Emotion and Value in Jane Austen and David Hume* by Eva Dadlez
9. *Comic Relief: A Comprehensive Philosophy of Humor* by John Morreall
10. *The Art of Videogames* by Grant Tavinor

THE ART OF VIDEOGAMES

Grant Tavinor

WILEY-BLACKWELL

A John Wiley & Sons, Ltd., Publication

This edition first published 2009
© 2009 Grant Tavinor

Blackwell Publishing was acquired by John Wiley & Sons in February 2007.
Blackwell's publishing program has been merged with Wiley's global Scientific,
Technical, and Medical business to form Wiley-Blackwell.

Registered Office
John Wiley & Sons Ltd, The Atrium, Southern Gate, Chichester, West Sussex,
PO19 8SQ, United Kingdom

Editorial Offices
350 Main Street, Malden, MA 02148-5020, USA
9600 Garsington Road, Oxford, OX4 2DQ, UK
The Atrium, Southern Gate, Chichester, West Sussex, PO19 8SQ, UK

For details of our global editorial offices, for customer services, and for information
about how to apply for permission to reuse the copyright material in this book please
see our website at www.wiley.com/wiley-blackwell.

The right of Grant Tavinor to be identified as the author of this work has been
asserted in accordance with the Copyright, Designs and Patents Act 1988.

Library of Congress Cataloging-in-Publication Data

Tavinor, Grant.
    The art of videogames / Grant Tavinor.
      p. cm. – (New directions in aesthetics)
    Includes bibliographical references and index.
    ISBN 978-1-4051-8789-3 (hardcover : alk. paper) – ISBN 978-1-4051-8788-6
(pbk. : alk. paper) 1. Video games–Philosophy. 2. Video games–Social aspects. I. Title.
  GV1469.3.T39 2009
  794.8–dc22

                                                                          2009009313

A catalogue record for this book is available from the British Library.

Set in 10/12.5pt Galliard by Graphicraft Limited, Hong Kong

01   2009

For Mum and Dad

.

CONTENTS

ACKNOWLEDGMENTS

I would like to thank Stephen Davies, who supervised my doctoral studies at the University of Auckland, and set me a model of academic excellence to aspire to.

Denis Dutton at the University of Canterbury in Christchurch has been of huge help in allowing me an avenue for developing my ideas by inviting me to read various papers at the Canterbury Philosophy and Religious Studies departmental seminar. This book owes its existence to a paper I read there in 2004, and that was subsequently published in *Philosophy and Literature*.

Thanks go to all of my colleagues in the Social Science, Parks, Recreation and Tourism Group at Lincoln University, who provided a lot of support for Lincoln's sole philosopher throughout the course of this research, and indulged my somewhat atypical research interests. I have learnt a great deal from being forced to confront the opinions of my colleagues who work in disciplines other than philosophy.

I would like to thank the editors of the Blackwell *New Directions in Aesthetics* series Berys Gaut and Dominic McIver Lopes, and Blackwell's acquisitions editor Jeff Dean, for seeing the potential in this topic and making the book possible. Thanks also to the two anonymous reviewers for their invaluable feedback on an earlier draft of this work, which allowed me to gain a helpful perspective on the ideas developed here.

I would like to thank all those fellow gamers that I have raced, battled, and fragged over the years, and especially those who have taken the time to discuss gaming with me. My brother, Lance Tavinor, has been a gaming companion ever since the days of Nintendo's *Snoopy Tennis*. Tama Easton has also been an invaluable source of gaming discussion.

This research was made a great deal easier by a research grant made by the Lincoln University Research Fund in 2008.

1

THE NEW ART OF VIDEOGAMES

I have a horrible secret to admit: I routinely carry out acts of murder and barbarism for fun. I have beaten up old ladies, run over pedestrians while driving recklessly on the footpath, and killed a multitude of gangsters, cops, innocent civilians, and sequined jumpsuit-wearing Elvis impersonators. In acts of gross animal cruelty, I've exploded numerous lemmings. I have even committed genocide, putting entire civilizations to the sword as I ravaged continents as a brutal militaristic tyrant. Worst of all is that though I presently find myself somewhat guilty and ashamed of my actions, at the time it was all great fun. There is no doubt that I laughed hysterically throughout many of my criminal and immoral adventures. I suspect that I am not alone in this concealed shame, and that readers will have similar guilty secrets about what they do in their spare time. Videogames, of course, are to blame for all these activities. Gaming has made me an immoral monster.

A philosophical exploration of the art of videogaming is overdue. In the space of little more than forty years videogames have developed from rudimentary artifacts designed to exploit the entertainment capabilities of the newly invented computer, into a new and sophisticated form of popular art. For many people, I suspect, the image of videogames is still one of rather crude digital entertainments: pixilated space invaders moving jerkily across a screen, yellow discs munching glowing balls, and tiny men climbing ladders and jumping barrels might come to mind. But recent times have seen the technical and artistic sophistication of games grow to an amazing degree. Many videogames are now simply stunning in their graphical and auditory depictions. In a manner similar to the development of representational techniques in other art forms, digital artists and craftspeople have explored the artistic potential of the new medium and are now producing results arguably equal to the other representational arts. All of these developments have been made in the space of living memory, and watching this evolution of the new cultural form has been an exciting experience. On a number of occasions I have felt the thrill of seeing something entirely new, a game that seemed suddenly to expand the horizons of art.

It is worthwhile pausing here to consider some examples of what this new art has become in so short a time. I cannot hope to convey a true impression of the artistic qualities of videogames here – there is no substitute for experiencing the games first-hand – but surveying some of the artistic highpoints of recent gaming is worthwhile nevertheless. No doubt anyone reading this book would benefit from playing the games mentioned and discussed in the text in conjunction with the reading. I suspect that most readers will be able to supplement these examples with their own anyway.

The 2006 fantasy game *The Elder Scrolls: Oblivion*, places the player, in the guise of a character that they have designed and named, into a massive and beautiful fictional province called Cyrodiil. *Oblivion* is a *sandbox* game, in that it represents an open fictional environment in which the player has a great deal of choice over exactly what they do: they can engage in one of the several narratives that span the world, take up the robes of a wizard and battle the evil influence of the necromancers in Cyrodiil, fight various foes as a warrior for hire, or merely explore the wilderness, ruins, and dungeons of the area. This is all run of the mill fantasy fare, but what makes *Oblivion* so engrossing is that the fantasy world is presented in an extraordinarily beautiful way and with such a complete freedom that exploring Cyrodiil is an engaging, emotional, and aesthetically rewarding experience.

The very beginning of the game bears out the beauty and freedom of the game. *Oblivion* begins with a short dungeon adventure in which the player constructs their character, including their name, race, appearance, and class, learns the controls and basic gameplay of the game, and also learns something of the narrative that forms the background to their involvement in Cyrodiil. This initial dungeon adventure is very much a *tutorial* for the playing of the game. Dungeon exploring has been a staple of role-playing adventure games since near the beginning of videogaming, and it is typically *linear* in that it forces the player down a certain path in which monsters must be confronted and defeated, and puzzles solved, before the player can proceed. Dungeon jaunts can also be aesthetically dismal, with the predominant textures being darkly rendered stone and rock passageways and tunnels. On exiting the dungeon, *Oblivion* sets both of these features – the linearity of the dungeon adventure, and the dismal appearance of the dungeon itself – in an abrupt juxtaposition with an open, unconstrained, and strikingly beautiful environment. Suddenly the player is in the open air, confronted with a wonderfully rendered pastoral scene including misty green hills, rippling water, and an enticing ancient ruin on a nearby shore.

Furthermore, where their progress through the dungeon was previously strictly guided, the player now finds that they are free to wander the environment as they wish, with only the briefest of prompts that there is a quest that they might take up. When I first emerged into the open environment, the freedom and expanse of the environment was a little bewildering: what should I do? Exactly what *could* I do? Was the game environment really as big as it looked? (It was.) Only over time – the game has literally hundreds of hours of gameplay – did I answer these questions through exploring the world and its potential for adventure. Cyrodiil also became a familiar place, populated by people I would get to know, and even favorite places that I would return to repeatedly to experience their beauty. This seems to be something new in art: the representation of the player, their agency, and their aesthetic experiences, *within* a fictional world – videogames seem to provide an active exploratory aesthetics.

Grand Theft Auto: San Andreas stands for many gamers and gaming critics as a significant achievement of modern videogaming. Like *Oblivion*, *San Andreas* is a sandbox game, though here rather than exploring dungeons and going on quests, players spend their time in various criminal activities such as carjacking, robbery, and, to put it plainly, murder. Set in a fictional version of the West Coast of the United States, and spread over a huge digital environment encompassing several islands and three distinctive cities and their outlying rural areas, the game involves the player – in the guise of urban gangster Carl "CJ" Johnson – in a fiction that is filled with remarkable characters and events. From the first frames the impressive style of the game is evident. The tone is set by the stylish introductory graphics: where other games rely on a flashy animated set piece for an introduction, *San Andreas* employs a graphically minimalist strategy of introducing the places in the game in pictures rendered in the style now distinctive to the franchise. The production quality of the game is striking, and though the polish on the graphics is inferior when compared to games in other genres, the depth and vivacity of the world of *San Andreas* both explains this, and makes up for it.

The game's narrative is at once archetypal and also agreeable in its arc and detail: CJ, the prodigal son, returns home to find his neighborhood now wracked by internal conflict and external threats. The game sets out his slow rise through the criminal ranks from petty crook to gangster kingpin, his reconciliation with his brother, and the eventual defeat of his enemies. Along the way CJ encounters Los Angeles style gang wars and riots, corrupt cops, drug dealers and pimps trying to muscle in on his territory, shadowy FBI operatives and paranoid conspiracy theorists, a secret military base in the middle of the desert complete with top secret technology, and the high life in a city of bright lights, gambling, and the aforementioned sequined jumpsuit-wearing Elvis impersonators. The characters are especially vivid: Officer Tenpenny is a corrupt city cop with a disposition for violence; Catalina is Carl's psychotic man-hating girlfriend; The Truth is an aging gnostic hippy with paranoid delusions and a large plantation of dope; OG Loc is a wannabe gangster and rapper working in a burger joint while dreaming of hitting it big. The gameplay that is set against this narrative, as infuriating as it can be, is also intensely satisfying, and often, giggle inducing. The sheer amount of gameplay – the main storyline, hidden mini-games, the many incidental tasks that must be completed – is immense. To do everything in the game can take weeks of fairly regular play.

Finally, elevating the game above many of its more mundane contemporaries is the sense of intelligent and subversive humor that pervades it. *San Andreas* picks up on the clichés of its setting – both those of the actual time and those funneled through the popular cinema and gangster rap of early 1990s California – to present a compelling and hilarious take on that period in history. The *Grand Theft Auto* series is frequently misunderstood by casual observers who see only the fictional violence of carjacking and murders, but miss the many signs that the games are black comedies in which the player takes the central role, exploring a fictional world, and through it, the human potential to be violent and immoral. *Grand Theft Auto: San Andreas* is undoubtedly fictionally violent, but it also seems a significant artistic achievement, despite this violence – or perhaps indeed because of it.

As a quite different example, the recent videogame *Portal* gives a tantalizing glimpse of how 3D space might be manipulated to produce mind-bending puzzles. *Portal* situates the player in a set of austere futuristic environments or *test chambers* built by the fictional military contractor Aperture Science within the extended *Half-Life* universe. The object of the game is to progress through the test chambers and reach the exit. The spatial puzzles presented by the game derive from the *portal gun* the player is equipped with. Firing the portal gun at a wall, floor, or ceiling, the player can open a portal to another spatial location in the environment through which they can step to access the new location. The player can open up to two portals at most – an orange and a blue portal – and entering one portal leads to the location of the other. So, for example, if the player wants to access a high ledge that they cannot climb, the solution is to open a portal on the ceiling above the ledge, and another portal on the floor in front of them, and simply step through to land on the ledge.

As the player moves through a spatial portal, from their new orientation they can often briefly see themselves disappearing into the portal they just entered, and this proves to be a very disorientating and disconcerting feeling, giving the game a very surreal character. Furthermore, travel though a portal preserves the momentum of the player-character so that if the player jumps into a portal they exit the second portal with their previous vector, though with the new spatial orientation: or as the game puts it, "speedy thing goes in, speedy thing comes out." The player can exploit this preservation of momentum to *fling* themselves around the environments: by placing one portal on the floor in front of a ledge, and another at the bottom of a pit, the player can jump into the second portal, emerge from the first now traveling upwards, and land on top of the ledge. The game exploits this potential for movement to present challenges that become increasingly complex and confounding. *Portal* is the game you would get if M. C. Escher took on videogame design.

As well as its excellent and innovative gameplay, *Portal* presents an engaging narrative. The player-character, almost entirely anonymous apart from her name, Chell, and her appearance that can be glimpsed though the portals, is guided though the test chambers by an artificial intelligence named GlaDOS (Genetic Lifeform and Disk Operating System). In the best of science fiction traditions it quickly becomes clear that GlaDOS is insincere, malfunctioning, and probably insane. GlaDOS makes promises of cake as a reward for passing the tests, and the player soon finds that they are not the first to be subjected to the challenges, with the discovery of broken and dilapidated areas of the test chambers where previous test subjects have taken refuge and scrawled their disturbed ramblings on the walls – including the recurring line "the cake is a lie." The player encounters deadly but apologetic gun turrets that when destroyed assure the player they don't hold a grudge, and a *weighted companion cube* the player must take with them through one level and then incinerate in a sentimental and particularly funny sequence. The game ends unexpectedly with a song sung by GlaDOS, where she recounts the events of the game in the deadpan dialogue characteristic of the game: when I played the game, the song had me in hysterics, but also gave me an overwhelming sense of artistic completion. The idiosyncrasies of the game were perfectly summed up by the unexpected and odd little song.

From just these three examples it is clear that videogames share many of their artistic qualities with other cultural forms – particularly in their graphical and narrative qualities – but they are also artistically significant in their own terms. *Gameplay*, which is comprised of the interactive challenges presented by games, has become an object of complexity and subtlety, calling in many cases for an artistic evaluation. The examples introduced above give some idea of the variety there is in gameplay: *Oblivion* sets the player on exploratory quests, battling monsters and gathering treasure. One might read about a quest in Tolkien's novels, but in a gameplay setting the player performs the quest. *San Andreas* asks its players to perform missions, some of them very much like the action set pieces of blockbuster movies, others involving collecting photos of landmarks or spraying graffiti to stake out gang turf. *Portal* engages the player with odd spatial puzzles. Puzzles have been around for a very long time, but in *Portal* the player encounters the puzzles within a fictional world that also involves a narrative providing their fictional motivation for interacting with the puzzles. This fictional first-hand experience of gameplay seems to give it an aesthetic edge, and indeed, when criticizing games, players and critics often turn first to the interactive and expressive qualities of the gameplay. Does it flow? Does it engage or immerse the player? Is it varied? How does it *feel*? Despite its interactive and gaming nature, gameplay seems to engage players in ways similar to other arts and that calls on a similar kind of interpretive and evaluative engagement.

Each of these games, though not entirely unprecedented, and not without flaws, struck me as a notable artistic achievement. Though in each case there are earlier games with similar gameplay and themes, all of these examples display a polish and depth that signifies their artistic worth and that extends upon previous achievements. In this they are symptomatic of a general trend toward the increased artistic and technical sophistication of videogaming. Some gamers and games critics argue that gameplay has shown little development in the past twenty years. But to say that videogames have not made significant strides across the full range of their artistic qualities is an untenable position. Even the claim that gameplay has shown little development seems dubious when one considers that *The Elder Scrolls* and *Portal* replicate earlier gameplay types only when they are characterized in the *grossest* terms as, respectively, a fantasy role-playing game and a puzzle game. It is the striking way in which the role-playing and puzzles of these games are presented that is a noteworthy development. The openness of sandbox games also seems to be a significant and mostly unprecedented recent formal development in the artistic qualities of gameplay.

Why are videogames displaying this trend toward artistic sophistication? A large part of this artistic growth has been driven by technology: the present is an age of next generation consoles and powerful personal computers – gaming devices that are able to create sophisticated, responsive, and increasingly beautiful fictional worlds into which players step in order to play games. The most recent batch of consoles – the X Box 360, Nintendo Wii, and Playstation 3 – are each technological marvels that bring real-time digital animation into the home where less than twenty years ago such animation was the exclusive domain of big budget film makers. This technology is a prerequisite for most modern gaming, and though other artworks such as popular film have felt the influence of the recent technological developments, none is so closely tied to digital technology as videogames. Games are now commonly played on the high definition digital televisions and monitors and through Dolby 5.1 home theatre sound systems, and these, in conjunction with platform developments of consoles and PC gaming, have had a significant impact on how modern games look and sound.

The Internet has also proved to be a significant technological impetus to gaming, both in allowing people to come together to play online, and in bringing gamers together to discuss games and to criticize them on the many gaming forums scattered around the net. These discussion boards have led to a level of gaming criticism and connoisseurship not previously seen. The Internet has led to the development of videogames with simply huge fictional worlds. *World of Warcraft*, for example, is a Massively Multiplayer Online Role Playing Game (MMORPG) that brings players from around the real world together to interact in a fantasy world, engaging in all the typical fantasy role-playing game fare of exploring dungeons, fighting monsters, performing quests, and some much more unexpected behavior to be discussed later (chapter 3). As of 2007, according to a press release from the game's developer Blizzard, the game had 9 million subscribers (Blizzard, 2007). Millions of players interacting in a virtual fantasy world is a stunning fact of both technological and artistic significance.

This last example is also evidence that videogames are now incredibly widespread, and are generating an evermore general appeal. The games industry is now by some estimates bigger than the movie industry, widely reported to be worth US$30 billion a year. Sales of the next generation of consoles number in the millions, and top gaming titles can sell tens of millions of copies: often with numbers in excess of the sales of music titles. *Halo 3*, released on the X-Box 360 in late 2007, took US$170 million domestically on its first day and US$300 million worldwide in its first week of sales: the latter amounting to 5 million units sold (Microsoft, 2007). *Grand Theft Auto IV* made an even more impressive US$500 million in its first week of sales in May 2008. These numbers dwarf revenues for recent releases from popular music, and all but the biggest blockbusters in film. This, arguably, is part of a trend that sees videogaming eclipsing film and pop music, the predominant popular art forms of the twentieth century. This commercial growth underpins the technological advances in providing an economic rationale for the research and development necessary for the gaming technology, and hence has a direct bearing on the current artistic sophistication of gaming.

Also relevant is the recent change in gaming demographics. Recent industry research carried out by the Interactive Entertainment Association of Australia finds that the audience for games is maturing and widening, showing the inaccuracy of the popular image of gamers as adolescent boys: the average age of gamers in Australia is 28, 41 percent of gamers are females, and 8 percent are seniors (Brand, 2007). Gaming seems to be growing up in a literal sense as its players get older. Arguably, the new and maturing audiences of gaming are demanding more variety and are also paying increasing critical attention to games, explaining something of the recent artistic developments. Admittedly, games still have a lot of growing up to do.

Gaming is not always seen as an entirely positive development: my mock shame in the opening paragraph of this chapter dices with a genuine moral difficulty. No doubt many have a response of immediate distaste to videogames, associating them with violence and aggression, and worrying about their effects on children and society. Videogames generate a host of moral worries that, like the artistic qualities discussed above, seem to be becoming more pronounced in recent times. The two issues seem related: because recent games are more artistically sophisticated, particularly in terms of their graphical qualities, the immoral content of games seems all the more lifelike and hence worrying. A game like the post-apocalyptic role-playing shooter *Fallout 3*, because of its graphical brilliance, can depict violence in a very visceral way, thereby making the images it presents all the more shocking: the game is filled with slow-motion shots of dismemberment and exploding body parts.

San Andreas is especially notorious for its immoral content. The game is filled with violent content and sexual themes, and in it the player controls a character that is quite obviously morally vicious. CJ, by any standard, is not a nice guy. In 2005 the game generated a considerable controversy when it was discovered that it could be modified by hacking its code to unlock a mini sex game that had not been included in the official release. CJ, it turns out, is able to partake in fairly explicit sexual acts with a number of girlfriends he has scattered throughout San Andreas. But even the official release of the game allows players to pick up prostitutes for sex, and then murder them. Though *San Andreas* does not give the player points for such actions – as sources in the popular media have suggested – the game could be conceived as rewarding the player for these acts, as after the murder players can take any money the prostitute had. Any particular game of *San Andreas* is likely to involve hundreds, if not thousands, of killings – the number of which is kept track of in the *achievements* menu. It is undeniable then, that the game involves its players in fictionally immoral activities. For many, this is a reason to think *Grand Theft Auto* and similar games to be morally suspect.

As well as involving its players in immoral fictions, some think *Grand Theft Auto* and other games like it are genuinely psychologically and behaviorally injurious to their players. Psychologist Craig Anderson begins one of his influential papers on the consequences of videogames for aggressive behavior by setting out the now familiar story of Eric Harris and Dylan Klebold, the perpetrators of the Columbine school massacre who were frequent players of the first-person shooter videogame *Doom* (Anderson and Dill, 2000). Retired army lieutenant colonel Dave Grossman thinks that videogames are "training" children to be killers (Grossman and DeGaetano, 1999). *Grand Theft Auto* has even been blamed for actual crimes. American anti-gaming attorney Jack Thompson has repeatedly appeared in the news media arguing videogames to be responsible for school shootings in Kentucky, Columbine, and Virginia Tech.

Beyond these specific claims, videogames have always had something of an image problem. Among the common charges are that videogames are a pointless waste of time, are offensive, misogynistic, immature, addictive, encourage sedentary behavior and hence obesity, cause seizures, dumb children down, hype children up, keep them up late at nights, cause occupational overuse syndrome, destroy the culture of reading, involve players with the occult, lead to suicide pacts, and attack the moral fiber of our society.

And yet, videogames are also increasingly morally aware. Having often been the subject of ethical criticism, gaming is now showing signs of taking itself seriously as an art form with moral implications. *BioShock* – a recent first-person shooter set, amusingly, in a world derived from Ayn Rand's *Atlas Shrugged* – puts the player in a position where they cannot help but ponder the morality of their actions. *BioShock* draws on the past, depicting its dystopia through the architectural and pop-cultural tropes of 1930s and 1940s America. Decaying art deco facades, faded Hollywood socialites, and echoes of Howard Hughes and *Citizen Kane* are combined with period music and philosophical and literary references to produce a coherent aesthetic statement that is all the more engaging because of the player's moral role within that world. The familiar task of harvesting resources from the game world is given a moral twist in that the resources are stored inside *Little Sisters*: cute little girls who have been genetically modified for the task of extracting the stem cells the player needs to complete the game.

Oblivion also offers the opportunity to pursue an irredeemably evil lifestyle – but one that is not without consequences, and indeed, occasional moral guilt on the part of the player. As a part of the assassin storyline, the player must kill a number of people who, unlike the cannon fodder in most other videogames, are given a back-story and characterization that shows them to be innocents caught up in the machinations of some evil individual – more often than not the player! Fictions have often been thought to provide opportunities for moral reflection or learning, and there is a large literature devoted to how (or indeed if) they can do this. But because of the interactive nature of videogame fictions – the player takes a part in the moral situations presented there, and whether or not the evil occurs is often up to them – the potential of games for the exploration of moral issues seems somehow more vivid: and perhaps more dangerous, where the game does not provide opportunities to put the content in a thoughtful or realistic context.

There is then, plenty of motivation for the theory of videogames, and a number of theorists have already taken up this concern. The growing academic literature on games and gaming – often referred to as *games studies* – has made some initial strides in the last decade. Games studies is an interdisciplinary field drawing mostly from the humanities, social sciences, psychology, and computer science, and which deals with a wide variety of issues ranging from technical inquiries into design principles, to theoretical examinations of the social significance of gaming. The field, though still in its early stages, has already led to a number of valuable new perspectives on videogaming.

My disciplinary orientation is rather different to that found in games studies, however. In this book I will situate videogames in the framework of the philosophy of the arts, a field that has almost altogether ignored gaming. Philosophical aesthetics, I hope to show, is ideally suited to providing an informative theoretical prototype for the study of videogames. Hence, I see this book not as one situated within games studies, but as a philosophical and humanistic work on the topic of videogames. This makes a practical difference in that the gaming examples I focus on, and the issues that I explore through them, will often not be orientated around the issues prominent in current games studies, but instead those to be found within the philosophy of the arts.

Gaming replicates many of the issues that have been the traditional focus of philosophical aesthetics. Theories that exist within the philosophy of the arts, designed to explain things beside videogames, often find a natural application in the case of videogames. Among the topics dealt with in the recent philosophy of the arts are the definition of art, the ontology of artworks, the expressive nature of artworks and our experience of their expressive qualities, the nature of narrative and interpretation, and recently, issues in cognitive science particular to the perceptual, cognitive, and emotional processes involved in the appreciation of art. A number of these concerns have their corollaries in videogaming.

Among the questions that will interest philosophers when they come to look at videogames are the following:

- Can videogames be defined?
- How do videogames sit in respect to earlier forms of art?
- How does the digital medium of videogames have an effect on their employment of narratives, fictions, and visual art?
- How does the player stand in relation the fictional worlds of videogames?
- How do videogames appeal to the player's emotions?
- What is the moral significance of videogaming?

- Can gamers be genuinely morally blamed for what they do in a fictional world?
- What is the locus of artistic interest in games, and how does this differ from other traditional forms of art?
- Finally, are videogames genuinely art, as I have unquestioningly and perhaps rashly claimed in this introductory chapter?

This book, split into nine chapters, is an attempt to address these and other questions concerning videogames and their relationship to art. In the next chapter I address the first issue on the list, arguing that we must turn our attention to the formal features of definition if we are to construct a definition responsive to the varied nature of videogaming. Chapter 3 discusses the fictional nature of videogames, drawing on the philosophical theory of fiction to establish that videogames are indeed *interactive fictions*. Along the way the concepts of virtuality and immersion are considered and explained in the context of the theory of fiction: videogames, I argue, are *virtual fictions*. Chapter 4 is comprised of a survey of the representational means of these virtual fictions, including the crucial role of the player-character as the player's *fictive proxy* in a game world. Chapter 5 looks at how these virtual fictions are ideal for situating games. Games, I will argue, are best seen as formal systems set in a framework of behavioral norms, and on both of these issues the theory of interactive fiction has something to contribute to the understanding of gaming. Chapter 6 discusses the nature of narrative in gaming, again arguing that the nature of videogames as virtual or interactive fictions has a significant impact on this issue. Chapter 7 presents a theory of how the emotions are involved in gaming, explaining what it is we become emotional about, and the role that emotions play in *connecting* us with game worlds. Chapter 8 looks into the obvious moral significance of videogaming. Many people are of the opinion that the violent content in videogames is genuinely worrying from a moral point of view; I assess whether these basic intuitions really are warranted, offering a partial defense of the disturbing content found in games. Chapter 9 turns its attention to whether videogames really are a form of art. Drawing on the discussion of the previous chapters, and philosophical theory about the nature of art, I hope the reader will come to agree with me that videogames are not only properly regarded as art, but as an art form filled with a potential for creativity, richness, and subtlety.

I suspect, for a number of reasons, that there might be some resistance to this last claim about the potential of videogames as art. Fans of high-art, in particular, may balk at comparing *Fallout 3* and *Grand Theft Auto IV* to *War and Peace*, *Les Demoiselles d'Avignon*, and the other pinnacle achievements of human culture to be found in the arts. Admittedly, videogames do not yet reach the heights of these great artworks. Though the ultimate justification of my application of philosophical aesthetics to videogames will be what success I have in my aims in this book, I will say a couple of things here. First, videogames are in their infancy, and have developed to their current level of sophistication in a very short time. The last fifteen years in particular have seen rapid maturation of the form, and I see signs in that growth that games are beginning to broach the concerns usually associated with serious art. Second, looking on games with a sympathetic eye already turns up impressive riches. In many respects videogames are a hard sell to culturally literate people: they have a bad image for any number of reasons. But pushing beyond this often unfair image, videogames do have much to offer in the way of aesthetic pleasures, and as such they are of intrinsic interest to philosophical aesthetics.

But besides allowing us to understand videogames themselves, a philosophical study of gaming also has the potential to shed new light on a number of the traditional issues within the philosophy of the arts. As a new form of art, a careful study of videogaming can allow us knowledge not only of videogames, but of the larger classes – popular art, fiction, visual art, narrative – of which modern gaming is an instance. Permit me to extend an analogy. For biologists, the discovery of a new species is exciting not only in the interest of the new species itself, but of the potential the discovery has to tell them about the rest of the biological world. The discovery of the platypus, for example, made a great many surprising facts known to eighteenth-century scientists, forcing them to revise many of the ideas they accepted about the world (Eco, 2000: 241–248). Some mammals, it turned out, not only lacked nipples, but also laid eggs, and so nipple-bearing and egg-laying could no longer be thought to be features that distinguished between reptiles and birds (sauropsids) and mammals. More significantly, the platypus served to make clear the aetiological links between mammals and the egg-laying creatures from which they were ultimately derived: platypuses seem from the previous perspective to be an uncomfortable middle point between reptiles and mammals, providing an important illustration of the continuities of nature (Dawkins, 2004: 238–242). Through the discovery and explanation of the platypus we learn something about the more familiar classes of which it is a member, and also of the basic nature of the biological world.

Videogames have the potential to be a *cultural platypus*. The general theme of this book is that videogames are a new form of representational art that employ the technology of the computer for the purposes of entertainment. They involve their audiences through structural forms – including visual representations, games, interactive fictions, and narratives – that have cultural precedents in other artworks and non-artworks. When represented through the digital medium of videogames, however, these forms are productive of new possibilities in artistic creation, some of them described above in the examples of *Oblivion, Grand Theft Auto,* and *Portal,* and others to be met through the course of this book. Equally, videogames also engage us in ways that are precedented in previous forms of culture and art: they inspire us to judgments of perceptual beauty, they involve us in interpretation, and they arouse our emotions. But they also modify this participation by representing the player and their agency within a fictional world. It may turn out that what we thought we knew about art, fiction, narrative, games, and the psychology of the arts, was really an artifact of what was already known to exist in those classes of things.

I am a gamer as well as a philosopher, and a lot of my discussion here will be informed and propelled by my own gaming experiences. This book is filled with anecdotes of my many adventures in game worlds. A number of the academic works about videogames give the unmistakable impression of really being about something else: many are merely surveys of the author's academic and theoretical preoccupations, with videogames employed as a subject matter to tease out the issues they find to be of real interest. When I began this work, I wanted to write a book squarely about videogames, because I think they are of intrinsic and not merely instrumental interest. I have sympathy for videogames, and if I achieve anything here, I hope it is to show how a sensitive look into gaming can uncover the genuine artistic richness of the new cultural form, perhaps even tempting some of the non-gamers who read this book to pick up a controller and play.

CHAPTER SUMMARY

Videogames are a growing phenomenon and influence in the modern world, and are displaying new levels of artistic sophistication. As such they seem to engage many of the same issues as do the traditional arts, raising questions about aesthetics, representation, narrative, emotional engagement, and morality, that have been the focus of the philosophy of the arts. Philosophical aesthetics promises to provide a unique window of understanding into videogames.

NEXT CHAPTER

Can videogames be defined? Exactly how do they relate to previous forms of art and entertainment? Videogames, I argue, are not characterized by any single distinctive trait, but instead are made up of a variable set of such conditions. Specifically, they employ new digital media toward the ends of entertainment, achieving that function through the representation of the traditional cultural forms of gaming, narrative, and fiction. Videogames differ to previous forms of art, mostly in their technologically dependent digital media, but also share profound continuities with earlier forms of art and entertainment in how they engage their audiences.

2

WHAT ARE VIDEOGAMES ANYWAY?

ON DEFINITION

An interdisciplinary field known as *games studies* has coalesced in recent times. One concern that has interested a number of game theorists is the question of exactly what games are. Indeed, this seems an obvious and foundational issue for games studies to tackle. Often the question of the nature of gaming is taken to ask which of the previous non-videogaming forms of culture videogaming most resembles. Three such approaches are salient in the literature: the *narratological* approach, where videogames are characterized as new forms of narratives or texts; the *ludological* approach, where they are seen as being principally games though in a new digital medium; and the *interactive fiction* theory of videogames that emphasizes their fictive qualities. The debate between narratology and ludology has taken a particular prominence in the literature and at recent games studies conferences (Frasca, 2003; Aarseth, 2004).

Though each of these approaches does see games and gaming as involving typical features, the theories do not come in the form of definitions. This seems to be partly explained by the disciplinary location of some of these ideas: current games researchers, often aligning themselves with critical theory and media studies and the theoretical equipment of semiotics and intertextuality, do not seem to have much interest or patience with formal definition. James Newman (2004) is one of the few researchers to confront the definitional issue head on, though even he does not seem to hold much hope for the prospect of defining videogames. Interestingly, both Katie Salen and Eric Zimmerman (2004) and Jesper Juul (2005) discuss a number of previous definitions of gaming in general, testing the applicability of the definitions to videogames. Again, these definitions are not worked out with any great philosophical rigor, and also, the focus on gaming in general means that their definitional concern is not with videogames *per se*, but with videogames *vis-à-vis* traditional gaming.

This lack of concern with definitions is unfortunate because dealing with the definitional issue in a forthright and clear manner at the outset has the potential to add significant clarity to what can at times be a very murky debate. It is often just not clear what it is that theorists are arguing games to be, and hence it is sometimes very hard to know what would support or falsify their theories. A successful definition of videogames would provide games studies with a target of explanation. But even if gaming proves to be beyond the scope of definition, the process of offering and criticizing definitions would nevertheless have practical and heuristic value in that we might learn a great deal about the category, including, perhaps, the reasons for its definitional recalcitrance. The very difficulty in defining gaming may account for the lack of enthusiasm for definitions, of course.

It is useful to compare the situation with videogames to that with the definition of art. Philosophers have struggled for a long time with the task of defining art, providing many definitions which have all in their turn seemed subject to serious doubts. A representational theory of art might define art as involving representation or mimesis, seeing art as a mirror on reality. Such a definition is easily falsified. Though a large proportion of artworks do involve representation, it quickly becomes clear that this definition is prone to examples of artworks that do not – pure orchestral music and some abstract art, for example – and objects such as billboard advertisements that do involve representation but which are nevertheless not artworks. For some, the history of the definition of art seems comprised of a succession of such definitions and their prompt refutations (Gaut, 2000). Though a number of thinkers have over the years disputed whether art can be defined at all (Weitz, 1956), the interest in the definition of art shows no sign of waning. Furthermore, the debate has been worthwhile despite the clear lack of agreement: along the way a lot has been learned about the genuine range of definitions that might be offered, and also about some tempting mistakes to be avoided. A great deal has also been learned about the formal, artifactual, social, and institutional natures of art, a fact easily proved by dipping into the rich definitional literature (Davies, 1991; Carroll, 2000).

What precisely is a definition, and what is it meant to achieve? It is clear that definitions can serve a number of different purposes and take different forms. One of these – and it is the version of definition that many of my first year students seem most drawn to when they begin their essays by citing a dictionary – is what we might call *nominal definition*. Nominal definitions attempt to chart the conceptual relations of words, often as they appear in everyday usage, and are definitions of the kind commonly found in dictionaries. Such nominal considerations are relevant here in that there clearly are variations in how videogames are referred to. *Computer game, electronic game, console game, PC game,* and *handheld game* have all been used to refer to videogames, or some class of them, and they are not strict synonyms. Indeed, the usage of these terms is far from univocal: *computer game* is sometimes taken to refer to games on a personal computer, but it is also used as the generic term; *electronic game* might also refer to toys as well as videogames; while *videogame,* as well as being a generic term, is sometimes used to refer exclusively to console games such as those on the X-Box 360 or Playstation 3. I have settled on *videogame* as the generic term in this book partly because it dominates current usage, partly because it does have a generic sense that cuts across the nominal variants just noted, and partly because it has the virtue of referring to the *visual* aspect of games, a fact which will assume importance later in this book.

Setting out the nominal bounds of a concept is not always sufficient for providing a real understanding of the term, however. Some everyday concepts, though proving perfectly suitable for the use to which people put them, fail to capture the real nature of the world. Consider as just one example the pre-scientific use of the concept *water*: people used the concept successfully for millennia before chemists discovered what water *really* was. As such, *water* could be defined nominally despite the lack of a real understanding of water, in that lexicographers could specify the way in which the concept was used. More worryingly, sometimes everyday concepts just get the nature of the world wrong, and so nominal definitions, though capturing the way the concept works, can incorrectly describe reality. One such example is the vernacular term *lily* which groups together biologically disparate groups because of the superficial resemblance of their flowers (Griffiths, 1997: 191). It is for reasons such as this that a more substantive sense of definition than nominal definition is often desired. We can call this substantive sense of definition a *real* or *empirical* definition. Scientists take a principal interest in empirical definitions because of their concern with discovering the real nature of the world, which may depart from how our nominally specified concepts tell us it is. The formulation of successful empirical definitions can also have a correcting effect on nominal terms.

In philosophy, such empirical definitions usually come in the form of *definition by necessary and sufficient conditions.* Such definitions attempt to explain, clarify, or even revise the conceptual status of a term in common usage and come in the form of a condition or set of conditions that are *necessary* and *sufficient* for x to be y. Water can be defined as H_2O, because water must have this makeup, and if a substance has this makeup, then that guarantees that it is water. In philosophical parlance, a substance is water *if and only if* it has the microstructural composition of H_2O molecules. The necessary and sufficient conditions are often thought to explicate the *essence* of the defined term, and so this form of definition is sometimes called an *essential* definition. Such essentialist definition is a substantive conception of definition in that it is an explanation of what it is (if anything) that makes all members of a given class – be it water, art, lilies, videogames – members of that class.

The definition proffered here *is* an attempt to capture the material nature of videogames: what it is about them that makes them all videogames, and makes them different to other cultural artifacts. But this ambition for realism needs to be tempered by the likelihood that games lack a substantive essence and that a nominal aspect to this definition is unavoidable: videogames may sit together in a category *in name only*. A great many of our concepts are resistant to empirical definition, because they are *merely* nominal, being coined to reflect our needs or perceptual dispositions, rather than any natural categories that exist in the world. The vernacular term *lily* is like this, in that it uses something that is particularly salient to us – a resemblance in the shape of flowers – to group together what are actually quite different things. And of course, there is nothing stopping someone arbitrarily collecting a group of things together under a concept: I might collect all of the things currently sitting on my coffee table into a nominal category, but it would be absurd to think that there is any *real* nature to that category other than the stipulated classificatory principle I originally used to group the items (that they all currently sit on my coffee table).

Videogames, of course, are quite unlike water in being a cultural invention. With cultural artifacts, such categorial nominalism can be even more striking, because the coining of a term to describe an invention can lead to the production of new instances of the kind. In popular music, the rise of the *album* surely had an effect on the types of music released, so that even today when the technological means that originally gave rise to the form – the long-player record – has largely disappeared and artists can freely produce music in vastly different forms, the album is still a concept through which musicians organize their musical activities. What this shows – and it is a point that will have consequences for videogaming – is that just which categories are coined to group cultural items together can have a significant impact on the kinds of things that subsequently get produced within those categories. It can even occur that artifacts are intentionally produced to expand or stress a category, or even merge categories, and as a result, our interests in defining cultural categories can become very complicated indeed, as the definition of art literature makes abundantly clear.

I think that for these kinds of reasons it is likely that *videogames* form a class in virtue of that very coinage, and that the terminological variations referred to earlier – *computer game, electronic game,* and so on – are equally plausible and motivated ways of cutting up videogames and similar artifacts into explanatory groups. This means that even a successful definition of videogames may arrive not at some fact about what videogames *really* are in the sort of robust sense in which water *really is* H_2O, but a specification that the term *videogame*, which is a fairly nominally contingent way of grouping a set of objects – but nevertheless a subsequently influential one on the development of the class – can be given a conceptual foundation in terms of necessary and sufficient conditions.

This nominalism does not mean the definition of videogames is unmotivated or lacks utility. The worth of such a definition will be adjudged not by how closely it corresponds to an underlying fact of nature (as in the case of water), but how useful it is in allowing us to explain where videogames came from, their similarities to other cultural forms, and how they function. The very nominal nature of the definition itself allows us to understand something very important about games; that is, their *continuity* with other cultural forms. Admittedly, this is a very pragmatic conception of definition that may not please everyone, but I think it will prove up to the task of providing a focal point for this study.

THEORIES OF GAMING

What do the currently popular theories of videogames assert about the nature of games, and how do these theories stand up to a definitional analysis of the kind just outlined? Inevitably, because of the failure of games studies to squarely approach the definitional issue, this section is something of a reconstruction of the literature. In their native forms, the theories discussed here are not formulated as necessary and sufficient conditions, but to see what can be made of them as definitions, I will treat them as such. It may be unfair to the authors discussed here to treat them as stand-in philosophers, but lacking a significant philosophical literature on these issues, I think this is the best way to make use of the genuinely important theoretical contributions these writers make to the debate. My argument is that when treated as proper definitions, narratology, ludology, and interactive fiction theories are all prone to examples of videogames that lack the purported characteristic feature, or of items that have it but are not videogames.

Narratologists argue that games are a new kind of the narrative structure seen in older cultural artifacts such as films and novels. Because of this, the theories that are used to explain those traditional forms of narrative can be adapted to explain videogames. Janet Murray (1998) discusses how games can be used to express narratives and stories even though their representational means differ to previous ways of depicting these things. A related approach sees games as being *texts*, and again, this means that games can be explained by adapting the literature used to explain texts in non-videogaming contexts (Poole, 2000). It is here that I must write the first of the promissory notes needed in this chapter so that I can suspend the real discussion of narrative in gaming until chapter 6. But even a cursory observation shows that many videogames do involve narratives. *Narrative* might be roughly defined as a representation of sets of events chosen for their contribution to an unfolding plot with a beginning, middle, and an end, and it is clear that many videogames involve such things. Narratives are more prevalent in some gaming forms than others: adventure and role-playing genres such as *Oblivion*, for example, often rely on narratives for much of their interest. But as shown with the case of *Portal*, even what is essentially a puzzle game might present a narrative.

But if we are to settle the question of the nature of gaming – the task I have set myself here – something stronger than the presence of narratives in *some* games needs to be shown: it needs to be shown that narrative is *essential* to videogames. Problematically, narrative does not seem to be a sufficient or even necessary condition of videogames. The presence of narrative is not sufficient to make an artifact a videogame because of the very obvious fact that non-videogames also involve narratives. Narrative constitutes the primary interpretive interest in television and film drama, and in a number of literary forms. In fact, videogaming often seems to be a *combination* of these media forms with a gaming element. As we will find, the narrative in many games is represented by pre-rendered videos that interrupt the gameplay proper, often effectively suspending it, and the narrative in a great number of games might actually be removed without detriment to the gameplay: and given how ham-fisted many gaming narratives are, one sometimes wishes this was the case.

Narrative is not even a necessary feature of videogames because many videogames lack it entirely. Though *Tetris* involves a represented sequence of events – namely, differently shaped blocks falling at regular intervals from the top of the screen – the events are not chosen for their contribution to an overall plot or story. Rather, the events occur simply to test the skills of the player. Dance and music games also tend to lack narrative structures, at least in their gameplay. Some theorists seem to be tempted to include such games as having narratives by broadening the meaning of *narrative* away from that supplied above. For example, a game like *Tetris* might be included in this narratological approach because it is comprised of a represented set of unfolding events in which the notions of success and defeat can be applied, something that Poole envisages being referred to as a "kinetic" story (2000: 108). Arguably, this would include *Tetris* within narrative theory only at the cost of making *narrative* vacuous in that it is now not clear what "represented sequence of unfolding events with a narrative" does *not* refer to: is a film of someone making a cup of tea a narrative? What about CCTV footage of someone parking their car? If we include these as narratives, the concept threatens to become uninteresting through its sheer ubiquity of application. The same arguably goes for the extension of the term *text* to apply to videogames and other items very unlike traditional texts. For all of these reasons it seems doubtful that narrative is by itself a constitutive feature of videogaming, but is instead a contingent aspect of some games. Still, the nature of narrative in videogames where it does exist remains an interesting issue, and I will have a great deal more to say on the topic in this book.

Ludology emphasizes the obvious gaming nature of videogames, and is sometimes seen in opposition to narratological approaches. The claim that videogames are principally games might seem self-evident because of the similarities videogames bear to non-digital games, a similarity which no doubt led to the coining of the term *videogame*. Exactly what this similarity amounts to – what makes a game a game – is an issue that will also be deferred (chapter 5), but some videogames are very obviously games, having only migrated into the digital setting after being invented in another medium: chess and card games are such examples. Sports videogames such as *Madden NFL* are digital forms of physical sports games, and in most cases stick close to the actual rules and objectives of their real counterparts, in this case American football, though in a simulated setting. Such "transmedial games" – games that migrate from one medium to another – give a very strong indication that ludology is the right explanatory approach for a great many videogames (Juul, 2005: 48). Other videogames do not seem possible except in the digital medium. *Tetris* is one such videogame that seems perfectly suited to this ludological theory in that it involves a set of rules (albeit programmed into a computer) and an objective that must be achieved through those rules (to fit the colored pieces together so as to avoid them reaching the top of the box into which they fall). Real-time and turn-based strategy games like *Age of Empires*, *Civilization*, and *Rise of Nations* also seem entirely appropriately characterized as digital games. While not strictly being transmedial games, these strategy games seem to have non-videogame relatives in strategy board games such as *Risk*, and the strategy war games that use small figurines to represent the positions of armies.

Espen Aarseth is perhaps the writer most commonly associated with ludology, though whether this is because of his opposition to narratology, or any substantive ludological theory of gaming that he has, is unclear. Aarseth has written at length about the function of games as a kind of "ergodic" item (1997). Aarseth thinks ergodic items – examples being role-playing games such as *Dungeons and Dragons*, the Aleatoric writing of the French surrealists, modern experiments in cyber and hypertexts, some of the more complex non-linear and experimental literature of the twentieth century, and videogames – demand "non-trivial" effort for the reader to "traverse the text" (1997: 1). Ergodic texts allow the possibility of multiple readings, allow the reader to instill in a text novel meaning, or place the onus on the reader to choose in which narrative direction a text goes.

I am not convinced that a new concept is useful or even needed for my analytic purposes here. Aarseth's introduction of the term *ergodic* is related to his evident general resistance to the term *interactive* (1997: 50; 2004). I will later argue that Aarseth's resistance to the term is unfounded and that interaction, a concept with which we are already familiar, can be given a perfectly good theoretical analysis that does an acceptable job in capturing this aspect of videogames (see chapter 3). But more important than the criticism of the very notion of a distinctive class of ergodic media are worries about its potential to be developed into a definition of videogames. Even if Aarseth has identified something that is distinctive of a range of textual artifacts, it is clear that this range is not coextensive with videogames, and Aarseth, in setting out the explanatory range of his theory, admits as much: ergodic properties, even should they exist, are not sufficient to make an item a videogame because they also occur in non-videogames such as game-books, *Dungeons and Dragons*, and hypertexts.

In many ways, Jesper Juul is a better choice of a theorist who attempts to explain how videogames instantiate traditional gaming forms, though his theory is complicated in that he holds that at least some videogames are not games, but rather fictions (2005). Juul links videogames to earlier forms of gaming, hoping to show that they replicate many of the properties of traditional gaming in a new digital medium. Juul draws on a number of earlier theories of non-digital games, attempting to illustrate how they converge on a basic prototype which he calls the "classic game model" (2005: 36–43). Without going into the details at this stage, this model defines traditional games as involving rules, variable and quantifiable outcomes, player effort and attachment to the outcome, and negotiable consequences. Videogames replicate these properties, and hence count as games. Juul's work is one of the best in current games studies, especially in the clarity of his comparison of videogames to earlier forms of gaming.

As with the concept of ergodic media, it is not clear that a simple use of the classic game model will allow us to develop a definition of gaming. To his credit, Juul accepts as much. The classic game model is clearly not a *sufficient* property, given that it was initially developed to define and explain non-videogames: the theory shows what is similar between traditional games and videogames, and not what is distinctive to the latter. Furthermore, for the conjunction of features in the classic game model to be a *necessary* feature of *videogames*, all videogames would have to fit under the classic game model, and as Juul himself admits, they do not. Juul notes that the classic theory of games counts such a seminal videogame as *Simcity* as a "borderline" case of a game because it does not involve a clear or quantifiable goal but rather is comprised of an open-ended simulation (2005: 43). *Microsoft Flight Simulator* is a similar case, in that the idea of *winning* such a game makes little if any sense. Juul's solution to this problem is to see *Simcity* and *Microsoft Flight Simulator* as videogames in virtue of being simulations and hence fictions, though like almost everyone else in the debate he does not go as far as formalizing this into a definition.

The two problems with Juul's theory are instructive: Juul has shown that some videogames share a set of formal properties with earlier games, but he perhaps does not attach enough significance to the *differences* in the media instantiation of videogames to their earlier and non-videogame counterparts, giving us a hint that one of the needed conditions of a successful definition of videogames will refer to their typical *media*. Second, Juul's admission that some videogames are not games but instead simulations, suggests that there might be more than one characteristic way of being a videogame. Suitably formalized, and with the nature of games and fiction properly explained, I will argue here that something like Juul's hybrid theory can be used to base a definition of videogames.

Thus a third theoretical approach is to characterize games as *interactive fictions*. Two immediate confusions need to be avoided here. First, there are at least two senses of the term *interactive fiction*. The term can be used in a narrow way to refer to the *genre of interactive fiction*, a type of interactive literature in both electronic and non-electronic media that reached its height of popularity in the early 1980s in videogames like *Zork* and in the various *Choose Your Own Adventure* style game-books, and which is still evident on the Internet today. Typically, such interactive literature sets out a story during which the reader has choices to make that determine the outcome of the fictive narrative: "if you would like to fight the goblin, turn to page 88. If you would like to run away, turn to page 52," and so on. This genre of interactive fiction in fact seems more appropriately described as *interactive narrative*. The use I intend to make of the term *interactive fiction* is wider and more encompassing than this genre sense, including interactive narrative, but also other kinds of interactive fictions. Some of the things I will refer to as interactive fictions, such as flight simulators, do not involve narratives of any kind, but nevertheless allow the player to interact with a fictive scenario. A second and related confusion is that the concepts of *fiction* and *narrative* often appear to be conflated in the games literature, with some writers seeming to use the term *fiction* to refer to a game's background narrative. Properly conceived, narrative and fiction are logically independent. Not all fictions are narrative in form, and equally, not all narratives are fictional.

I have argued elsewhere that if one is careful in specifying exactly what it is that is interactive about interactive fictions, then videogames can often be counted as such things (Tavinor, 2005a). Though again we will have to wait for another chapter (3) for the real justification and explanation of this claim, here we can pause briefly to consider the interactive fictive elements of videogames. *Oblivion* represents a fictional world filled with ogres and goblins, and it is fictional of the game that you interact with these things. I have never fought a goblin in real life, though fictionally I've fought many of them. Some fictional worlds are more similar to our own world than Cyrodiil is, and even reproduce parts of the real world: the car racing game *Gran Turismo*, for example, represents a number of real race tracks such as the excellent Nürburgring Nordschleife from Germany, and California's Laguna Seca. Even though the fictional setting has a real-world counterpart, the activities that the player is represented doing in the world are fictional: I have never driven a Toyota Supra around Laguna Seca; it is only fictional that I have done this.

Unfortunately, videogames cannot be defined as interactive fictions. Being an interactive fiction cannot be a necessary condition of videogaming as it is not clear that *all* games really are interactive fictions, or involve fiction at all. This seems to be the case with some transmedial games. The primordial videogame *OXO*, videogame chess, *Sudoku*, and solitaire do not seem to present a fiction that one is playing these games in the sense that *Oblivion* presents a fiction that one is fighting a goblin. Rather, they merely allow one to play a *digital version* of tic-tac-toe, chess, *Sudoku*, or solitaire. Admittedly, many chess and card videogames do seem to represent chess boards and pieces and playing cards in a visual way. But these representations owe to the *virtual* representational configuration of modern computers (see chapter 3). It is not clear to me that moving a symbol from a material to a virtual medium is sufficient to make it a fiction. Similarly, *Tetris* does not seem to be a fiction, because it is no part of that game that we imagine a corresponding fictional world; arguably, the game is just comprised of the real manipulation of virtual representations or symbols on a screen. Later, when I turn my attention to the theory of fiction (chapter 3), I settle on a robust meaning for the term, where fiction is something more than this symbolic activity: it is where representations are used as props for envisaging a world with an imagined existence only.

James Newman makes a different objection to the idea that videogames are necessarily interactive fictions by noting that much of the fictive activity involved in gaming is distinctly non-interactive (2004: 75–76). For large stretches of many games one is merely viewing pre-rendered videos in which the player has no ability to act. And being an interactive fiction cannot be a sufficient condition of videogame-hood, as pen and paper role-playing, military or commercial flight simulators, the *Microsoft Word* paper clip character, and childhood games of pretense are all interactive fictions while not counting as videogames.

A DEFINITION OF VIDEOGAMES

If the above analysis is correct, when treated as essentialist necessary and sufficient condition definitions, narratology, ludology, and interactive fiction theory fail to pick out all and only videogames. It is probably not fair to attribute this failure squarely to these theories given that they usually have no such intention to be so treated. But these failures do clear the way for me to offer my own definition of videogames. It is clear that games are not *simply* narratives, games, or fictions. What, then, are they?

The definition I propose here involves a slight emendation to what I said earlier about the nature of definition. There I assumed that a definition is made up of a set of conditions that are individually necessary and jointly sufficient for *x* to be *y*. When formalizing narratology, ludology, and interactive fiction theory in this way, it became clear that none really worked out as a real definition because there were obvious counter-examples of videogames without the specified feature, or items with the specified feature which were nevertheless not videogames. Perhaps, though, the fault lies not with the theories themselves, but with the way in which I formalized their content into a definition.

In the definition of art debate, a number of recent philosophers of the arts have argued that an essentialist mode of definition is not the only definitional game in town: *disjunctive definitions* are also possible (Davies, 2004; Dutton, 2006). A disjunctive definition is one that includes at least one disjunctive (*either/or*) clause among its conditions. To drastically simplify matters, it may be that

X is art if and only if it has property A *or* property B.

In this case a set of properties may be individually or jointly sufficient for *x* to be a videogame, but it is not specified that they are individually necessary for *x* to be so. In the case of theories of the arts, such definitions are often meant to capture the intuition that there may be more than one way to be art (Dutton, 2006). To revisit the earlier toy definition of art, we might define art as involving representation *or* expression of the emotions: some artworks may lack representation, but count as art in virtue of their emotional expression.

Perhaps there is more than one characteristic manner of being a video-game. I have already noted that Juul has this intuition about the hybrid or disjunctive nature of videogames. A disjunctive definition might be used to explain how, even though they fail to have a *single* set of necessary and sufficient properties, videogames can nevertheless be defined. Indeed, this would be a way to reconcile the theoretical divergence of ludologists, narrato-logists, and interactive fiction games theorists, while retaining the valuable contribution these theorists do make to the understanding of videogames. Though not describing some aspects of games that can be developed into a successful definition, each theoretical vantage point isolates a characteristic that genuinely exists in videogames.

In my view, videogames can best be defined by providing a set of con-ditions, not all of which are individually necessary, but when combined in an appropriate way are sufficient for an artifact to be a videogame (Tavinor, 2008):

> X is a videogame if it is an artifact in a visual digital medium, is intended
> as an object of entertainment, and is intended to provide such entertainment
> through the employment of one or both of the following modes of engage-
> ment: rule and objective gameplay or interactive fiction.

This definition differs from a purely disjunctive definition in that there are at least two necessary conditions needed to distinguish videogames from their conceptual precedents and relatives: being an artifact in a visual digital medium, and being intended as an object for entertainment. The invention of the computer, including its crucial visual display elements, stands as a historical prerequisite for videogaming, and gaming exists as an employment of that technology for the purposes of entertainment. It is obvious that videogames also employ non-visual representational means, but the visual display has always seemed prominent or central to the form. One of the very first games, Willy Higinbotham's *Tennis for Two*, ran on an analogue computer and used an oscilloscope as a visual display. Higinbotham's game was developed in 1958 to entertain visitors to the Brookhaven National Laboratory where Higinbotham worked. Modern games have thankfully moved on from the oscilloscope: I currently do most of my gaming on a Playstation 3 running through a 32-inch high definition LCD television. But the basic prototype – entertainments in a visual digital setting – can already be seen in *Tennis for Two*.

Despite their almost self-evidence, the media-based conditions need to be included in the definition because a number of videogames are structur-ally very similar to non-videogames, differing only in their representational medium. This is the case with the *transmedial* games that have migrated into a digital setting, an issue that was touched on earlier in terms of the videogame versions of chess, card games, and *Sudoku*. These games can become *videogames* in virtue of their transfer into a digital setting. Without the necessary condition specifying the computational and visual medium of videogames, the above definition would also apply to these games in their non-digital form.

The reference to visual representation in particular is needed because there are a range of toys and electronic games that would otherwise be included under this definition. *Computer Battleship* – the 1980s Milton Bradley version of the pen and paper game – is an example of an electronic game that does not count as a videogame because it does not have a computer visual display; rather, the players themselves display the state of the game with small ship models and pegs on a plastic grid. Videogames exist as a species within the wider class of *electronic games*, allowing us to understand the connection between the clearly related kinds, however. Videogame versions of *Computer Battleship* have been produced, adding to the electronic games a visual depiction of the game state, including animations of the battle. They also add the possibility of playing against a computer opponent.

One point of clarification is needed: the visual medium condition is not a claim that videogames are always *pictorial*. Though almost all recent videogames are pictorial – indeed, 3D representation is now the norm – this has not always been the case. Many early videogames such as *Hunt the Wumpus* and *Colossal Cave Adventure* were text-based games. In these games, the visual screen is used to represent text, and the interaction that the player has with the game typically utilizes text as the player types their move as a command using a keyboard. Some might think that these text-based games, because they could be played in non-computer settings, are not really videogames at all, and that genuine videogames involve the manipulation of pictorial representations. But to make this conclusion would unsatisfactorily exclude from gaming an important kind of early videogame that has had a persisting influence in the form of the textual aspects still evident in games (see chapter 4). What we should say, I think, is that these text-based videogames have potential transmedial forms in non-digital media.

It is with this visual media condition that the nominal aspect of this definition is most evident. This visual condition seems almost *stipulatory* owing to the fact that there just is a nominal variant that refers to videogames/computer games/electronic games in virtue of their visual qualities. One potential counter to my definition is that it counts out games without visual display elements. *Metris* is a computer game that is structurally similar to *Tetris*, but which uses musical tones and phrases where *Tetris* employs geometrical shapes. It might be claimed that *Metris* is a videogame while lacking one of the necessary conditions of my definition, hence falsifying it. The obvious counter to this is to deny that *Metris* is a *videogame*, instead being some other clearly related kind: and it is surely a *computer game*. I could have orientated this book around computer games, and so included *Metris*. This would not evade the definitional problems being encountered here of course; in fact they would probably be worse given that the category of computer games seems even harder to pin down than videogames. All that can be said here, I think, is that *videogame* just is in this respect a nominal category, and that the suspicion that *Metris* might act as a counter-example to the present definition makes the mistake of crediting such cultural categories with a real existence they just do not have.

The entertainment condition of the proposed definition is needed to distinguish games from similar artifacts that have purposes besides entertainment, and so do not sit comfortably under the classification of videogame. Examples of artifacts that have similar digital and visual media to videogames are military and commercial flight simulators, virtual museums, and computer desktop applications that involve fictive aspects such as the aforementioned paperclip character who offers advice – moreover proves to be an annoyance – in some versions of *Microsoft Word*. The representational abilities of the computer that give videogames their potential to entertain also have a host of more utilitarian functions. Simulations in particular, because they are able to present in a virtual manner an activity that would be either dangerous or costly in reality, are valuable tools in learning and training. This entertainment clause needs to be prefixed by "intended" both because some non-game artifacts might prove to be entertaining or used to provide entertainment while not being intended as such, and because some games, while intended to be entertaining, actually turn out not in the least entertaining just because they are so bad.

The disjunctive aspects – the *either/or* clause – of the definition are needed to cover the ways in which videogames have characteristically provided entertainment. I am in general agreement with Juul's game-fiction hybrid theory of videogames in picking out games and fiction as the crucial entertainment forms. Where I differ to Juul is in formalizing these conditions as part of a disjunctive definition. The gameplay and interactive fiction conditions of the definition are needed to distinguish ways in which digital visual media have been employed for entertainment purposes that do not constitute videogames, examples being Internet sites and videos, and digital television. While these artifacts do entertain and do share the media of videogames – and so meet the necessary conditions of the definition – they differ in how they engage their audiences. Digital films may involve fictions, but not the interactive ones characteristic of videogames. Non-gaming Internet sites are interactive, at least in some sense of that term, but do not always involve interactive fiction or gameplay; where they do, they are rightly counted as online videogames. It seems a matter of historical contingency that videogames have employed one or both of these modes of engagement.

That an artifact involves rule and objective gameplay is a condition that is sufficient, given the presence of the two necessary conditions of this disjunctive definition, for an artifact to be a videogame. *Tetris, Pong, Pac-Man*, and transmedial games such as chess and card games count as videogames in virtue of this condition. In a later chapter I will develop this condition into a fully-fledged theory, providing the real justification for seeing videogames as being games. It already seems clear, however, that there are some crucial differences between games in the setting of videogames and non-videogames. In particular, the nature of the rules in videogames seems quite unlike that in traditional games, existing not as explicit linguistic formulations about legal moves and objectives, but as possibilities for interaction and goals to be achieved. In fact, many videogames do not even inform you of the rules and objectives of the game prior to play, these only being discovered as one plays.

Not all videogames involve rule and objective gameplay, and so the second characteristic way in which an interactive entertainment can be a videogame is its employment of interactive fiction. Fiction by itself is not sufficient, because as noted, this would include within the class of videogames many fictional Internet videos and films in a digital medium. The idea of interactivity must hence play a crucial role, and this explanation is to be taken up in a later chapter. Interactive fiction comes in a number of forms – including simulations, world-exploring or world-building fictions, and interactive narratives. These fictions are surely one of the principal interests to be had in videogames, both in their playing and their study.

My claim here, then, is that videogames can be best defined by a conjunction of two necessary conditions – the *digital/visual medium* condition and the *entertainment* condition – and a disjunction that summarizes how the former necessary condition instantiates the latter: *rule and objective gameplay*, and *interactive fiction*. An important motivation for the disjunctive aspect of this definition of videogames is that it explains some of the links that videogames have to earlier forms of culture, in particular, games and fiction. These features are clearly seen in other media, and it is these similarities that have tempted games theorists to characterize games in terms of those previous forms. Videogaming is essentially a manner in which these traditional forms of entertainment have been implemented in a new technologically derived medium.

Though the disjunctive aspect of the definition is needed to allow that there are videogames lacking either games or interactive fictions, but not both, it is surely the case that the majority of videogames involve *both* disjunctive features. The examples with which I introduced this book – *The Elder Scrolls: Oblivion, Grand Theft Auto,* and *Portal* – certainly contain interactive fictions *and* games. As do many of the classics of videogaming such as *Pac-Man, Space Invaders,* and *Donkey Kong.* Though it would not be suitable as a definition, I do not think it is too far from the truth to say that typically, videogames are *digital visual entertainments that employ games in a fictive setting.* Thus the disjunctive aspect of this definition, though important from a definitional point of view in allowing the definition to capture a category that does not seem monolithic, may not amount to all that much when it comes to the *explanation* of games. In the following chapters, as I relax my analytic tendencies, this rough categorization of videogames as being *games through fiction* will bear the main weight of the theory offered here. At the same time, the definition offered here should serve to remind us of the difficult and atypical cases that do exist.

It is worthwhile covering some potential objections to this definition. It might be argued that the definition offered here is *too inclusive.* Are transmedial videogames like chess and *Sudoku* really videogames, or normal games in a video setting? Chess can be played on a board using pieces, by correspondence, and on a computer. It might be argued that the latter media change is not sufficient to make chess a videogame. Genuine videogames such as *Tetris,* it might be claimed, cannot be played *except* in their digital medium. If the intuition is correct that medium transposition is not sufficient to make non-videogames such as chess or *Sudoku* videogames, the proposed definition includes artifacts that are not genuinely videogames.

There are some obvious responses to make to this argument. First, there are unequivocal cases where non-videogames are adapted into videogames, such as videogame football or cricket. Playing videogame football is not merely *playing football in a video setting.* We are already familiar with transmedial forms of chess, and so our initial temptation is to see videogame chess as *just* chess in another medium. Given their unfamiliarity, transmedial sports games make the categorial effects of media transposition more obvious. Chess is also such a representationally minimal game that it is very easily shifted between media (including into a purely mental/linguistic medium, as in *blindfold chess*). Modern videogame football, on the other hand, needed the technology to support 3D graphics before it could be created, and even now the form we have is only a rough approximation of the game.

Second, I think that if chess had originally developed as a computer game and had subsequently been shifted to a board game setting, our intuitions would tell us that a videogame had become a board game. Indeed, there are cases where videogames have moved to a board game setting that have had this categorial effect: as Juul (2005: 50) notes, in the early 1980s Milton Bradley produced a number of adaptations of popular videogames, including board game versions of *Pac-Man* and *Frogger*. These examples show that media transposition can change whether or not something is a videogame or a board game. To explain this intuition, we might say that there is a genus/species relationship here, with board games and videogames being instances of a more inclusive category of games *simpliciter*. Movement from a board game to a videogame is dependant on a change in representational media (and so explaining the necessity of the media condition of the definition being offered here). There is a real sense of game identity at the genus level, however, so that videogame and board game chess or *Frogger* can still count as the same game in different media.

It could also be claimed that my definition is *too narrow* in excluding those games that have intended uses besides entertainment. Defining games as "intended as an object of entertainment" might seem to exclude games used in learning and instruction, such as mathematics and spelling games, or used in advertising or public relations functions, as with *America's Army*, a first-person shooter aimed at increasing army recruitment. Surely the proposed definition would not allow either kind of case to be counted as a videogame given their intended respective educational and public relations functions?

My response is that these are clearly videogames with *extended* functions. Artifacts can have a host of functions and their categorial identity can change depending on which function we pick out for attention: videogames and can-openers can both function as saleable items, but they also sit within the narrower categories of videogames and can-openers in virtue of the function – providing entertainment, and opening cans, respectively – on the basis of which they garner a commercial interest. *America's Army* is a videogame in virtue of its local function of being an object of entertainment, and because it is a videogame it is apt in serving the extended function of public relations. If *America's Army* was not first a videogame, then it could not have this further function.

Another example that shows the need for the entertainment criterion are artifacts in a digital medium that have as their extended aim learning or education, but which are not videogames because they do not use the local function of entertainment in achieving this aim. A medical simulation aimed at training laparoscopic techniques would be an example if the simulation did not intentionally engage and motivate its users by means of entertainment. It is sometimes argued that *Second Life* – a virtual world in which participants can engage in activities besides those of entertainment – is not a videogame in virtue of lacking this condition. The entertainment condition of the disjunctive definition – framed in reference to the local function of an artifact – is needed to distinguish such cases.

A final potential problem arises when we question if this disjunctive definition could be turned into a simple necessary and sufficient condition definition by characterizing the disjunctive aspect of the definition in a more encompassing manner. Videogames could be defined as *interactive visual digital entertainments*, with *interactive* seen as a term that captures the nature of both interactive fiction and gameplay modes of engagement. Unfortunately, *interactive* is unsuited to the task of defining videogames because a sense of interaction wide enough to capture both interactive fiction and gameplay would include other things besides. If *interactive* is taken to refer to audience participation, the definition would probably stretch to include interactive DVDs, television on demand systems, various non-game Internet activities, and toys with digital and visual display elements. If the sense of *interactive* was specified more restrictively, so as to capture the ways in which videogames are interactive, but to exclude other interactive artifacts, it is not clear that the term could stretch to cover all and only videogames because the interaction involved in the various kinds of videogames seems quite diverse. *Tetris* is interactive in virtue of being a challenge to sensory-motor abilities set within a goal-directed framework. *Microsoft Flight Simulator* is interactive in the sense of allowing the player to explore and interact with a fictional world through simulated flight. It is not clear that these two games share a sense of *interaction* that is not also shared by non-gaming Internet activities or other interactive digital media.

I have claimed that a potential benefit of defining games is the instrumental effect this would have on the theory of videogaming in clarifying the topic and setting out new avenues of study. Here then is the payoff for this rather technical and dry chapter: the definition provided here sets the scene for the following explanation of videogaming. In the coming chapters I will explore the conditions specified in the above definition, showing how each condition exists in a distinctive manner when employed in a videogame setting. Much of the philosophical interest in videogaming will derive from how these conditions interact to produce new possibilities of artistic creation, and also new tensions, given that the definitional characteristics do not always sit comfortably together in their new setting in videogames. Enough of definition; it is now time to move on to the explanation of videogames.

───────────────── CHAPTER SUMMARY ─────────────────

Previous theoretical approaches to videogames do not hold much promise when formulated as definitions. Rather, to define videogames, we need to look into the formal possibilities of definition itself, and construct a definition that offers the possibility that there may be more than one way to be a videogame. Thus, X is a videogame if and only if it is an artifact in a visual digital medium, is intended as an object of entertainment, and is intended to provide such entertainment through the employment of either rule and objective gameplay or interactive fiction. This definition promises to provide a focal point in this study. Also, it allows us to reflect on the continuities between videogames and previous forms of culture, connections that will be explored in the coming chapters.

NEXT CHAPTER

There is an immediate plausibility that videogames are fictions or represent fictive elements. The many goblins that I have fought while playing *Oblivion*, for example, have an imagined existence only. Still, videogame fictions seem different to other kinds of fiction in allowing the player to adopt a fictional role and so to interact with a fictional world. I draw on the philosophical literature on fiction to explain the nature of game fictions, and also to explore the notions of virtuality and immersion, and how these relate to fiction. Videogames, because of their robust and contingent digital media, are interactive fictions in two senses: their props engage players in an ongoing physical interaction, and they allow the player to fictionally step into an imaginary world.

3

VIDEOGAMES AND FICTION

FROM TENNIS FOR TWO TO WORLDS OF WARCRAFT

Videogames have involved fictions from very early on in their history. The origins of the videogame are complicated, with gaming arguably being invented independently a number of times; Steven Kent (2001) is one of few writers to explore the history of gaming. Several very early games seem particularly significant in terms of setting a precedent for games as fictions. In the late 1940s and early 1950s, researchers at MIT working on *Project Whirlwind* – originally an attempt to create a functional flight simulator but later to lead to the first real-time digital computer – made a rudimentary videogame employing an oscilloscope as a display unit, which involved bouncing a crudely rendered ball into a hole (Woolley, 1992). In 1958 Willy Higinbotham created the oscilloscope tennis game already mentioned. In the mid-1960s Ralph Baer, an engineer with the military electronics company Sanders Associates, conceived of a range of television games, including handball, car racing games, and ping pong, eventually being marketed as the Magnavox Odyssey, the original home games console. In 1962 several MIT students including Steve Russell created the videogame *Spacewar* on the newly developed Programmed Data Processor, or PDP1.

All of these early games involve the rather simple display of fictive elements that it is the player's purpose to manipulate with a goal in mind. The games are fictional in that the oscilloscope patterns and pixel displays are meant to represent states of affairs having no real existence: a game of tennis, a space battle, and so on. These fictive scenarios are subsequently used to represent games with possible moves, and objectives to achieve given those moves. In *Tennis for Two*, the idea is to return the ball across the net so that the other player cannot also return it. The ball is represented by a moving dot following an arc over a net represented by a vertical line. The fiction of *Tennis for Two* – like the later *Pong* – is extraordinarily rudimentary: the representations could fictionally be of any number of ball games.

Spacewar is a little more determinate in terms of exactly what kind of fiction it represents in that the spaceships look somewhat like spaceships. In the center of the screen is a star that exerts a gravitational force on the two spaceships – one controlled by each player – so that they respond to the gravity of the central star. The spaceships are armed with torpedoes, represented as tiny pixilated blips that shoot out from the front of the craft. If a torpedo hits the other ship it is destroyed; if the two ships collide they are both destroyed. The object of the game is to avoid the other ship and the central star, while attempting to get close enough to the opponent to destroy it with the torpedoes. Though both games represent a fictional world, *Spacewar* has the more sophisticated world both because of the detail of its two-dimensional representations and the fact that the spaceships are subject to rudimentary laws of physics in the form of a fictional *inverse r squared* force – *Spacewar* has a Newtonian universe.

Other early games utilized different means to represent their fictional worlds. *Colossal Cave Adventure* is a text-based adventure game that involves the player exploring a cavern where they attempt to find as much treasure as possible and return to the cave's entrance. Text-based games involve prewritten particles of script that are displayed to the player conditional upon the player's previous moves in the game, which are also text-based in that the player types in commands on a keyboard. Another text-based game, *Hunt the Wumpus*, involves navigating an environment and attempting to shoot an arrow into the deadly wumpus, *whatever that is*. Again, the player performs actions by typing in commands, and is warned by the computer of the dangers of the fictional world of the game: "Bats nearby," or "I smell a wumpus!" The resemblance of these early games to game-books and pen and paper role-playing games is no surprise, given the historical links between role-playing and videogaming (King and Borland, 2003).

Recent times have seen an incredible growth in the sophistication of the fictional qualities of videogames. Just one example should bear this out. *World of Warcraft* is a massively multiplayer online role-playing game that depicts a large fictional world, in this case called Azeroth, much like that of *Oblivion* in having various fantasy elements, but involving multiple players. Players pay for subscriptions to the game and enter its fictional world through the guise of a *player-character*. The objective of the game is to *level up* the character to gain access to further fictional abilities, skills, equipment, and other unlockable game content. Leveling up is initially easy, but becomes incrementally more difficult as one progresses. In this, *World of Warcraft* is similar to many other videogames which motivate the player by offering them fictional items and abilities in exchange for completing tasks; in this case, very involved and even difficult or laborious ones. Players can band together into groups to tackle the more difficult challenges offered by the game, and some unlockable content can be accessed only in this manner. A group of players might join together to explore a dungeon or battle foes that would be unrealistic for a single player to confront. Players can then split any treasure and equipment that is found.

The fictional currency in Azeroth is copper, silver, and gold. Currency can be collected by gathering resources, killing monsters, or performing quests, and then spent to acquire new spells, weapons, armor, steeds, and other items. The fictional gold is even subject to real financial transactions, with players buying and selling amounts of fictional gold, thus taking a shortcut to the more inaccessible items the game offers. Some have the intuition that this amounts to cheating (Consalvo, 2007), and the developers of *World of Warcraft*, Blizzard, have attempted to deter the practice within the game. The trading of fictional commodities has also led to *gold farming*, where particularly industrious players have found ways to play the game efficiently to generate large quantities of gold that they can then sell on for a real profit. Farming usually involves performing game events such as repetitively killing a monster or collecting resources; such repetitive games activities, characteristic of a lot of the gameplay in *World of Warcraft*, is also called *grinding*. It has frequently been reported in the popular media that companies have been set up, often in China, and reputedly involving very poor working conditions, to farm for gold in a commercial way – the popular media has occasionally dubbed these "sweatshops" (Barboza, 2005). The gold is then sold on the Internet, sometimes advertised through spamming subscribers to the game. Again, Blizzard has attempted to regulate against the practice, in many cases banning subscribers suspected of the activity. Fictional financial transactions are precedented outside of videogames – the fictional money in *Monopoly*, or the pretend money used by children in games of make-believe – and people have long traded in fictions. But in the *World of Warcraft* the financial transactions are represented with such a depth and consistency that what one is fictionally doing – killing a respawning monster to generate fictional amounts of gold – can lead to a real saleable item.

World of Warcraft also depicts global events in which the player might take a role, such as an invasion of Azeroth by otherworldly creatures, or even wars between political or racial factions – though fictional ones. The world is ultimately split into two warring factions: the *Alliance* and the *Horde*. One of the most interesting of such fictional events to occur in *World of Warcraft* was largely unintentional. The *corrupted blood* incident occurred when new content was introduced to the game through an update patch.

The new content came in the form of the dungeon of Zul'Gurub designed for large groups of players. The ancient Blood God Hakkar the Soul Flayer inhabited the cave acting as a *boss* for the level, and was able to cast a spell – or *debuff* – against the players called the *corrupted blood* spell. The effect of the spell was to damage the player's life points, while infecting anyone standing nearby. Dungeons like Zul'Gurub (called *instances* in *World of Warcraft*) are intentionally isolated from the main game world so that multiple groups can tackle the same dungeon, and so that the events that occur in the dungeon have only a limited effect on the main world. The corrupted blood spell was thus intended to remain within the dungeon. Unfortunately, the designers of *World of Warcraft* failed to take into account the ability of non-player-characters and pets to catch the curse and then spread it to players outside of the dungeon.

Very shortly after the release of the Zul'Gurub content, on September 13, 2005, the virus spread to the main game world, apparently through non-player-characters and the pets of player-characters, causing a virtual epidemic. The corrupted blood curse spread especially quickly in the densely populated cities such as Ironforge and Ogrimmar, killing many characters with low hit points. The plague was eventually "cured" by a later patch that changed the nature of Hakkar the Soul Flayer attack. This event is a measure of how rich with possibilities the fictions of videogames have become. A number of scientists have even seen the potential in this event for some sort of study on the way that epidemics affect behavior in populations (Balicer, 2007). The game's epidemic does seem to have interesting parallels with real-world behavior, in particular the malicious spreading of the virus observed in the game that involved an *exploit* (a manner in which players might take advantage of the unforeseen design consequences of a game to have an effect on the game world) in which players intentionally spread the disease by summoning their infected pets into the main game world.

Things have come quite a way since the oscilloscope depictions of *Tennis for Two*. *World of Warcraft* represents a particularly robust fictional world in which all sorts of complicated events become possible. Where *Tennis for Two* seems so rudimentary that the representations could correspond to any number of fictional scenarios – handball, volley ball, tennis, ping pong – the representations in *World of Warcraft* are rather more explicit, so much so that unforeseen practices and events such as commercial activity or epidemics can occur in the game's fictional world. And yet in these examples we can still see the basic form discovered in the late 1950s and 1960s: a fictive scenario used to situate a game. What has changed is the richness and depth of the representations, and subsequently, the variety of ways in which players can interact with the fiction.

IMAGINARY WORLDS AND WORKS OF FICTION

This aspect of videogames – that they depict worlds in which events occur and in which characters might act – has been prominent in the previous games literature, though it has hardly ever prompted a discussion of the fictional nature of videogames. One already noted exception is Juul (2005), though he does not go into great depth in his discussion. It will be worthwhile spending a little time here exploring the nature of fiction so that my later discussion of the fictive nature of videogames has a firm foundation.

What are fictions, anyway? In short, though the term has a variety of meanings, fictions are representational artifacts that depict situations with an imagined existence only. It is this aspect of fiction that is developed in the theories offered by the philosophers Kendall Walton (1990), Greg Currie (1990), and Peter Lamarque (1996) that will form the basis of my theory here. These recent philosophical theories of fiction argue that fiction is characterized by considerations of *pragmatics*. In the philosophy of language, pragmatics refers to the study of how language is *used*, as opposed to language's formal or referential qualities, which are covered by syntactics and semantics, respectively. For example, the basic meaning of the sentence "I love coffee" should be relatively clear from the reference of the words – I, love, and coffee – and the method of their combination, in which *I* am the subject doing the loving, and the *coffee* is the object that is loved. But the pragmatic context in which this sentence is uttered might make it clear that what I *really mean* – the pragmatic use to which I am putting the sentence on a particular occasion – is that I would be pleased if you made me a cup of coffee. Similarly, fictional sentences such as "Gollum was once very much like the other hobbits" can have an obvious meaning, as well as a pragmatic use. Specifically, fiction is a classification that depends on the intention with which a representation is produced and used for the purposes of *imagination*. "Gollum was once very much like the other hobbits," when uttered in a fictional mode, is an invitation to imagine that this is the case.

The usual way of showing that facts of pragmatics determine whether something is a fiction or not is to reflect that a single utterance or representational item might count as a fiction or a non-fiction depending on the circumstances surrounding its creation and intended use. Imagine two texts, one written to recount the life of an actual person, the other a work on the life of an imaginary person, but that happens by extraordinary coincidence to replicate the former text word for word. It is not the media or representational form – in both cases, written biography – that makes one fiction and the other non-fiction, because they share a representational form; rather, it is a fact about their intended function that distinguishes them, a fact which surely has to do with what the author had in mind when writing the text: the fictional work is written to be used as a prop for the imagination.

Gaming gives us a parallel and indeed more credible example of how fiction derives from pragmatic considerations. One disturbing thing to come out of the most recent war in Iraq was how much like a videogame some aspects of the fighting looked. One piece of footage I saw on the nightly news showed the crew of an M1 Abrams Tank engaging the enemy at night using night vision technology. The gunner was able to draw a crosshair over a target using, for want of a better term, a *joystick*, and shoot the enemy soldier with the press of the trigger. It is not much of a stretch of the imagination to conceive of an identical engagement with a screen and joystick happening in the context of a videogame. In fact, *Call of Duty: Modern Warfare* has an interlude in which the player acts as a gunner in an AC130 Specter gunship, similarly picking out targets using night vision in a sequence unnervingly reminiscent of the real footage. The reason why one case is really deadly and the other only fictionally so cannot be traced to their representational media, but to the context in which they occurred, including the intentions of those involved: the military joystick and display screen were intended to mediate an involvement with reality, the latter, with an imaginary world.

Hence, fictions invite their appreciators to psychologically engage with a world existing only in the imagination. There are various theories on offer to explain the exact nature of this imaginative involvement with fictional worlds, though there is also an immediate pitfall to sidestep. If people are aware at all of an attitude we take in regard to fictional works, they will tend to see it as involving the *suspension of disbelief*, the idea originally expressed by Samuel Taylor Coleridge in the philosophical and autobiographical work *Biographia Literaria* (Engell and Bate, 1983). This idea does not get us very far. In fact, appreciators of fiction never suspend their disbelief in fictional scenarios when they encounter them, as this would in most cases generate behaviors on their part that we do not observe. Because beliefs are characterized through their impact on behavioral dispositions, to really suspend my disbelief in *Grand Theft Auto* and other fictions would cause me to perform some pretty bizarre behavior: at the very least running out of the room screaming every time someone aimed a rocket launcher at me. Further, and more importantly, the suspension of disbelief simply does not do the theoretical work demanded of it here. What is needed is not a temporary lack of relevant beliefs, particularly that what is being observed is not real, but a new set of beliefs or belief-like states that what is being observed is a fiction and hence demands the adoption of the new and differing behavioral repertoire appropriate to fictions. As such, many philosophers of the arts now think that the attitude should be positively couched as not merely a lack of a belief, but as a cognitive and pragmatic attitude distinctive in its own right.

Peter Lamarque (1996) calls this attitude a "fictional stance"; both Roger Scruton (1974) and Noël Carroll (1990, 1998a) take the cognitive attitude to be comprised of "unasserted thoughts"; Susan Feagin (1996) thinks that appreciating fictions involves our natural cognitive ability to make "mental shifts and slides" akin to those associated with the familiar Necker cube and duck/rabbit picture; for Currie and Walton, the appreciative attitude is seen as "make-believe" (Currie, 1990; Walton, 1978, 1990). Though they differ in the detail of exactly how all this works out, what all of these positions have in common is that they are comprised of an ability to hold representational content before the mind, not so that it is believed, but so that it is subject to quite a different type of attitude, with behavioral consequences quite different to those normally associated with belief.

All of these theories depend on the basic portrayal of fictions as *representational artifacts that depict situations with an imagined existence only.* Fictions depend on some very basic abilities that we humans have. Thoughts, language, and pictorial representations can be used in hypothetical ways, not to pick out the way things are, but how they could be, and this surely stems from our ability to imagine situations that have no real existence. This pretense aspect of the imagination is almost certainly a key part of our rational abilities to think about the future and about the effects of our actions there. The ability to imaginatively conceive of hypothetical situations also shows itself in the make-believe games that children play. A rich part of the philosophical literature on fiction is an attempt to connect these hypothetical abilities to their nature in cognition and the brain (Currie, 1995; Nichols and Stich, 2000). What exactly the cognitive basis of make-belief or pretense is, especially in its basis in the brain, is not something that I can say a great deal about in this book, and so my reference to it will remain mostly in functional terms. Whether it involves *mental simulation* and *mirror neurons,* and how closely it resembles our everyday representation of the world, there is some functional aspect of the mind that allows us to imagine that things are not the case.

Walton's (1990) theory of fiction seems particularly useful for explaining the fictive nature of videogames. He argues that fictions are meant to engage us in "games of make-believe" that often involve linguistic props such as in novels and short stories, but also involve works of visual art and even sculpture (1990: 63). *Make-believe* as a concept has many associations: we speak of worlds of make-believe; make-believe is a common childhood game most of us can probably remember indulging in or that we see our children involved in; and the term also implies that there are things called *make-beliefs.* Walton employs all of these associations in his characterization of the nature of fiction, and though his theory is not without detractors, I think it does an excellent job of allowing us a purchase on the slippery issues surrounding fiction.

The notion of *play* holds an especially important place in Walton's explanation. Walton asks us to imagine a particular game that involves children treating as bears any tree stumps they discover (1990: 21ff.). As the children explore the forest and come across stumps, it is true in the game that they explore the forest and wander across the path of bears. The children act accordingly: they run from the bears, warn others of their presence, or perhaps throw stones at the bears. Interestingly, the children also seem to become excited and even frightened by the discovery of the bears. But what is really occurring is that the children are pretending that the stumps are bears, and this is at least in part comprised by adopting a specific set of *make-beliefs*. It might be noted, though, that Walton is somewhat coy about getting into the psychological details of what exactly make-beliefs are (1990: 190).

In Walton's example the nature of the stumps influences the games that are played with them. Thus, when a child comes across an extremely large stump, it is true within the game that they have just stumbled upon an extremely large (and probably ferocious) bear. The features of the stumps make certain facts in the world of the game *fictional*. This aspect of fictive practice is something that Walton calls "reflexivity" (1990: 210). Non-fictive properties of the stumps *project* into the game of make-believe. This reflexivity allows Walton to explain how fictive appreciation is enriched by participation with physical "props" (1990: 21). Props ground, prompt, and advance games of make-believe. In the children's game above, the stumps are props that stand proxy for real bears. Walton notes that children often use such props in their games of make-believe as a method of making the games more interesting and vivid, introducing an element of fictive content that is out of their control. Note that this also means that if the prop has features that are apt for physical involvement – a stump that might literally be wrestled with – then the game that involves the prop may also allow fictional physical involvement: the bear for which the stump stands proxy might fictionally be wrestled with. This idea will turn out to play an important role when I come to explain the interactive nature of videogames in the last section of this chapter.

The imagination gives rise to sophisticated fictions like novels and films when artists create props to depict hypothetical situations in an enduring, robust, and detailed way. A novel, for example, builds on a basic imagined scenario by adding descriptive detail so that readers can get a vivid sense of the people, places, and events that have no real existence; a film employs visual and auditory imagery to do much the same, though filling in more graphical and auditory detail. The philosopher Greg Currie thinks that works of fiction "make it easier for us to weave together a pattern of complex imaginings by laying out a narrative; they give us, through the talents of their makers, access to imaginings more complex, inventive and colourful than we could hope to construct for ourselves" (Currie, 1997: 53).

In their dealings with traditional narrative fictions that constitute sophisticated adult games of make-believe, audiences treat the senses of the propositions within fictive works as true in a manner analogous to that in which children take stumps to be real bears. They pretend that the descriptions found in a fiction describe an actual state of affairs, and that the pieces of dialogue found there are actual utterances of actual people. Just as children, in a game of make-believe, apply expectations, understandings, and actions to the stumps that they might apply to real bears, appreciators of fictions apply similar things to the representations found within fictive props. Thus, corresponding to a child's running from a bear, or wrestling with a bear, as appreciators of traditional narrative fictions, participants engage in complex elaborative and interpretive cognitive practices concerning the fictional people and situations that constitute the premises of these fictions; they follow, interpret, and emotionally respond to the story.

Such props – novels, film reels, and so on – also seem to be the source of the apparent enduring nature of *fictional worlds*. Childhood games of pretense usually are fluid or even solitary interactions where the worlds imaginatively interacted with might change at the whim of the participants. It is for this reason that the scenarios of childhood pretense are prone to changing so rapidly and arbitrarily: "This is boring! Let's play doctors instead!" The worlds of these games "exist" solely in the practice of the game, and hence are almost always transient affairs. However, the premises of these games can be documented and thus externalized, and so children might conceivably write out some of the details and history of their fantasy kingdom so that the game might be picked up again later. In doing so, however, this act of documentation cuts loose the pretenseful scenario from an actual instantiation or game, and means that it can be the base of a new game in the future, whether involving the original participants or a new group.

This formalizing act comprises the origin of fiction in a culturally transmissible form, though the detail of exactly how the pretense scenario is formalized – whether by a lone author in the case of a novel, or even generations of a culture, as in folklore – will differ from instance to instance. This formalizing or externalizing process also lends the fictional worlds and characters of these games an apparent *existence* that they do not have when confined to isolated games of make-believe. It becomes possible to return again and again to a single fictional world, or revisit a fictional character on a number of occasions. This, I believe, is the origin of the *apparent* ontology of fictional worlds such as Middle Earth and Liberty City. For Walton (1990: 57), talk of such *fictional worlds* is indispensable in the theory of fiction, even though it has the potential to give rise to ontological confusion if we credit them with any sort of real existence.

Walton contends that the fictional worlds detailed by fictive works are *nested* within a wider interpretive fiction that involves the audience. This is expressed through the concepts of "work world" and "game world" (1990: 58–59). Distinguishing between the work world and the game world of a fiction allows us to draw the distinction between what is fictional of the work itself, and what is fictional of the interpretive game that appreciators play with the work. Take as an example the fiction of *Star Wars*. All the things that *Star Wars* invites us to imagine as fictional – that Luke Skywalker lives on Tatoonie with his aunt and uncle, that the Rebels are at war with the Empire, that Darth Vader wears an exceedingly shiny suit – constitute a fictional work world (Walton, 1990: 58). The work world of a given fiction will be the same for different appreciators, ignoring for the moment cases of potentially ambiguous fictional worlds such as Henry James' *Turn of the Screw*. That Luke Skywalker lives on Tatoonie with his aunt and uncle was also fictional of the world that you observed when you watched *Star Wars*, assuming you did.

It is necessary to differentiate the "game world" from the "work world" because there are many things that are fictional of our dealings with fictions, yet which may not be true of the work world of the fiction (Walton, 1990: 59). Nothing in *Star Wars* implies anything about me as an appreciator, and yet I do relate myself in a fictional way to *Star Wars*. I describe myself as afraid for Luke, or surprised to learn that Vader is Luke's father. According to Walton, given that in reality I do not even believe that Vader or Luke exist, it cannot be straightforwardly true that I am afraid or surprised concerning things they do. Rather, Walton claims that it is *fictional* that I believe that Vader and Luke act in such and such a way, and that I am surprised or made afraid by these fictional events. Specifically, these things are fictional of the game world, a wider fiction that encompasses me as observer of the fictional events of *Star Wars*. Whereas what is fictional of the work world is identical for appreciators, the game world of two appreciators may differ significantly: maybe you were not surprised by Darth Vader's admission in *The Empire Strikes Back*.

Some philosophers are tempted to deny the existence of this wider participative fiction and claim instead that it is non-fictionally true that we understand that Darth Vader is Luke's father, feel surprised by this state of affairs, or feel sad for Luke's plight (Carroll, 1990: 73–74; Lamarque, 1996; Yanal, 1999: 52). But that some aspects of our participative relationship with fictional worlds need to be characterized as fictional seems inescapable: what would we say if someone claimed, while gazing up at the cinema screen, to *see Darth Vader*? We all know that what the observer is really seeing is an actor dressed up as Darth Vader (with the further complication of being represented through the visual medium of film). Darth Vader does not exist. It is true only in the wider interpretive fiction or game world that they *see Darth Vader*. I will have more to say on this issue in chapter 7, on emotion in gaming.

FICTIONAL OR VIRTUAL?

I claim here, then, that videogames just are representational artifacts that depict situations with an imagined existence only, and that they rely on our cognitive abilities to imagine such things. And yet, some writers are actually opposed to the idea that videogames are fictional, preferring some other term such as *virtual worlds*, *simulations*, or instances of *cyberspace*, a term owing to the fiction of William Gibson. In a paper on fiction and virtuality in videogames, Aarseth (2005) seems to challenge the idea that games are fictions by claiming that some of the apparent fictive elements in videogames – dragons, doors, mazes – are not fictional but instead *virtual* items. Edward Castronova (2005), in a very similar conclusion about the status of game worlds, classifies them as "synthetic worlds." I also claim that our cognitive attitude toward videogames is comprised of make-believe; but here too there is a competing explanation in the literature: *immersion*. In this section I will address these apparently alternative approaches, offering a conceptual resolution that sees the virtual and the fictional as somewhat overlapping categories and that reconciles make-believe with immersion.

Aarseth argues that "Game worlds and their objects are ontologically different from fictional worlds" (2005: 1), by which I take him to mean that games belong in a different cultural category to fictions. His argument notes a number of key differences between videogames and traditional fictions and infers from these differences that videogames are not fictions. Referring to a difference between the dragon Smaug in Tolkien's *The Hobbit*, and a dragon as represented in the videogame *EverQuest*, Aarseth notes that the former "is made solely of signs, the other of signs *and* a dynamic model" (2005: 2). It is relatively clear that the claimed difference between Smaug and the dragon in *EverQuest* is in terms of *media*: one is represented through signs, and the other through these things and a dynamic 3D model. Because of its dynamic model, the *EverQuest* dragon makes possible a number of modes of engagement that Smaug does not: "Simulations allow us to test their limits, comprehend causalities, establish strategies, and effect changes, in ways clearly denied by fictions, but quite like reality" (2005: 2). Virtual objects "can typically be acted upon in ways that fictional content is *not* acted upon" (2005: 1). This seems, for the most part, to be true: videogames do involve their players in forms of engagement that are quite different to those involved in traditional literary fictions such as *The Hobbit*.

EverQuest is quite different to *The Hobbit*, but I am not convinced that Aarseth has established that these differences are sufficient to make *EverQuest* something other than a fiction. A minor revision allows us to escape Aarseth's conclusion: *EverQuest* allows the player to interact in ways that are clearly denied by *most traditional forms of fiction*. Furthermore, the robust props seen in videogames and their accompanying modes of interaction do not as a matter of fact distinguish videogames from fictions, because these things can also be seen in uncontested fictions. Fiction covers a wide range of artifacts, from novels, television programs, plays, and films. Many of these include the representationally robust props that Aarseth thinks count videogames outside of the category of fiction. Thus, if representational robustness is to count against videogames as being fictional, it also counts against uncontested fictions like plays, special effects-laden films, and television drama.

To illustrate the commonalities that motivate extending the concept of fiction to cover the representationally rich and responsive artifacts seen in videogames, let us imagine a fiction in which it is the case that a man named Liberty Valance is shot with a gun. In a short story about these events, the gun is referred to through the descriptions in the text. This kind of linguistic fictive *prop* uses descriptions to depict the gun, and relies on the reader's imagination to fill out the representational gaps; subsequently, different readers might imagine the gun in quite different ways. The same or similar fiction might be represented through a picture book: in this case simple line drawings are used, in addition to the text, to represent the gun. But though the gun is now given a much more determinate appearance – it is now clearly a six-shooter, perhaps – it is no less fictional in having no real existence. Now imagine the same fiction in a movie setting. The fictive representation is now film footage of an actor holding a prop gun, and so the fiction has become even more representationally robust than the picture book, so much so that the gun might obviously be a Smith and Wesson six-shooter. In fact, the movie drama might not even use a filmed physical prop gun to represent the gun, given that computer graphics might be used instead, as they have increasingly been used in many recent movies. Nevertheless, whether the gun is depicted by a physical prop, computer graphics, or even a real unloaded gun, the gun that shot Liberty Valance is no less fictional because it is only imaginary that Liberty Valance was shot.

Next, imagine a videogame based on this fiction, in which the player-character is the man who shot Liberty Valance. The gun in this case is one of the dynamical graphical models that Aarseth refers to, and in this case, the player uses it to shoot Liberty Valance. Note that the videogame gun is very similar in terms of media to a computer-generated film gun, so on Aarseth's logic – where *virtual* is seen to rely on an artifact being a dynamic graphical model – if one is to be virtual so should the other. But there is absolutely no temptation to think that the gun in the film is virtual *rather than* fictional because we can clearly see that its only difference to a traditional prop gun is in terms of its representational medium: both artifacts represent an event that is only imagined to exist, though one is made of wood and metal, and the other of *polygons* (see chapter 4). Perhaps we might say that the virtuality of the computer-generated gun derives directly from its medium, and so that computer-generated guns are virtual *as well as* fictional. But what this would show is that *fictional* and *virtual* are non-contradictory categorizations, in that a computer-generated film prop can be both fictional and virtual. Shortly, I will argue for such a conceptual relationship between the terms *virtual* and *fictional*.

Note also that the principal difference that there is between the videogame gun and the computer-generated gun in the movie fiction is *who* is in control of the events depicted. In the movie the audience has no control over how the gun is used, in that the control of the fiction is in the hands of the writers, directors, actors, and computer graphics artists, whereas in the videogame the player is in control of the representations through their playing of the game. Indeed, we might think this is the location of the key difference between videogame fictions and (most) traditional fictions: whereas in a computer graphics movie the audience encounters the fiction after it has been rendered, in videogames the player joins the process before that point, having a (partial) input into exactly what is rendered on the screen. Some of the fictive control usually allotted to the writer, director, or production crew is ceded to the player. This difference in who is generating the content of the fiction does not seem to motivate calling one a fiction and the other not, rather it seems to have a bearing on videogames being distinctively *interactive* (see below). Note also that this demonstrates the falsity of Aarseth's claim that the elements in videogames "can typically be acted upon in ways that fictional content is *not* acted upon": filmic content is acted on in much the same way as videogame content is acted on; the difference is exactly when it is acted on in the two cases and by whom. In the former, the interaction occurs during the process of production of the fictive artifact by actors, writers, and directors, in the latter, during the audience's engagement with the fictive artifact.

Finally, imagine a stage drama of the Liberty Valance fiction. In this case, like the film, the prop gun is a physical object appearing very much like a gun; it might as well be a genuine gun loaded with blanks. Clearly, the stage drama gun is even *more* representationally robust than the videogame gun, but equally as fictional as the gun depicted in the movie and the story book: hence, representational robustness does not motivate the claim that videogames are non-fictive, because it does not motivate the claim that the events depicted in plays are non-fictive. In fact, the stage prop gun can be used in a way that is even more substantial than the gun in the videogame, in that the fiction might easily be adapted – through improvisation – into *the man who pistol-whipped Liberty Valance*. Videogames will allow this fiction only if it is previously programmed into the interactive potential of the game. What this shows is that another of the putative differences that might motivate distinguishing videogames from fictions – their interactivity – might exist in *improvisational theatre*, again strengthening the ties between videogame fictions and uncontested cases of fiction.

Perhaps it might be claimed that the stage gun is *simply real and not fictional* and hence this example does not have the implications I have claimed it to have. What the stage gun example shows, it might be thought, is that some aspects of stage plays are simply real, perhaps leaving space for us to conclude that some aspects of videogames are similarly real (or virtual) rather than fictional. Certainly, a real gun might be used as a stage prop. But the stage prop gun is simply not *the* gun represented in the fiction, no matter how much it might appear to be a gun, indeed even if a real gun loaded with blanks is used. The gun represented in the play presumably has as one of its identity conditions "the gun used to shoot Liberty Valance," but no such real events occur, even if the substituted real gun is accidentally used to shoot the actor playing the part of Liberty Valance. What is real in this case is the prop, and the events that involve the prop, and not the fiction that it is used to represent. What is common to all of these cases of prop guns is that the representational prop stands *proxy* for a fictional object having no real existence: there really was no gun used to shoot Liberty Valance. This commonality across all these cases motivates extending the classification of *fiction* to videogames, though they are clearly of a different kind of fiction in being representationally robust and interactive in a way that many typical fictions are not.

In fact, Aarseth warns against the conclusion that these differences merely make videogames a *different kind* of fiction:

> Of course, it can be argued that the fictionality of Tolkien's dragon lies in the fact that it simply has no counterpart in reality, and not in the material way it happens to be presented to us in games or stories. In other words, the argument would go, both dragons are equally fictitious, they just happen to be presented in different media. (Aarseth, 2005: 2)

In response to this, Aarseth notes that dynamical graphical models can also represent non-fictive things, and that our intuitions about such cases make it hard to sustain the fictive/non-fictive distinction in the case of videogames. A picture of our real Uncle Oswald, Aarseth contends, might be materially similar with a still from a film like *Captain Blood*, but non-fictive in that it is clearly meant to represent our real Uncle Oswald; but what of a *simulation* of Uncle Oswald? Surely, Aarseth implies, our intuitions tell us that such a dynamic graphical model of Uncle Oswald is not equivalent with the picture of real Uncle Oswald *or* the picture of the fictional Captain Blood, because unlike the former it is interactive, and unlike the latter it is non-fictional. The simulation of Uncle Oswald must be something other than real or fictional: it is virtual.

Unfortunately, Aarseth's intuitions about this case only work because he has failed to connect his examples to the relevant examples from fiction and non-fiction. Aarseth asks whether a simulation of Uncle Oswald would "be real or documentary, like his photograph, or fictive like the picture of Captain Blood" (2005: 2). But this is simply a false dichotomy: the simulation is not real like the picture, or fictional like the picture of Captain Blood, rather *it is real like* a graphical model of a real place such as the city of London, or *it is fictional like* the depictions of Lyndon Johnson, John F. Kennedy, and John Lennon in the movie *Forrest Gump*. A simulation of Uncle Oswald could be fictional *or* non-fictional. If it was just a dynamic model of Uncle Oswald it would simply be non-fictional in depicting a real person and that person's qualities; but if it was used to depict events which Uncle Oswald had not actually engaged in, it would become *a fiction involving Uncle Oswald as a character*. In *Forrest Gump*, through the use of special effects techniques, real historical figures are depicted in a fictional interaction with Forrest, and though they are real people, the events that are depicted in the movie are clearly fictional in having no real existence. *Forrest Gump* is not an isolated case: there are many examples from traditional fiction of real people being depicted in fictions, and being depicted doing fictional things. Acknowledging these cases undermines the distinction between fiction and simulation Aarseth attempts to make.

We obviously need to reconsider the conceptual relationships between fiction and virtuality. I contend that the terms are not opposed, but rather that they are somewhat overlapping. It might be profitable to subject the term *virtual* to a closer consideration, just as I did with the concept *fictional*. What does the term *virtual* really mean? Clearly, the word has a number of senses, and it is used in a number of distinct domains. One sense of the term is simply a generic reference to the new kinds of technology made available by computers. Perhaps we would be better to use the word *digital* here – as I have done throughout this work – given its established use in referring to digital watches, cameras, and other new technological artifacts.

But *virtual* also has an ill-defined sense that conflates the issues discussed above, and which adds to the confusion about the fictional status of videogames. *Virtual* in its original sense means "being such practically or in effect." A virtual disaster is an event, which for most purposes can be considered an effective disaster. In computer technology, this term entered the lexicon through reference to virtual computers and virtual memory. A virtual computer, often used in the early days of computing when computer hardware was expensive and rare, involves running a computer program on pen and paper rather than on actual hardware. Given that the pen and paper process can mimic the same rules as an actual hardware running of the program, for functional purposes the virtual computer can be treated as an actual program. Similarly, virtual memory gives the impression of being continuous memory, but instead is merely apt to be treated as such for practical purposes because it replicates the functional features of continuous memory.

Virtuality also now clearly refers to media representations. Drawing from the narrow sense of *virtual* referred to above, I might define a *virtual representation* as one that is capable of reproducing structural aspects of its target, so that it can be treated, for some purposes at least, as a proxy for the target. A virtual representation such as a 3D model of a city can be treated like the real city because it replicates features of the city (such as geography, street layout and addresses, and so on) in a symbolic form. As such, it is as good as the real city – or even better than it, in some respects – for learning the city's layout: practically, one might treat the representation like the thing it represents to achieve some goal (orientating oneself, or learning where to go to find a given street address). This definition of *virtual*, incidentally, does not restrict virtual representations to digital media; I think that a paper map might quite properly be referred to as a virtual representation.

On this reading of *virtual*, there is a clear sense in which virtual representations can present real *and* fictional things. An example of a non-fictive virtual artifact can be seen in the city model discussed in the paragraph above, but also in the dynamic graphical models used to represent car racing tracks such as one might see in coverage of Formula 1, or the graphical models used in the real-time television coverage of America's Cup yacht racing. Such computer simulations also seem to have important potential in investigation and explanation: a computer simulation of the last moments of an airliner crash might use the information gleaned from the black boxes to depict in a graphical way what happened to the aircraft. But often simulations and virtual worlds are used to represent fictional places and events, and this is typically their nature when they are used to represent videogames. Consider the difference between the example above of a simulation used to depict the final moments of a real air crash, and a gamer playing *Microsoft Flight Simulator* having a near-identical crash. Though the two graphical artifacts might appear very similar, they differ in that one virtual world represents events with a real existence, and the other represents events that are entirely imaginary and hence fictional. The reason for this is that the two representations exist in differing pragmatic contexts, the fact that I earlier argued has a bearing on whether a given representation is fiction or non-fiction.

One problem with my application of Walton's theory is worth mentioning at this point. Walton uses the term *fiction* in a rather wider stipulated sense than I intend here. For Walton, even road signs and ornamentation like patterned wallpaper are fictions because they engage us in limited games of make-believe (1990: 276–281). Walton seems to think that make-believe is crucial to our ability to understand pictures and symbols. On this view, I think that most things represented in computer visual displays, such as *Tetris* and 3D virtual models, would count as fictions. Hence, virtual representations might be counted for Walton as fictions in virtue of their symbolic capacities. But I want to employ the term *fiction* in a more robust sense, such that it is meaningful to think of a graphical model or symbol as representing something in the real world and hence non-fictional, something with an imaginary existence only and hence fictional, or simply *as symbols* unconcerned with their real or imagined reference. I ascribe our ability to perceive pictures and symbols to our symbolic capacities, which though no doubt related to the imagination, span our abilities to represent real and fictional things because of their varied pragmatic uses.

I suspect that somewhere along the line virtuality also began to be used in media studies and related disciplines to refer to these fictional issues, so that a *fictional world* became a *virtual world*. The upshot of this was a great deal of confusion about the ontological status of what is depicted in virtual representations, and the nature of virtuality itself. To avoid these kinds of problems, we need to be more careful in our use of these key terms. *Virtual* should be restricted to the narrow sense identified above: a virtual representation is one that, because of its structural features, is apt to be treated as its target for some given purpose. A robust sense of *fiction* refers to the pragmatic location of a representation, and determines whether what is represented is claimed to really exist, or to have an imagined existence only. Decoupling virtuality from fiction, I suspect, will also go a long way to addressing some of the widespread metaphysical confusion that exists in the literature on virtual worlds and cyberspace (Heim, 1991; 1993; Woolley, 1992; Wertheim, 1999).

Videogames are thus often *virtual fictions*. Characteristic of such virtual fictions is their richly contingent representational media, their responsive nature, and their consequent interactive opportunities. In videogames, this virtuality allows the player to fictionally move through, explore, and interact with an environment, for representational reasons we will discover in the next chapter; nevertheless, the circumstances they depict are no less imaginary in the sense of having no real existence. This reformulation of the concepts of *fiction* and *virtuality* as having a contingently overlapping rather than oppositional relationship accounts for the media differences between videogames and other fictions, but does not lead us to reject the very strong intuitions that games – with their goblins, dragons, Russian civil wars, and ghosts – are fictional.

Just as the games literature has characterized the ontology of videogames as virtual, if there is an explanation inherent in the games literature as to how we become psychologically and behaviorally engaged in these virtual worlds, it is likely to be through the concept of "immersion" (Murray, 1998; Newman, 2004: 16). The idea of immersion has also worked its way into the popular and critical lexicons: both players and critics talk and write about how immersive or lacking in immersion a given game is. So, just as the concept of *virtuality* might seem to compete with the application of the concept *fiction*, so *immersion* might seem to preclude the need to invoke *make-believe* in the explanation of videogame cognition, there already being a suitable concept in place. However, as an explanation of the cognitive engagement players adopt in regard to videogames, immersion is unsatisfactory. What it is to be immersed in a videogame is ambiguous, conflating at least three identifiable aspects of gaming cognition and practice, which though related, are conceptually distinct. Because of the multiple conceptual strands in the concept, without specifying exactly what one takes the term to mean on a given occasion, *immersion* is only of limited theoretical use. Furthermore, analyzing the various meanings of the term provides further evidence for characterizing videogames as a species of fiction.

First, *immersion* seems to refer to some of the *behavioral norms* involved in gaming. In chapter 5 I will discuss how games are often characterized as separate from reality, unproductive, or otherwise set aside from everyday concerns. Playstation once had an advertising campaign which referred to gaming as "the third place," distinct from work or home life. The language of *immersion* or *becoming immersed* does seem to align with removing yourself from your everyday concerns and engaging with another form of life. Similarly, people might be said to become immersed in their work, or in their home life (particularly in its problems). What this sense of immersion means is that one sphere of life dominates over others. It is certainly the case that many gamers allow themselves to become immersed in gaming in this sense, and sometimes to the detriment of other spheres of life. Obsession and addiction are particularly acute and harmful forms of such immersion.

Second, *immersion* seems to refer to the idea of *flow*: how players can become so engrossed in actual episodes of gaming that they lose their sense of time (Csikszentmihalyi, 1990). This attentive capacity is sometimes referred to by psychologists as *absorption*, and is a concept discussed throughout the games literature. Absorption is not particular to videogames, and is a common experience while driving, reading, watching movies, or any other activity that takes a hold of a person's attention, and all of these instances would likely share a psychological explanation. Immersion might thus amount to little more than a distinctly concentrated or attentive manner of playing games. Given that a gamer could presumably be less than attentively immersed in a given game and still manage to play it, absorption seems a contingent fact about some game playing, rather than a general theoretical posit that explains the cognitive engagement behind all gaming.

A third sense of *immersion* seems to refer to the ability to *step into* fictional worlds, which, as I will argue here, depends on the cognitive attitude of make-believe and the interactive nature of the fictive props in videogames. The real problem for the characterizing of fictional gaming is not how players become immersed in videogames in an *absorption* sense of the term, but how they play them at all, attentively or not. This is especially evident when we consider that the worlds that players become immersed in – Cyrodiil, Liberty City, Azeroth – do not actually exist! Thus a third sense of *immersion* – and it is a sense also obvious in previous games theory – concerns exactly how it is that gamers become involved in virtual fictional worlds, or how their characters inhabit fictional roles.

I suspect that the vagueness of the term *immersion* hides a serious theoretical hole in many of the works that employ it, especially in allowing theorists to avoid or become entirely oblivious to the fact that videogames often involve apparent interaction with fictional worlds. For example, in Newman's deliberately "contextual" study of videogames, much is made of how structural, political, social, and gender considerations impact on the playing of games, and of their "intersubjective relationships" with other media forms (2004: 96), but the actual cognitive activity or stance involved in playing the games is passed off as involving players becoming "immersed" in a game world (2004: 16). Newman thinks that a concern with the inherent psychology of gaming would commit the fallacy of "internalism" by attempting to explain a cultural form by its intrinsic features. Newman is correct that the intrinsic features of an artifact underdetermine its cultural properties; but proceeding to ignore the intrinsic features of games or gaming activity, as he arguably does, would be equally problematic. In the rest of this work, when employing the concept of immersion, I will try to specify exactly which of the three kinds of immersion I intend to refer.

INTERACTIVE FICTION

I can now develop the general theory of fiction to apply more specifically to videogames. Despite some of the noted resistance to the term, I believe that videogames are, at least in part, *interactive fictions* (Tavinor, 2005a). With videogames and their attending games of make-believe, the props are the complex electronic modal representations stored on electronic media, accessed via a computer program and hardware, and the representational potential of these things generates quite novel fictive games. Videogames provide a prop that not only depicts vivid imaginative worlds and narratives, but worlds that respond in various ways to the interaction of the player, so that if I manipulate the controller in such and such a way, a new fictional event is depicted in the world of the game: the slash of a sword, the casting of a spell, or the grappling of a mutant humanoid. In watching the movie *Star Wars*, the audience has no effect on the events of that fictional world, but in playing one of the many *Star Wars* videogames, the player takes an active role. Nowhere is this interactivity clearer than in the *Grand Theft Auto* series, which is immensely popular largely because of the range of fictional actions it makes possible: as well as the morally suspect behaviors noted in chapter 1, the player can spend their time driving taxis for cash, flying aircraft, sky diving, mountain biking, exploring the large wilderness areas, interacting with pedestrians, going on dates, shooting pigeons, swimming in the sea, playing basketball, and even fictionally playing classic arcade videogames.

The meaning of *interactive fiction* is ambiguous, and I believe that this ambiguity has given rise to some of the resistance to the idea that videogames genuinely are interactive fictions. This ambiguity is owing to variations in the pragmatics of fictive language, that is, what it is that given sentences about videogames are intended to communicate. A non-fictional mode of utterance might be employed to refer to what is true of a fictive work, such as in the utterance:

> *Grand Theft Auto: San Andreas* is a sandbox game that was released in 2004.

This sentence is straightforwardly true, and if we were to look for what makes it true, we would refer to an aspect of the real world. Language in a fictional mode might refer to what that work makes fictional:

> CJ has just stolen a helicopter from Area 69.

Rather than referring to some actual state of affairs, this sentence is used in the offering up of content for the imagination or make-believe, and thus describes what is *fictional*, rather than straightforwardly true, of *San Andreas* (Walton, 1990: 35). This pragmatic difference, of course, is what I earlier argued to be at the core of the fiction/non-fiction distinction. In fact, such idioms are almost always used in close connection with each other, and often a single utterance can be a mix of the ways of speaking:

> The sandbox videogame *Grand Theft Auto: San Andreas* allows the player to fly helicopters and fighter jets.

Here the utterance refers to both the non-fictional and fictional aspects of the game. The mixing of such idioms means that great care must be taken with attributing genuine existence to the apparent commitments of fictive utterances: the above sentence does not imply that *Grand Theft Auto* really allows gamers to fly helicopters and jet fighters.

Because of this linguistic distinction, the term *interactive fiction* can imply at least two things, which are of very different significance. First, the phrase could signify that a given fictive work is a physically responsive thing, apt to be interacted with in the course of its appreciation. All fictions involve some form of this interaction: the pages of a novel must be turned if one is to read it. But videogames do seem to provide a much more robust sense of physical interaction than other fictions because of the distinctive nature of their props. In this sense, for example, videogames are certainly more interactive than television fictions, the latter being notable for their passivity. The physical interaction with a television is minimal: one merely turns on the television and sits on the couch viewing the fiction unfold before one (even though the TV fiction will demand various amounts of *interpretive participation* from the viewer). But videogames are *played* rather than merely *watched* as television programs are, and the player is in a constant state of physical interaction with the gaming hardware and peripherals. The closest television comes to this kind of interaction is *channel surfing*, a practice driven by the usually forlorn hope that there might be something actually worth watching on another station.

Most often, this physical interaction with a videogame involves a controller, keyboard, or joystick, but the gaming can even involve vigorous physical movement, as in dancing games such as *Dance Dance Revolution*, or the recent musical game *Rock Band* where players simulate musical performances by strumming prop guitars and hitting prop drum kits. Recent developments in motion-sensing game control, particularly from the Nintendo Wii, have expanded on this potential for physical interaction. While playing a tennis game in Nintendo's *Wii Sports*, the player might actually move the controller to simulate a tennis shot. In *Resistance: Fall of Man*, a first-person shooter on the Playstation 3, the motion-sensing capacity of the game is utilized so that when the player is attacked and grappled by one of the grotesque zombie-like *menials* in the game, the player must hurriedly shake the controller to fictionally shake the creature off. I found that this particular case of gaming physicality provided an almost panicked engagement with the fictional world of the game, given the unexpectedness with which the menials would latch on to me.

This physical interaction is possible because unlike traditional narrative fictions, such as novels, films, and television fictions, the representational props at the basis of videogames are able to represent content that depends on a player's physical input, and so the content of the fiction varies according to how the player of the game manipulates the controls of the game. The principal reason for this is the technological basis of gaming fictions: games consoles and personal computers might in many regards be thought of as *fiction machines*, producing fictive content given the initial state of a fiction, and how the player responds to that fiction. Thus, one sense in which videogames are interactive, and certainly more interactive than many other fictions, is that their physical props sustain an ongoing physical engagement through the course of the fiction.

But second, and already obvious in the above descriptions of *shaking off mutants* and *making tennis shots*, to say that a videogame is an interactive fiction can imply that the appreciator adopts a fictional role – acts – in the fictional world of the game. This latter sense seems to be the key issue in terms of the fictional activity that is the subject of this chapter. It is in this sense that the player of *World of Warcraft* might contract the corrupted blood curse, or that the player of *Resistance*, while shaking the controller, might *shake off a mutant*. This second sense of fictional interaction is a much more conceptually difficult thesis to substantiate than the former sense of fictive interaction. Just what is it to interact with a fictional world? Obviously, there is no real interaction going on, given that fictional worlds do not exist to be interacted with: there really are no mutants involved in playing *Resistance*. This might lead us to doubt that there really are interactive fictions in this second sense. This apparent difficulty is resolved by acknowledging it is *only fictional and not real* that gamers interact in the worlds of videogames: Walton's theory of make-believe is in part aimed at avoiding this kind of ontological mystery by distinguishing what is real from what is fictional.

The two senses of *fictional interaction* – interacting with a gaming console and interacting with a fictional world – are intimately connected: it is because videogames allow more complex and responsive physical interaction that they enable augmented fictional interaction. Because the motion-sensing technology of the Playstation 3 Sixaxis controller is able to sense the movement of the player and feed this into the representational prop underlying *Resistance*, rendering that fictive prop so as to acknowledge the player's input, that prop can represent that player as shaking off the mutant. The representations of other fictions – descriptions, pictures, and moving images – are mostly insensible to the audience's presence, having been rendered before the audience engages with them, but videogame representations can integrate the actions of the player into the fiction they depict because the effects of the player's interaction are rendered on the screen. Videogames augment fictional interaction because of the stunning developments in computer technology.

Indeed, we can further frame the fictive interactivity of videogames by drawing on Dominic Lopes' theory of digital art (Lopes, 2001). Lopes argues that a number of recent artworks, exploiting the representational potential of computers, allow appreciators modes of interactive engagement that "no other art media can enjoy" (Lopes, 2003: 112). Lopes' theory, developed to address digital artworks, promises to apply to videogames because he sees traditional game activities as a paradigm of the kind of interactivity now seen in digital art. Distinguishing between "strongly interactive" works and "weakly interactive" ones, he claims:

> Games are "strongly interactive" because their users' inputs help determine the subsequent state of play. Whereas in weakly interactive media the user's input determines which structure is accessed or the sequence in which it is accessed, in strongly interactive media we may say that the structure itself is shaped in part by the interactor's choices. Thus strongly interactive works are those whose structural properties are partly determined by the interactor's actions.
> (Lopes, 2001: 68)

Lopes concludes that much of what is referred to as interactive in the digital realm is only weakly interactive because it involves an appreciator merely navigating their way through a predefined structure. Games like chess, however, are strongly interactive because they involve the player shaping the course of the game by making decisions within the framework of the game's rules. Lopes thinks that this characterization of the strong interactivity of games can be applied in the case of many interactive artworks because they share a productive *algorithmic* structure with games. When the interactive object in question is an artwork, the structures in question are those that are behind "whatever intrinsic or representational properties it has the apprehension of which are necessary for aesthetic engagement with it" (Lopes, 2001: 68).

It seems clear enough that videogames often do count as strongly interactive in Lopes' sense: videogames do not merely involve choosing the order in which the representational structures of the videogame are experienced, but involve the player having an effect on just which potential structures of the game are depicted, and how those structures are depicted. Furthermore, the principal structures affected in the videogames under discussion here are fictive ones. Again, games are interactive fictions in a theoretically substantive sense.

Walton's distinction of "work worlds" and "game worlds" is crucial in explaining this potential for fictional interaction. In videogames, the distinction between work worlds and game worlds plays out differently than it does with the traditional fictions that Walton discusses, thus showing how interactive videogame fictions differ to most traditional fictions. When appreciators interact with videogame fictions, the game world effectively *projects* into the work world of the fiction because the work is only rendered after the game has been played. In traditional fictions such as the film version of *Star Wars*, my game world leaves the fictional world unchanged, and what is fictional of the work is true for all appreciators. Furthermore, the events of the work world almost always leave my presence as an appreciator unacknowledged, though there may be a limited kind of exception to this idea in cases where fictional characters directly address the audience, or otherwise acknowledge their presence. This anomalous situation – *breaking the fourth wall* – is found in fictions from Shakespeare's plays to Mel Brooks' *Blazing Saddles*.

Nevertheless, in most traditional fictions, the barrier between the work world and the game world is permeable in one direction only, with material implication running from the former to the latter. Though what is fictional of a work world has an effect on what is fictional of the game world, the converse is not the case. Even in the case where a fictional character addresses the audience directly, the audience usually cannot respond, apart from the case of pantomime, which indeed can profitably be compared to videogaming in this regard. With videogames, because of their interactivity, the game that I play with the work clearly feeds into the fiction as it is represented. In a game like *Mass Effect* that involves dialogue, the player *can* respond to a fictional character's utterance by picking their desired response from a number of listed options.

In fact, videogames may give extra evidence for Walton's theory of participative game worlds, at the very least showing that such participative game worlds exist in the case of videogames. It is very obviously not the case that I can really have a lightsaber battle with Darth Vader, even though it may be possible to fictionally do so in a videogame such as *LEGO Star Wars*. Hitting Vader with a lightsaber is not something that the player really does, rather it is something they *fictionally do*, and hence a part of the game world of the fiction of *LEGO Star Wars*. If we are tempted to say that we really hit Vader with a lightsaber we are merely confusing the two linguistic idioms that I have argued are essential to appreciating the significance of language about fictions: the player *really* manipulates a controller, but only *fictionally* swings a lightsaber.

On closer inspection, videogames seem to undermine the distinction between game worlds and work worlds because the game world so significantly determines what happens in the fiction. Videogames contain the *bones or possibility of a work world*, and demand more than mere interpretation of this work world, as most traditional fictions do. They necessitate that the player adopt a role in that fictional world, or at the very least manipulate the fictional world so as to achieve the goals of the game. The fictional worlds of these games are only actualized – more correctly, *fictionalized* – once a game is played with them. Unless I actually play the game and strike Vader with a lightsaber, no such event occurs in the fictional world; indeed, the game might make it possible to avoid the lightsaber battle by some means. One of the reasons why *Grand Theft Auto* is so popular is that it does allow players to come up with novel ways of succeeding in missions. Thus, different worlds may often be fictionalized by the same prop. The fictional world of my playing of *Grand Theft Auto* may be a more violent one that yours, for example, if I engage in more fictionally violent behavior than you do while playing the game.

And yet the notion of a work world/game world distinction is still useful because there does seem to be a sense in which two different players might step into the same fictional world. If you have played *San Andreas*, there seems to be an intuitive sense in which we did enter the same fictional world, even though the particulars of our involvement in the world may have differed in various respects. This probably depends on the fact that there are still standard fictional features of any playing of the game. In any game of *San Andreas*, Carl Johnson returns at the beginning of the game from his sojourn in Liberty City, for example. But at the very least, the increasing freedom with which players might determine their own activities in sandbox games shows that videogames are eroding the control that the author has traditionally held over the imaginative scenarios presented in works of fiction.

Hence, we might also say that there is a kind of work/performance relationship occurring here (Smuts, 2005a). In many performing arts, the artist produces a script or a score which is used by performers to produce an instance of the artwork, and that performance may involve a greater or lesser degree of input from the performer. It is tempting to see the relationship between a videogame and its playing in a similar light. The videogame might be a kind of algorithmic script from which the player extracts an object of appreciation though their playing. One potential difference between the cases, however, is that it is not entirely clear that the playings of a game really are apt to be judged for their aesthetic merits in a way that the performances of symphonies, dance pieces, or jazz standards are. One may certainly relate to others what one got up to in a game world and how it was pleasing, but when critics evaluate games, they tend to refer to features that are likely to be standard to a large range of playings, and not those specific to a single idiosyncratic playing. This is quite unlike aesthetic evaluation in other performance arts, where it is the unique aspects of a performance that are one of the principal targets of evaluation. Another related difference is that with videogames it is usually the one person who is at the same time the performer and audience of the work (although some games do lend themselves to being viewed by third parties). This conglomeration of issues surrounding game authorship, performance, ontology, and aesthetic evaluation is certainly one that could be further explored. Dominic Lopes (2001) has made excursions into the area in his work on the ontology of interactive art.

Videogames are not alone in their fictional interactive potential, with improvised theatre, pantomime, pen and paper role-playing games, and childhood games of pretense being other cases where participants may play an active role in a fictional scenario, that is, where the game world fictionalizes much of the content of the fictional world. These are structural precedents for, and hence relatives of, videogames. Indeed, they sometimes share the disjunctive aspects of my definition of gaming – being interactive fictions and games – but differ in their representational media. In videogames, the fictional premises that are represented through the informal speech acts and physical gestures of the participants in childhood pretense and role-playing games like *Dungeons and Dragons* are given a more substantial basis in the representational means of modern digital technology: the player's fictional actions and the fictional world in which they exist are represented via a graphical model. What was only imagined or *rendered* in the mind of the player of pen and paper *Dungeons and Dragons* – the look of their character, the sound of their sword cleaving into a goblin – is given a substantive representation in the videogame *Dungeons and Dragons: Baldur's Gate*. This may explain why videogames have all but supplanted pen and paper role-playing, in that the very imaginative nature of pen and paper role-playing both restricts its interest to particularly imaginative people, and gives it a very childish or geeky image. But the general lesson here is that developments in computer technology – principally the ability of machines to create responsive fictive representations in real time – have led to corresponding developments in fictive practice; and so, not for the first time, a technological development has opened up the possibility of a new artistic medium.

CHAPTER SUMMARY

Videogames are fictions because, though differing in representational media to previous forms of fiction, they share a pragmatic context with those earlier forms: they seek to depict situations with an imaginary existence only. We can employ the philosophical literature on fiction, with its details of how fictions engage their audiences, and how authors build props to represent fictional worlds in enduring and rich ways, to explain how these things occur in the context of videogames. Fiction and virtuality are not opposed, but are overlapping concepts, and videogames are often virtual fictions, because their props exploit the possibilities of new digital media to allow for interaction on the part of the player. The player of a videogame, compared to the reader of a novel, has a much greater role in determining the fictive events that occur; this is because the prop renders the fictional world only after the player has encountered it. In fictively rich games, this allows the player to adopt a fictional role in the game world of a videogame fiction. Videogames are interactive fictions.

─────────────── NEXT CHAPTER ───────────────

Many modern videogames employ their virtual props to present visuospatial fictional worlds in which the gamer can interact, explore, and play games. This is largely due to stunning advances in digital graphics technology that allow the fictional worlds of videogames to be, not only functional, but also aesthetically rich fictional worlds. Just how videogames represent their fictive details is an often unique employment of the visual, audio, and even haptic potential of digital technology. Crucial to the function of videogames as fictions is the player-character: the player's fictional proxy in the world of the game, allowing them the ability both to perceive and to act in the world of the game.

4

STEPPING INTO FICTIONAL WORLDS

WELCOME TO RAPTURE

In the evocative opening sequence of *BioShock*, the player discovers a mysterious island, and on that island, a building with darkened passages leading to a bathysphere. Entering the bathysphere, unaware where it will take them, the player is suddenly transported to the underwater city of Rapture, which opens out before them as an art deco wonder. Rapture is filled with horror and strangeness, but also significant beauty. The metaphor of being *immersed* in a fictional world is surely not accidental – *BioShock* is self-aware in a way that draws attention to its nature as a videogame and as a fictional world into which players step as actors.

But how do videogames represent these robust and participative fictional worlds? This is really to question exactly what kind of *fictive props* are involved in gaming. Orientating this discussion around the graphical depiction of game worlds seems inescapable given the prominence of visual qualities in videogaming. Videogames are not solely visual items – they are *modal* representative props, like movies, depicting their fictional worlds through a variety of representational media. *Modality* is a technical term, of which one of the many senses refers to the various forms of sensation – vision, hearing, taste, smell, touch – a given representation employs. Videogames engage at least three of the sense modalities, but their visual nature seems altogether more pronounced than the other representational facets. Perhaps this is partly an accident of the visual technology at the basis of computer gaming, but it surely also derives from the fact that our spatial representation of the world is biased toward a visual format, in that of all the senses it is vision that gives us the greatest spatial information about our environment. One could potentially play most videogames without their auditory or haptic elements, but playing almost any game without its visual elements would seem impossible. Videogames, at least of the three-dimensional variety most familiar from modern gaming, are *visuospatial fictions*. This chapter is devoted to explaining how videogames develop these visuospatial fictions so that they can ground the fictive epistemic and behavioral engagement that is a prerequisite for their nature as games.

A couple of provisos about the limited scope of the discussion are appropriate here. First, what I say here is geared toward showing how the representational props of videogames allow players to generate a visuospatial game world though their interactive involvement, especially where there is a *player-character*. Thus, I do not intend to give a full discussion of the representational potential of videogames. I think this limited focus is justified because the issues that arise from a consideration of the representation of the player-character in a fictional environment are the most interesting in terms of the existing philosophical debates about art and fiction with which I have orientated this book. The theory being presented here can be generalized to cases without player-characters with appropriate modifications. For the most part, the difference will be that in games without player-characters, the player directly manipulates the fictive qualities of the game without taking on a role in that world.

Second, though the representational abilities discussed here depend squarely on the technological capacities of games hardware and software, technical issues for the most part are outside the scope of the philosophical theme of this book. The focus here is not on the actual nuts and bolts of game design and representational technologies, but rather the *functional* contribution these make to representation in games: this book is on the *art* rather than the *technology* of videogaming. But ultimately, of course, the props underlying videogames are computer programs implemented on gaming hardware. The program of a game, mostly hidden from the player's view, coordinates the representational aspects of the gaming prop because, being a computer program, it is ideal for making representational changes contingent on how it is interacted with.

As such, a crucial part of the representational potential discussed in this chapter, and also the game functionality of videogames, is the *game engine*. The game engine is part of the software of a videogame that is responsible for organizing structural features of the game, including cueing artificial intelligence, threading, management of the memory of the hardware, collision detection, physics, and the final graphical rendering of the game. The game engine is also responsible for combining the various representational threads discussed in this chapter into a rendered prop that is apt to base a participative fictive game. Interesting in its own right, the history and function of the game engine is not something I can go into in great depth in this short survey; its importance in the functioning of videogame props cannot be underestimated, however. Any number of books or manuals in the game design literature can be referred to for the technical details of the representational techniques that are only briefly described here, though it should also be noted that the state of the art is developing very quickly. The games magazine *Edge* is an excellent source of games writing, covering the more usual magazine fodder of reviews and previews of games, as well as valuable articles on game design and theory.

The earliest games used the available graphical means to represent their fictive worlds. As already noted, Higinbotham's *Tennis for Two* utilized an oscilloscope as its display device. The representations of *Tennis for Two* are rudimentary, and the resemblance to tennis, and hence the appropriateness of the prop for representing a fictional game of tennis, largely comes from the movement of the "ball" through the two-dimensional space of the oscilloscope screen. As computer graphics have advanced – employing bitmapping, vector graphics, and the sophisticated range of current techniques – the fictive representations of games have become much more detailed and fictively determinate. The representations of tennis in the recent *Wii Sports* are rather more obviously representations of fictional tennis.

The difference between bitmapping and vector graphics seems crucial in explaining the development of three-dimensional graphics, which are central in the ability of modern games to represent their interactive fictional worlds. A bitmap is an array of pixels where each pixel has a defined color value in terms of its red, blue, or green content, so that patterns or pictures might be represented by various arrangements of pixels. Some classic videogames, such as *Pong* and *Pac-Man*, are comprised of relatively simple bitmapped representations. Bitmapping lends itself to two-dimensional representations, and hence to two-dimensional games such as the original platforming genre, in that a change of *perspective* on objects represented through the means of bitmapping is only achieved with difficulty. A bitmap conveys information about what is rendered on the screen, and not about the geometrical content to which that representational surface might correspond. Changing perspectives on or animating an object represented as a bitmap involves animating that change frame by frame by changing the pixel array using much the same method as traditional non-computer animation. This is an expensive and informationally demanding procedure. Videogames graphics still involve a form of bitmapping or *rasterization* in the final rendering stage where the picture is displayed on a screen; the modeling and animation of the three-dimensional elements of videogame graphics now depend on the principles underlying *vector graphics*, however.

Vector graphics is the system whereby geometrical primitives composed of various vector functions represent picture elements. The primary bonus of vector graphics is that the image produced is transformable by further algorithmic operations so that it can be rotated, skewed, stretched, or enlarged, and thus modified in terms of two-dimensional space. The initial use of vector graphics in the 1970s game *Space Wars* had a significant impact on how videogames looked. Visually, vector graphics appear as objects drawn in clean lines, the movement of which does not have the jerky or dotted appearance of earlier bitmapped videogames (the graphics may still appear pixilated due to the bitmapping involved in the rendering stage). Most imporantly, vector graphics allow for the development of graphical models that can be animated more easily. This is because such graphical representation no longer involves animating a scene frame by frame by changing the color values of individual pixels, but by performing transformative operations directly on the geometrical figures in the picture – a much less informationally demanding procedure.

The major graphical development sparked by vector graphics is wire-frame or polygonal animation, a style that led directly to the three-dimensional representation of modern videogames. Polygonal representation takes the geometrical primitives of vector graphics and combines them into complex three-dimensional wire-frame shapes. *Polygons* – closed two-dimensional geometrical figures – are joined together into three-dimensional polyhedrons to construct wire-frame objects. Four polygonal triangles might be built into a tetrahedron, which can be stretched, skewed, rotated and so on by performing operations on the geometrical primitives. Increasingly complex shapes can be built by adding sides to the building-block polygons and polyhedrons, and by joining different sized and shaped geometrical units together. Representations of almost any object or environment – from a gun to an entire dungeon – can be created via such a method. In many early games the polygons are left bare, so that the objects of the fictional world appear to be wire-frames rather than solid objects. In later games the polygons are shaded in so that the object previously existing as a wire-frame now gives the appearance of being a solid object. Textures can be mapped to the surfaces of the polygons to further the realistic impression. With the increased processing power in modern personal computers and games consoles, more and more polygons are now being used to draw the objects and graphical environments of videogames. Game objects can thus appear more realistic or organic because the greater number of polygons used to construct the model, the smoother and less angular in appearance the model can become.

Such three-dimensional polygon configurations can also be animated by algorithmic operations on their vector primitives, so as to represent *dynamic objects*, like player and non-player-characters, monsters, and the other furniture of the fictional worlds of videogames. Essentially, these digital elements are *articulated fictive props* in that they can be manipulated – by the game designer during production of game worlds and cut-scenes, and by the player during the playing of the game – to generate fictional events. For the production of convincing characters and monsters, the principles used to animate these representational figures range from *key frame* animation where the movements are animated frame by frame by manipulating the model, to *motion capture* where the movement is based on the recording of the body movements of an actor, to the new method of *procedural animation* such as that used by the Euphoria engine employed in *Grand Theft Auto IV*, where the articulated prop is given an internal anatomical structure so that its movements develop naturally and convincingly. Such procedural content generation seems a potentially important method of adding fictive richness to videogames; moreover, fictive richness that arises quite naturally out of the system and that does not need to be animated or scripted in advance: essentially, a way in which a fictive prop can be designed to generate its own novel content.

These three-dimensional models or articulated fictive props also allow for the depiction of complex physics, and physics is now a crucial part in conveying realistic fictional worlds. As we saw earlier, *Spacewar* involves a rudimentary two-dimensional physics in that the spacecraft in the game are drawn to the central star. The three-dimensional models involved in modern games allow for much more convincing depictions of physical forces. In *Oblivion*, casting a fireball spell in a room full of clutter sends the various items flying in all directions. When the affected model is an articulated one, the physical effects can act independently on the various body parts, and the interaction of these parts can generate quite sophisticated physical effects. *Resistance: Fall of Man* involves a lot of explosions which have a nice physical effect on the characters who get too close to them: firing a rocket at an adversary will see that adversary *rag-doll* away in a physically convincing manner. Most stunningly, when a *procedural behavioral regime* is added to the model – for example, in giving the model a motivation for self-preservation – the fictive prop can respond to the situation it is involved in. The character models driven by the Euphoria engine can thus shield their heads from damage with their arms while they are rag-dolling. What all of these physical elements really amount to, of course, is that the graphical elements of the game's fictional world are subjected to representational transformations that give the impression of physical forces and internal motivations acting upon the fictional bodies in the game: the graphical appearance of the articulated prop makes it appropriate to imagine the existence of physical forces acting on those fictional bodies, and in the case of the Euphoria example, the agent attempting to protect itself. The modeling of fictional physics on bodies with their own instinct for self-preservation, all in real-time animation, is surely a representational aspect that signals videogaming's genuine technical significance.

Once these objects – constituting characters and their adversaries, monsters, and the other furniture of fictional worlds – are placed in a similarly constructed environment, the representation of this world to the gamer is achieved by placing a visual perspective within the environment. The "virtual camera" (Poole, 2000: 91–97) is an important part of the graphical representation of the fictional worlds of videogames, and especially of the epistemic and behavioral roles that players take within those worlds. Literally, videogames do not involve cameras. Rather, *virtual camera* is an idiom employed by games designers to describe key aspects of three-dimensional representations (Kerlow, 2000: 88–91). In line with the discussion of virtuality in the previous chapter, a virtual camera is a representational device apt to be treated as a camera for certain practical purposes. In particular, the virtual camera is crucial in opening up the possibility of three-dimensional spaces, and allowing a character to move through those spaces. Alongside polygonal 3D objects, the virtual camera seems to be one of the key developments in virtual representation.

Original platform games like *Donkey Kong* represent the action from a static position, and the action itself is confined to two dimensions: Mario gets to climb and jump vertically and run horizontally in reference to the game's screen. A platform side-scrolling game such as *Sonic the Hedgehog* adds to this representational potential by moving the camera horizontally or vertically, tracking the game's action through a fictional world; the game still allows only vertical and horizontal character movement, however. An awkward middle ground between two-dimensional and three-dimensional representations are *isometrically* represented games such as *Civilization* and *Simcity*, where though the game world is represented as having three dimensions, allowing the fictive elements of the game – be they characters, armies, or roads and water pipes – to move through those dimensions, the perspective of the gamer on that environment is fixed in this isometric orientation (though the game may allow a number of different fixed or scrolling isometric perspectives so that the player can get a good view of the game world).

In genuinely three-dimensional games such as *Crash Bandicoot* or *Wolfenstein 3D*, the virtual camera is allowed to move *into* the environment, both showing the game world's depth, and also opening up to the character further freedom to move around in the environment and to explore new areas. Of course, it is not really the case that the virtual camera is *moving through an environment*, given that what is really happening is that the program is performing transformative operations on the polygonal objects and environments so as to give the impression of movement: this vividly shows that much of the language of game design is couched in virtual fictive idioms. Movement in many early games was quite limited: parts of *Crash Bandicoot* and similar platform games are *on rails*, in that the virtual camera takes a pre-defined path through the fictional world, curtailing the detail with which the environment must be depicted. In modern sandbox games like *Grand Theft Auto IV* the character can freely move in any direction allowed by the fictional features of the environment essentially because they are given control over the orientation of the virtual camera. The virtual camera thus defines a *point of view* on the representation, so giving the player a spatial orientation in the fictional world. Though there is a considerable variety of ways in which this point of view is used to depict the action of a game – in particular, I will note the difference between first-person, third-person, and cinematic views – the virtual camera is a crucial development in the evolution of the modern visuospatial fictions that comprise many videogames.

Once the virtual camera is in place, a number of other representational factors come into play, including occlusion and lighting effects. The virtual camera represents the view from a defined location in the geometrical space of the polygonal environment, and occlusion or hidden surface removal is subsequently important so that parts of polygonal forms can be obscured depending on where the camera is placed in relation to the figure. Lighting of an environment is now also common so that objects are suitably shadowed to be convincingly three-dimensional. In animating scenes, light sources are placed in different positions in the three-dimensional space of the game world, adding functionality and atmosphere to the game world. Haze for more distant objects, glare from light sources, and even focal depth blur might be added to provide a more convincing or stylish visual scene. A number of these effects are added in the final stage in videogame graphics (rasterization), which takes three-dimensional geometry and renders it to be displayed on a two-dimensional screen. Rasterization has become a complicated process where *shaders* are able to add in volumetric, color, lighting, and geometric detail to the rendered scene as a part of the so-called *graphics pipeline*. In this way, three-dimensional videogame representations have come to look very like the real world – even though graphics are not always used to render highly realistic scenes, with many games, such as the fantasy game *Folklore*, portraying stylized or fantastical visual worlds.

The principal fictive props of *Oblivion* and *Grand Theft Auto IV* – the fictional worlds of Cyrodiil and Liberty City – are essentially very large graphical models built up by these basic methods of 3D graphical depiction. Liberty City in particular is a stunningly sophisticated graphical model, both in its sheer size, and in the level of detail that the games designers have invested in the environment. Liberty City brims with detail, from newspaper boxes that erupt in a flutter of paper when run over in a car, to all sorts of junk lining the city's polluted harbor and rivers. The procedurally generated citizens also add a huge amount of depth and realism to the game world. Part of the success of Liberty City as an environment is its disheveled and grubby look, which is ultimately attributable to the finesse with which games designers can create realistic 3D objects through the means of polygonal models. This interest in creating a more realistic and detailed graphical fictional world – in essence depicting a dynamic modern city in a virtual way – is also one of the reasons that games like *Grand Theft Auto IV* should be considered art (discussed in chapter 9).

Even so, the fictional worlds portrayed by videogames are often very limited or lack obvious detail; sometimes, they can even seem *incoherent* (Poole, 2000: 63ff.; Juul, 2005). Most evidently, the worlds of videogames are sometimes hemmed in by invisible borders: in a fantasy game like *Baldur's Gate*, small hillocks or water barriers cannot be crossed, and the player must often take linear winding paths though gaming environments. Sandbox games attempt to avoid such artificial constraints by representing very large and open environments, and they do mitigate some of the fictive limitations, but even in the largest sandbox games such as *Oblivion*, the player is hemmed in by impassable mountains or even invisible barriers. Furthermore, there are still many fictive limitations *within* these fictional worlds: in *Grand Theft Auto IV*, very few of the buildings in Liberty City can be entered. Obviously, many of these limitations derive from the sheer expense of the graphical worlds of videogames. The fictional environments of videogames such as *Grand Theft Auto IV* are very expensive props, and represent an enormous investment of labor and capital: this is reflected in the movie-size crews and budgets such games are increasingly gaining: *Grand Theft Auto IV* is widely reported to have cost around US$100 million to produce. This cost really is evident in the detail and size of the game's environment.

These costs are amplified by the fact that graphically intense representations cannot skimp on the details at the risk of introducing material holes into the fictional world. Where the lack of representational detail in a written narrative fiction is not a major problem – the author can rely on the audience to *fill in* much of the imagistic detail of the fictional world – because videogames are interactive and visually rich, the representational gaps are likely to be more troublesome. In some badly executed games, there are literally *holes* in the environments of the fictional worlds where the graphical model has been poorly constructed. A common point in videogame criticism is that the *textures* of a particular game are too bland and repetitive. This is really a complaint that the game is not graphically rich enough in some areas, merely displaying the fictional world via a set of generic texture maps. To save the expense of representing different areas of the fictional environment, standardized textures are used to represent walls and other features of the fictional environment. That some games are excessively modular, in representing the fictional world via a set of repeating modules, is a similar problem.

The rendering of these large environments also makes enormous computational demands on gaming hardware. Portions of the environment not presently represented need to be buffered so as to be available when that area is entered, a problem that is compounded in sandbox games where the player can move in any direction they want (in *Oblivion*, at least my copy as played on the Playstation 3, this leads to a certain stutter in the animation as the player-character enters new areas, especially while running or riding a horse). In many games this problem is solved by breaking up the game environment into sections interspersed with loading screens, though this is frequently and increasingly seen as a flaw in game design. Thus, graphical fictive richness may add to the immediate impression and feeling of depth in a fictional world, but the costs of this graphical richness are artificially circumscribed game worlds. Still, the last ten years have seen the detail of these graphical fictional worlds grow at an astounding rate. Later, in chapter 5, I will argue that there is a second kind of constraint on the fictive richness of game worlds: open, rich, and most of all, *realistic* fictional worlds are somewhat inconsistent with the function of graphical worlds as the setting of games.

Recent games have made quite spectacular advances in their graphical qualities. Just one general example will bear out the advances, and also hint at the artistic significance they have. The graphical representation of water has taken enormous strides in recent times. Indeed, there almost seems to be a game of one-upmanship occurring in the representation of water as games developers strive to top the water effects seen in previous games. Again, the reader will be in the best position to judge the artistic worth of these water effects by seeing the effects for themselves. *Oblivion* makes good use of its convincing water in adding to the aesthetic appeal of its game world. In *Unreal Tournament 3*, a cartoonish and ultra-violent first-person shooter, I recently found myself stopping in the midst of a frantic death match to appreciate the particularly nice water effects depicted in one level. In *Grand Theft Auto IV* the early morning sunlight sparkles very naturalistically, and beautifully, off the surface of the Humboldt River. *Drake's Fortune*, though, strikes me as having some of the most convincing and aesthetically engaging water effects, especially in one sequence on a jet ski where the physical mass and power of the flowing rapids, as well as the water's sparkling surface, are captured in a very compelling way. *Drake's Fortune* also does a convincing job with depicting the wetness of characters when they emerge from the water (and even acknowledges its success in a nice aside from Nathan Drake). Arguably, the graphical representations seen in videogames are one of their most important aesthetic achievements, and they seem immediately comparable to representational advances seen in other art forms through-out history. The stunning representational advances may also provide one of the most compelling reasons to see videogames as a form of art.

MEET NIKO BELLIC

A key part of many of these interactive game world fictions is the *player-character*. So that the player can adopt a *role* in the fictional world of a videogame, many videogames represent the player as a character within that world, making the game world fictions that Walton argues can be seen in all fictions much more representationally robust in the case of videogames. Characters are an important part in almost all fictions, but they take on a distinctive nature in videogames because of the interactivity there. In most fictions the audience is not at all represented in the fictional work world, barring some famous cases from painting such as Van Eyck's *The Arnolfini Marriage*, which depicts a figure in a mirror standing in the position we would expect the viewer of the scene to stand in, or *Las Meninas* by Velasquez, where the viewer may stand in a position of the subjects that the painting depicts Velasquez as painting. Videogames expand on this representation of a *perceiving self* within the fictional world, also allowing the subject to act.

The term *player-character* will be familiar to those who have played fantasy role-playing games, and videogames have borrowed much from these games in this regard. *Avatar* is another term used to refer to the player-character. I favor *player-character* here because it seems more descriptive and so more apt for my purpose of detailing the *fictive* nature of games; unlike player-characters, avatars are often used in non-fictive connections such as Internet forums. I do not think the change in terminology amounts to much, however, as both terms have an established use in the context of gam-ing. Note that *player-character* explicitly refers to the real player and the fictional character – the player is real, the character only fictional – so bridging the idiomatic ambiguity discussed earlier. Also note that it explicitly refers to the dual aspects of *gaming* and *fiction* in videogames, again emphasizing the explanatory theme of this book that videogames are *games through fiction*. The relationship between the player and their character does seem to be one of *identity*: if asked of a number of characters on a screen "Which one are you?" gamers do not hesitate to pick out their character. The character is the player's *fictional proxy* in the game world.

The principal difference between the player-character in a non-digital environment such as *Dungeons and Dragons* and within a videogame usually amounts to the graphical robustness of the character, and the fact that the character's abilities are encoded in their fictional affordances for action rather than in a set of stats and descriptions written on a sheet of paper. Both differences are due to the robust representational medium of videogaming compared to non-videogame role-playing: parts of the fiction that are given only linguistic representation in a fantasy role-playing game are represented via a graphical 3D model in a videogame.

The player-character is still seen most vividly in the fantasy role-playing genre of videogames such as *Oblivion* and *World of Warcraft*. In these cases, the player gets to have a great deal of input into the features of the character. In the tutorial section at the start of *Oblivion* referred to in chapter 1, the player chooses the race, sex, player class, physical appearance, and special abilities of their character. To choose the appearance, the player uses option buttons and sliders to change various aspects of their character's face, the color of the hair and eyes, the hair style, the complexion, and the age of the character. In *Oblivion*, the character is the focus of gameplay, and playing the game amounts to adding to the character's qualities, both in terms of personal history through the quests that one plays, and in terms of the additional abilities and powers that the player achieves as they ascend through the character levels.

The character plays an equally significant role in genres other than role-playing. In *Grand Theft Auto IV* the player-character is Niko Bellic. Bellic is not only an articulated fictive prop in the form of an animated 3D model, but also an epistemic and active point of view on a fictional world, and an individual with a fictional history and personality which we learn a great deal about through the game, and which we also add to through our interactive choices. For example, the Niko that arises through my games of *Grand Theft Auto* has a particular history, which though sharing a great deal in common with other players of the game because of the set narrative and missions of *Grand Theft Auto IV*, also has idiosyncrasies due to my playing of the game. For example, my Niko spent a lot of time early in the game trying to get to the other islands and subsequently seeing how long he could evade the police given the high *wanted* level that Niko immediately gains by entering Algonquin and Alderney early in the game. The branching narrative of *Grand Theft Auto* also allows for Niko's life history to diverge in interesting ways. I also have to admit that my Niko is also an *extraordinarily* violent Niko.

In *Uncharted: Drake's Fortune*, the player-character Nathan Drake is represented via a third-person perspective, and has animated movements that seem convincingly real. Even though Nathan performs physical feats beyond the capacity of any real human – *Uncharted* is a videogame after all – his body gives the impression of having the articulation and mass of a real human body in motion. His running gait is not the unnatural cartoon-like movement of earlier games, but of a human body exerting effort to move through an environment: it is irregular and even labored. Nathan's jumping animations are also especially physically convincing, so much so that *Drake's Fortune* now brings into sharp relief the unrealistic nature of the movement of characters in earlier games: the character animations in *Oblivion*, in comparison, are laughable. To achieve this representational veracity, the game's designers, Naughty Dog, included an unprecedented number of movement animations for Drake, often employing motion capture techniques to model the basic movements. Exactly how the player manipulates Drake through the game, cues the different dynamic animations and Naughty Dog have done an admirable job with making these animations both smooth and responsive to play – the latter is an important contributor to the success of gameplay, as the realistic effect of the movement would be altogether spoiled if the player did not have an immediate sense of control over the character.

Games do not always involve player-characters, however, and in some cases where there are characters they are minimally detailed, or even fictively problematic. There seem to be at least four cases of this *character attenuation* in videogames. The first case is where the game is simply not a fiction. If *Tetris* is not a fiction, then it is no part of the game that the player is fictionally manipulating blocks; rather, they are really doing so. The case may be similar with videogame chess: it is not fictional that one is playing chess; rather, it is simply that one is playing chess in a videogame setting. Compare the case to one in which the player actually is represented as a character playing a game. I am not aware of an example of a character fictionally playing chess within a game world, but *Grand Theft Auto*, where the player is represented as a character playing pool and videogames, gives a parallel case. These, I think, illustrate what it would be to be fictionally playing chess within a videogame fiction rather than merely playing videogame chess.

Secondly, even where it may be the case that the game is a fiction, the player often remains unrepresented in the game world because the player manipulates the fiction of the game in a way in which no character could. In *Age of Empires* and *Rise of Nations*, the player manipulates a civilization though the course of history: in *Rise of Nations* the game spans the ancient world to the information age. The player is not represented as any particular character within the game world, and their role of guiding a civilization seems to defy such a characterization. In these cases the fictive role can best be thought of as a set of impersonal forces that exists to facilitate and motivate gameplay. Conceivably, one could consider the player a *god* in the game world – the genre is sometimes called *god gaming* – but this does not seem to square with the fiction as it is actually presented. There *are* games that really do represent that player-character as a god, such as *Black and White*, but I suspect that *Rise of Nations* is not such a case and that it and similar games are other instances where the player directly manipulates a fictional world without the pretense that they are a character in that fictional world.

The third case is related, and is one in which the character is apparently referred to, but where the role is not entirely consistent with the game's fiction. In *Simcity* the player is given the fictive characterization of being a mayor, but this fictive description is not apt in all regards: mayors, to my knowledge, do not have godlike forces that enable them to call down natural disasters and alien invasions on their cities, and they do not endure for the time periods represented in *Simcity*. The description of the player as a mayor thus seems inconsistent with the fiction of the game, but rather is a partial fictive gloss that relates the player to the fictional world and characterizes their manipulative role in it. Furthermore, because the fictions of videogames are not always the stories of people or other beings, and because these fictions when they do exist are often superficial glosses that exist to implement the structures of gameplay, the game world characters are not always the roles usually occupied by traditional fictive characters. Most bizarrely, in the Japanese game *Katamari Damacy* the player adopts the role of a large sticky ball that rolls around different environments sticking to and picking up a variety of objects!

Fourthly, it should be noted that many player-characters are extraordinarily minimal. *Pac-Man* is a little yellow disc with a rudimentary mouth that is continually munching. There is not much of a game world fiction to *Pac-Man*, and this fits with the very game-like nature of *Pac-Man* compared to the more extensive fictions found in videogames such as *Oblivion*. In car racing games the player takes on the role of the driver of the car, but often nothing is known of their personal characteristics or appearance: all that may be seen is a pair of hands grasping a steering wheel and a name in a list of starters. Another very obvious case of the representationally minimal character is the first-person shooter, where the player is sometimes represented only as a set of arms holding a large gun. In *Call of Duty: Modern Warfare*, for example, the player-character Soap McTavish is a very minimal character indeed, having no back-story or fictional attributes other than those the player can see from their first-person perspective. Chell from *Portal* is another mostly anonymous videogame character.

I see two principal reasons for this minimal character nature, and they relate back to the dual aspect of videogames as *games through fiction*. First, character attenuation is often desirable for the immersive fictive qualities of the game, allowing the player to more easily adopt the role of the character. That Soap McTavish is so minimal may allow the player to more easily project themselves into that role and identify with the character without a detailed fiction to get in the way of that process. Many games – including *System Shock 2* and *Grand Theft Auto III* – leave the player-character's identity relatively obscure in such a way. Some videogame characters have become extraordinarily fictionally complex, as should be obvious from my earlier discussion of *Oblivion*: what is significant about the fictive complexity in *Oblivion*, however, is that the player chooses much of it for themselves, perhaps aiding their identification with the character. Secondly, the attenuation of the character derives from the character's game function as a *shell* that facilitates gameplay. As I will argue in chapter 5, the games of videogames are usually encoded in their fictions. The lack of fictive detail in some videogame player-characters may simply derive from the fact that these games do not need very rich fictions in order to function as games.

The fictive role of the player-character, where one exists, should be clear enough: the character is the method via which the player has an effect on the fictional world of the game and so *is the player's fictional proxy in the game world*. It is essentially the way in which players fictionally step into and interact with the fictional worlds of videogames, and in this it is a way in which the game worlds seen in fictions generally have become more robust and detailed in the case of videogames.

EXPERIENCING GAME WORLDS

The modern graphical advances of videogames have allowed games designers to construct complex visuospatial fictions for the purposes of situating games, simulations, and narratives. In all of these activities the player has an *epistemic* interest in the fictional world: successfully playing the game, interacting with the simulation, or interpreting the narrative all demand that the participant is able to access what is fictional of the world. Here I will discuss the role of the player-character as an epistemic agent in the visuospatial worlds of videogames. One interesting and important theme seen throughout the following discussion is that some ways of gaining knowledge about the fictional worlds of videogames are themselves given a fictional rendering – they are attributed to the fictional epistemic nature of the *character* – while others are clearly non-fictional in merely providing the *player* with access to the facts of a fictional world. This is to say that some aspects of game epistemology are *diegetic* and imagined to exist within the game's fictional world, while others are not apt to be characterized diegetically. This fictionalization of the player's epistemic access to the fictional worlds of videogames again bears out the robustness of the participative game worlds of videogames, as we will see.

The virtual camera – defined as a point of view on the visuospatial worlds of videogames – clearly plays a role in the epistemic access the player has to such fictions. Most obviously, the first-person camera style, as employed prototypically in *Wolfenstein 3D* and *Doom* and now in very many first-person shooters, places the camera into the spot fictionally occupied by the player-character's eyes. The player sees much of what the character fictionally sees – the field of vision is constrained, however, and in many games the only visual evidence the player has of their own body is a set of arms and a very large gun before them. In this case, the virtual camera is essentially an embodiment of the player-character's spatial position within the fictional world. In the third-person camera, employed most often in action and platform games, especially those that involve jumping and climbing where an external view of the character's orientation in their environment is necessary, the camera views the player-character from either a fixed or player controllable external perspective. A single game might involve both first-person and third-person cameras, such as *Grand Theft Auto*, where the camera switches in and out of the different representational styles depending on what the player is doing. Both virtual cameras represent a fictional point of view, placing the character within the fictional world, and providing them with a perceptual access to the fictional world in which they are acting, though the first-person view more closely corresponds to what the character *fictionally sees*. Thus, unlike many fictions where the fictional point of view is that of a narrator or character internal to the fiction with which the audience is not meant to identify, gamers do often identify with the point of view in videogames. Moreover, the point of view in videogames is rather more literally *visual* than in traditional fictions, in that it is comprised of an orientation on a visuospatial world.

The visual means of representation in videogames is not restricted to the virtual camera. Games also involve *head up displays* or HUDs, which include control aspects on the game screen such as mini-maps, target crosshairs, and player scores, and these provide another key part of the visual representation of a game and its fictional world. These are often referred to as *2D visual elements*. Sometimes these 2D elements represent fictional facts of the game world, such as in the first-person shooter *Half-Life* where the on-screen HUD is a fictional HUD built into the survival suit that the game's player-character Gordon Freeman wears: the HUD in this case is *diegetic*. Often, though, the HUD is not meant to be imagined as something in the fictional world of the game, but merely represents functional aspects of the videogame in a non-fictional way: it is surely not the case that the character in the fantasy game *Oblivion* has a head up display, but rather that the on-screen elements there are diagrammatic representations that are not themselves fictional of the game's world. There is a great deal of ambiguity in particular cases, however, in that the fictionality or otherwise of the HUD is not always made clear. Some recent games have rejected such on-screen elements altogether, seemingly in the hope of greater realism. *Peter Jackson's*

King Kong – a game released to coincide with the motion picture – does not include a HUD. In *King Kong* the functionality usually supported by the HUD is generated by other means: the player-character's health is not represented as a number or a green bar, as is traditional, rather the screen appears washed out when the player is injured. *Call of Duty: Modern Warfare* uses a similar effect, though in this case the screen goes red when the player is injured.

Games are modal fictions – they are far from solely visual items – and so a lot of the epistemic access that players have to the fictions of videogames depends on the other senses. The visuospatial fictions of modern videogames are now combined with other representational formats – including acoustic, linguistic, and haptic representations – to further the representational robustness of these fictional worlds. Sound was introduced fairly early on in the history of videogames. In the 1970s gaming sounds were mostly comprised of crude electronic bleeps and blips. Anyone who visited games arcades in the 1980s will have memories of the cacophony of electronic effects and melodies such places involved: the soundtrack to *Pac-Man* in particular became an item of pop cultural significance. Later, more sophisticated means of acoustic representation such as digital sampling would be used. In *Gran Turismo* the recording of an actual car such as a Nissan GTR might be used to represent the sound of that car when fictively represented in the game. Recent games combine a variety of impressive sounds, often rendered in 5.1 Dolby audio, in their complex aural environments. Much of the experiential impact of a game derives from the quality of its acoustic environment.

Sound plays at least two roles in videogames, as it does in other fictive forms: one a fictive representation proper, and the other as an expressive accompaniment to the action of the fictional world. The first is comprised of the diegetic sounds of the events in the fictional world. The squealing tires of *Gran Turismo* and the booming explosions of *Unreal Tournament 3* are of this form. These are representations of the content of the fictional world of these games, as they signify fictional events and properties of those worlds. Such acoustic representation is extremely important in the functioning of many games, especially in stealth games such as *System Shock 2* that demand the character sneak through the environment while avoiding detection. Listening intently is a good way to derive information about the fictional environment. In *System Shock 2* you can often hear the enemies before you see them, and each has a distinctive sound that warns of the impending danger. The sound both allows the player to navigate the environment – enabling them to avoid the enemy, or preparing them for combat – and adds to the emotional experience of the game in that hearing a new and unfamiliar sound can lead to an anxiety about the nature of the sound's source. Players must also be careful of how much noise they make in the environment, because if enemies are close by, they will hear the noise and come running; a dropped wrench at the wrong time will alert the mutant hybrids to the player-character's presence in the fictional world.

Thus something analogous to the virtual camera exists in videogames where they represent sound spatially, both in terms of the player's ability to sense the environment, and their effect on the acoustic environment. Most simply, this *virtual listener* is represented to the player where the spatial pan of the stereo refers to the spatiality of the game environment, locating the player in a fictive position. The sound of gunfire can thus be represented as coming from a particular direction, enabling the player's response to the event. Movement through virtual space can be made to cue different aural domains, so that, for example, moving into a concrete building or bunker will give the sharp echoing ambience characteristic of such environments. *Grand Theft Auto IV* makes exemplary use of such acoustic modeling: a simple example occurs when the player exits their car and closes the door on the acoustic space within, and the car stereo now sounds muffled as though coming from within the car. These sorts of naturalistic and subtle acoustic spatial effects can add significant impact to the fiction. With more sophisticated means of audio representation being designed into modern games, the auditory environment will more realistically place the player within a fictional environment, adding to the art of those games.

The second kind of acoustic representation in games involves properties that are not meant to be imagined as fictional of the game's world, in much the same way that graphical head up display elements are not always to be thought of as part of the fictional world. Games often involve musical soundtracks. The *Medal of Honor* series, a first-person shooter set in World War II, is particularly good in this regard, being accompanied by a rousing orchestral score reminiscent of those in classic war movies. In *Oblivion* different musical styles are cued to different game events or situations such as dungeon exploring, combat, and peaceful exploration, giving these events an extra expressive element. A pastoral scene might be accompanied by music in a pastoral style, emphasizing the beauty of the fictional province of Cyrodiil. The sudden change of style also alerts the player to events in the game world: the combat music can tip the player off to the presence of an adversary before the adversary is seen, and as such makes a functional rather than merely expressive contribution to the game.

Many of these musical accompaniments are not strictly fictive representations, because in most cases appreciators are not licensed to imagine that the music on the soundtrack is a feature of the fictional world of the game. The musical pieces are, rather, an emotionally evocative supplement to the fiction in the mode of film scores. There are exceptions to this – as there is in film – where the music is fictional of the world. A notable gaming example of music being represented as fictional of the game world is the *Grand Theft Auto* series. In *Grand Theft Auto* many of the vehicles are equipped with radios that can be tuned to one of the many fictional radio stations of the city the game is set in. *Grand Theft Auto: San Andreas* makes effective use of the gangster rap of the early 1990 West Coast United States, but if one conducts a carjacking in the rural areas of the game, classic country music is likely to greet them as they enter the car, again, providing a distinct expressive nature to these portions of the game. Various hilarious advertisements and disc jockey banter can also be heard on the radio stations, and add further fictive content to the game's already detailed world.

Another mode of representation of the fictional worlds of videogames is the linguistic representation seen in many traditional fictive forms such as novels and plays. The early text-based games *Colossal Cave Adventure* and *Hunt the Wumpus* were exclusively linguistic in displaying their worlds through portions of text, but text survives even in recent games: again, *Oblivion* is an obvious example, where text is used in menus, subtitles, and in an interesting variation, books found within the game that the player can read to learn more about the fictional world. The game menu is a key part of the functionality of almost all games, and menus are usually represented at least in part textually. *Oblivion* includes detailed text in the menu to keep the player up to date with what is happening within the game world, particularly those parts of the game world that have a bearing on the player's present quests. Though this represents what is fictional of the game world, arguably it is not itself meant to be imagined as fictional in the sense of being part of that game world: the menu in this case is just a prompt to remind the player of the events relevant to gameplay. Potentially, this aspect of the game could be a character diary, but this is never made clear.

Contrastingly, *Oblivion* does have linguistic artifacts such as books, scrolls, and scribbled notes, accessed through the game menu, that are imagined to be part of the game's fictional world. A number of these contain mission relevant detail, though the gameplay hardly ever depends on you reading and understanding the text: it is usually sufficient to only *fictionally read the text* by opening the book in the game menu with the press of a button; the game then tells you the relevant details with a linguistic prompt. The content of the various books and notes does add depth to the game's fictional world, and the player might spend time interpreting the detail – there is a great deal to be experienced and learnt by doing so, including a number of good *in-jokes* – but the reading is not often necessary for achieving the goals of the game's missions.

Much of the linguistic access to the worlds of videogames is comprised of the conversation and verbal interactions that a player can carry out with the characters of these fictional worlds. Indeed, a great deal of some games is made up of such conversational dialogue: *Mass Effect*, referred to earlier, involves the player in discussions through which they are able to learn a great deal about the fictional world they are involved in. Such dialogue is almost always fictional of the game world, but again, like game music and text, the dialogue can be either functional in terms of gameplay or merely expressive. Lucas Arts' *Escape from Monkey Island* demands that the player converse with the eccentric characters on the island to discover hints for solving the difficult puzzles that exist in the game. Often, what the characters say will be inconsequential to the puzzle-solving but will still add to the vividness of the fictional world.

In *System Shock 2* the verbal interactions come in the form of emails and logs from other characters, and both provide information that progresses the narrative and facilitates gameplay by providing hints for completing the various tasks. If you do not listen carefully, you will not know what to do, although the messages are archived on the menu. Part of the brilliance of *System Shock 2* is that these logs add to the mystery narrative of the game, because something of a twist on the *untrustworthy narrator* technique seen in conventional narratives exists in the game. Interestingly, the representation of language in videogames does not always come in the form of linguistic representations: in *The Sims*, for example, the conversations that the fictional characters have are represented through a kind of gobbledygook accompanied by speech bubbles with pictures of the general themes of the discussion. This illustrates the point that, though it often does, the representational prop *need not* replicate the qualities of what it represents as being fictional.

Videogames also involve *tactile* or what we might call *haptic* representation of their fictional worlds. Force-feedback controllers provide the player with information about the fictional world of the game via tactile sensation. In first-person shooters, the controller might vibrate when a weapon is fired, when an explosion occurs nearby, or when the player is hit. In driving games the force-feedback can provide information about the road surface. In *Gran Turismo 3* the vibrate function of the controller gives a different (and uncanny) feel to various road surfaces, including gravel surfaces, tarmac, curbs, and ripple strips. Some arcade games, such as the influential *Sega Rally*, not only vibrate, but also jerk the controls out of the player's hands. These features essentially comprise novel ways in which the fictional worlds of videogames are represented to the player.

ACTING IN GAME WORLDS

The player-character's epistemic access to the facts of a fictional world is essential to their interaction with that world. It is also, as can be seen in the

previous section, itself an important part of their agency in that world: looking, listening, and talking are all *epistemic actions*, ways in which the player
actively discovers the nature of the world in which they are involved. It is
necessary here to discuss how it is that players have this active involvement
in the fictional worlds of videogames. The possibility of fictional action
comes about when various elements of the fictional environment are given
the potential to cue game events: or what we might call *affordances for action*.
Responsive parts of the environment are as simple as doors that can be opened,
mounted guns that can be used to shoot at a shambling Nazi-zombie horde,
or the ubiquitous crates that can be climbed to access higher areas, or smashed
to reveal their contents. Other affordances, as we will find, are more complex in being comprised of apparent intentional agents. Such affordances are
essential to the participative fictive game worlds presented by videogames in
that they ground the fictive behaviors and hence roles that player-characters
adopt in those worlds.

This use of the term *affordance* is obviously related to a use we might
make of the term in respect to the real world, referring there, simply, to
the things we can *do*. A *fictional affordance* in the case of a videogame is
thus an interactive aspect of a fictive representation that determines what
a player can *fictionally do*. The most basic affordance available to players is
the ability to look around and move in the fictional worlds of videogames.
In first-person games this movement is represented by the change in orientation and movement of the virtual camera through the graphical model
representing the fictional environment. A third-person game will animate the
character actually moving through the environment, with the virtual camera
adopting a *chase view*. To move their character, the player inputs directional
control into the control pad or keyboard. The epistemic role of such movement is obvious: a key part of many videogames is the exploration of a fictional
world. Such exploration is needed to discover the game-relevant features –
the spray shops, airports, gun stores, and safe houses in *Grand Theft Auto*,
or the keys and doors in *Wolfenstein 3D* – and over time and through repeated
exploration the player becomes familiar with the layout of the fictional world,
though in games with environments as large as those in modern sandbox
games this can take some time.

Fictive affordances also ground the interaction with objects discovered
in the worlds of videogames. In very early text-based games, such affordances are represented by a branch in the *text tree* that comprises the game.
In these early games, the program was able to parse very simple verb-noun
commands, such as "use key" or "open door," and so the affordances of
such environments were very limited. Things are much more complicated in
the case of modern 3D graphical games, but the principles are still the same.

In three-dimensional games, particular locations and visual orientations in fictional space are designed to cue the possibility of interacting with the world in some respect. These visual orientations will often pick out particular kinds of objects in the world, and so it is imagined that it is the object itself that can be interacted with. Fictionally looking at a key allows the player to pick up the key, to be subsequently used to open that end-of-level door.

Often, the affordances of a videogame world must be *tagged* so as to make their potential for interaction obvious to the player. This is usually because only a limited portion of the game world's objects lead to affordances. In *Oblivion* the affordances are signified by the change of the crosshair icon depending on what the crosshair picks out in the fictional environment. If the crosshair alights upon a book, it turns into an iconic book, signifying that the book can be read. In *Grand Theft Auto: San Andreas* not all of the buildings in the game can be entered, and those that can are tagged with a floating yellow pointer. Glowing items are also a ubiquitous way of tagging affordances for interaction. Sometimes such tags can lead to fictional incongruities, in that it is surely not *fictional* that there is a glowing pointer in front of some of the doors in *Grand Theft Auto*, but rather that the pointer represents that a building offers the affordance of being entered and explored.

This example illustrates two important points about the affordances offered by videogames. First, the affordances of games are often represented by functional devices such as icons and pointers that are not themselves fictional of the game world. Second, videogame affordances clearly represent an impoverished subset of the action affordances of the real world (though they also involve a number of affordances not allowed in the real world, such as the ability to take multiple hits from a high-powered assault rifle, survive, and be completely healed by walking over a health pack).

Fictional interaction with a world ultimately depends on real interaction with some form of controller. Usually, such physical interaction is achieved through the manipulation of a joystick, a keyboard and mouse, or a gamepad. In most of these cases the control movements are not apt to be assimilated into the fictional game world: the double tapping of an x button to perform a high jump in *Unreal Tournament 3* is not something that bears a great deal of resemblance to the action it controls, and so is not obviously apt to be described as fictional of the game. Videogames are increasingly allowing players to engage in *simulated* physical movements to represent their actions in a fictional world, however. As noted, *Resistance* allows its players to shake a motion-sensing controller as a means of fictionally shaking off a mutant. Even more vividly, the Nintendo Wii allows players to simulate tennis shots, punching in a boxing match, and so forth, by moving in ways that (roughly) represent those actual activities. In these cases, unlike the button presses in *Unreal Tournament*, the player's movement does seem to fictively correspond to their fictional movement in the world of the game. Such simulated actions also seem to illustrate the clear link between these participative game worlds and childhood pretense where participants often represent their pretended actions by simulating physical movements associated with those actions. The difference between videogames and childhood pretense is that the videogame player's movement – recorded by the motion-sensing controller – is given a robust graphical representation by the fictive prop.

The menu is an equally important way in which games represent their affordances for fictional interaction, though menus also support aspects of game functionality such as loading and saving, mission selection, control schemes, graphics and audio adjustment, and so on. The issues here are similar to the game functional HUD and its occasional fictional or diegetic representation, discussed earlier. Like the HUD, the menu often sits alongside the fiction and is not itself imagined to be part of the fictional scenario in which the gamer is playing: it is merely a non-fictive way to control or represent aspects of the game. Increasingly, though, game menus do seem to be represented as a part of the fictional world. *Grand Theft Auto IV* moves a lot of the menu into the game world by representing it in the form of a fictional mobile phone. Mission selection is fictionalized as a matter of accepting a mission offered to the player via a text message or call on the phone. *Assassin's Creed* goes a step further and portrays its game scenario – an assassin in the Middle East during the Middle Ages – as being *nested* in a further fiction that allows for the fictional explanation of almost all of its menu and on-screen HUD elements. The HUD elements and menu in this case are parts of a near-future science fiction world that allows the player to interact with the historical world in which the gameplay occurs. Given that players are quite accustomed to accepting the non-fictive and functional aspects of videogames, is such a fictionalization of a game's functional aspects really necessary or desirable? Audiences of traditional fictions are also asked to put certain factors out of their minds when appreciating fictions, of course: the opening credits are usually no obstacle to film audiences engaging and enjoying the fictional content of a movie. Arguably, whether or not a given fictionalization of game functions is warranted will come down to the success of individual cases, and whereas *Grand Theft Auto IV* is quite successful in its fictionalization of the menu as a mobile phone, *Assassin's Creed* seems a much less convincing example.

As noted earlier, conversational interaction with game characters provides an important mode of epistemic access to some game worlds, and this is also thus an important kind of affordance. A player's verbal participation in fictional worlds of videogames is usually mediated by a non-verbal means, by picking a sentence from a menu. However, some games have attempted to allow players to literally talk to games, such as the Sega Dreamcast game *Seaman*, which involves voice recognition technology. In this case, the player fictionally converses with what is essentially a digital pet by actually conversing with the digital prop, again illustrating the potential of videogames for richly represented participative fictions.

Such conversational affordances are only one of the ways in which *non-player-characters* constitute a particularly important kind of affordance. These aspects of videogames provide their own challenges in terms of representation given that their affordances for interaction are by their nature much more complicated than the inert furniture of fictional worlds such as doors and keys. Such intelligent agents differ to the more inert parts of a visuospatial world by representing a greater range of affordances for interaction. Whereas pot plants merely have to move around when you push them, or shatter when dropped or shot, an intelligent agent needs to be able to respond with more complex behaviors. Sometimes, especially in multiplayer first-person shooters or real-time strategy games, these agents are called *bots*, and in this case are little more than things to shoot at and be shot by. The bots in *Unreal Tournament 3* have to be able to represent the actions of an agent capable of playing these games. In the *Call of Duty* series – a squad-based first-person shooter where the player collaborates with non-player-characters – the bots need to be able to cooperate with the player.

Thus, non-player-characters have more complexly responsive dimensions programmed into their props so that the character can be predicted or at least be explained in terms of the *intentional idioms* often discussed by philosophers (Dennett, 1987). This feature of videogames is referred to under the rubric of *artificial intelligence*. The intelligence of agents within games – or more usually the lack of intelligence – is a crucial part of gaming criticism. Even though artificial intelligence in games has improved, personal experience informs me that enemies and even allies still blindly run into your line of fire, walk into walls, shoot their companions, or even madly run around in circles – things that intelligent agents in the real world tend not to do. Despite their relative sophistication, the squad members in *Call of Duty: Modern Warfare* are still pretty stupid. The problem of artificial intelligence in games does seem to be a partial version of the general problem of artificial intelligence seen in philosophy and cognitive science, but partially differs, I think, in that game designers seem not to aim for intelligence, but for a *predictability* that allows the non-player-character to function as a part of the game.

Both epistemology and action within a game world presuppose the enduring existence of a fictional world, and moreover a world that is predictable and somewhat coherent. As we have seen, the representational modalities of videogame fictions are discrete three-dimensional models, animations, physics protocols, environmental sounds, music tracks, pieces of dialogue, and so forth. For comparison, a movie is a modal prop and in this case the process of *editing* performs the function of rending the discrete representational threads into a fictional, narrative, and stylistic whole. But because they are interactive fictions, the fictional worlds of videogames are only rendered once they are played, and this demands a representational prop capable of combining the representational threads of a given game in *real time*. In videogames, it is the game engine that binds these disparate representations of content together into a coherent whole that it becomes appropriate to characterize as a fictional world. As I noted earlier, the game engine deals with game functions besides those that directly contribute to the fictional coherence of a videogame world, such as memory management and threading. But at least part of its function is to provide a sense of order and predictability for the fictional worlds of videogames, for example in binding animations, sounds, affordances, collision detection, and physics into a coherent whole that is apt to support the fiction of Niko Bellic exploring Liberty City. The nature of the fictive props at the basis of fictive videogames, then, is of a world-generator that holds a fictional world in limbo, existing as a network of representational possibilities to be fictionalized once a player takes up the controls to explore, act, and most of all, play a game. It is to the topic of gaming that I move in the next chapter.

CHAPTER SUMMARY

Modern, fictively rich videogames such as *Grand Theft Auto* and *Oblivion* allow their players to step into a visuospatial fictional world in the guise of a player-character. The player-character is the player's epistemic and behavioral proxy in the game world, allowing them to discover the many facts of the fictional world, and to act in that world. The representational developments that allow for this fictional interaction – in particular 3D representational space, the virtual camera, game menus, head up displays, acoustic environments, and haptic elements – have seen significant developments in a very short time, and are now able to depict game worlds in aesthetically rich ways. Functionally, these representational techniques, and their foundations in the game engine, serve to buffer a robust fictional world apt to support various entertainment functions.

NEXT CHAPTER

Chief among the entertainment functions of the virtual fictional worlds of videogames is gaming. Games can be usefully characterized as artifacts that involve the formal qualities of rules and objectives set in a framework of pre-scribed behaviors. Both these formal and situational aspects of videogames seem heavily dependant on the nature of videogames as virtual fictions, and so we can profitably explain the gaming aspect of videogames in terms of their fictions. Using an actual example of gameplay, I explore how videogames employ rich interactive fictions to depict game rules and the prescribed interactions of players. But characterized in this way, some of what is routinely called gameplay actually involves things other than playing a game: most importantly, freeplay, or the mere toying with or exploring of a fictional system.

5

GAMES THROUGH FICTION

THE NATURE OF GAMING

We have seen how videogames are often comprised of robustly represented interactive fictions in which a player-character takes on a perceiving and active role. Usually, though not always, these fictional worlds are created with the intention of situating a game. The gaming nature of videogames looms large in their playing and appraisal, frequently trumping other considerations in criticism: a game can fail despite displaying a convincing interactive world, flashy graphics or an engaging narrative if its gameplay is unappealing or otherwise flawed. *Myst* is perhaps the most famous example of a graphically excellent game that was criticized from a gameplay perspective.

In what ways do videogames count as games? What is a game anyway? This, as many will be aware, is a question with a philosophical heritage in playing the role of an incidental example in Ludwig Wittgenstein's philosophy (Wittgenstein, 1968). The definition of gaming need not detain us here, however: it is not important whether the entire range of things that are called games can be given a definition, but rather that uncontested examples of games can be given satisfactory explanations that when transferred to videogames also prove to be satisfactory there. Even if games cannot be given an essentialist definition, we can at least compare videogames to traditional games such as chess, rugby union, tic-tac-toe, asking in which ways they are similar, and how they differ to these non-digital precedents.

The gaming nature of videogames is most obviously referred to by the term *gameplay*. What is gameplay? How are games played? I could approach these questions with a near vacuous definition of gameplay as *the interactive involvement typically associated with videogames*, that is, the activities that occur when one *plays a videogame*. This initial characterization of gameplay rides carelessly over at least two important variations in gameplay. First, if gameplay signifies how videogames are interacted with, then it includes the following of narratives, empathizing with characters, an aesthetic appreciation of graphical depictions, and a great deal else that does not seem typical of traditional forms of gaming, but rather derives from the partial nature of videogames as narratives, fictions, and graphical artifacts. As argued in my earlier definition, videogames have a mix of artifactual functions, and this has an impact on how they engage their players. Playing videogames, it turns out, does not necessarily amount to *playing a game*.

Second, even when it comes to more clearly *gaming* aspects of what can be seen in videogames – those activities that can also be seen in cases of traditional non-videogaming – there is an important variation seen in the game activities that players engage in. Chess, we might initially think, is a pretty good example on which to base our understanding of games and how they are played. In chess we see the key role that the ideas of legal moves and objectives play. The game provides an area of play divided into spaces, a number of legal and illegal moves for each piece, a starting configuration, and an objective that the players must aim for if they are to win the game. In chess we also see the role of player investment in the outcome, and competition between different players. But unlike games such as chess that are structured around rules and objectives, player investment and competition, some of the things we call games encourage *freeplay*. In freeplay there are no pre-specified objectives, but rather the player *fiddles* or *toys* with the game, mostly unconcerned with some desired end state, perhaps even specifying their own goals along the way. *Play*, in this case, seems to be much closer to the sense in which children might play in a sandbox, using various toys to play out a fictional scenario or participate in games of make-believe. We can see this type of play in videogames such as *Simcity* and *Microsoft Flight Simulator*, where players engage with a fictional world or system for the purposes of entertaining themselves with its details and possibilities. Though they also involve aspects of rule and objective motivated gameplay, free-gaming is also seen in sandbox games such as *Grand Theft Auto* and *Oblivion*, thus explaining that idiom. A source of great fun in *Grand Theft Auto* in particular is exploring and interacting with its detailed fictional environments, perhaps even ignoring the objective-driven activities or *missions* that are represented within that world, or even setting the terms of your own missions: how long can I avoid the cops if I enter this restricted area? James Newman (2004: 20) calls this freeplay aspect of videogaming "paidea," contrasting it with "ludic" games such as chess where there are pre-specified goals and objectives.

Thus videogames might count as games in a *strong* and *weak* sense. A strong sense of *game* is the rule and objective based ludic gaming in which it makes sense to say what it is to win a game or to ask what the rules or possible moves are. The weaker sense – drawing from the phrase "to make a game of something" – refers to those cases where videogames encourage freeplay, exploration, and imaginative involvement in much the same way as toys and some fictions do. Juul (2005) sees this latter form of gaming as having a particularly strong fictive component, allowing his theory to cover games that do not sit squarely within the traditional rule and objective conception of gaming, or "classic game model." Indeed, if we characterize freeplay as the playing with a fictional world or system, as I think is justified, then these two activities – objective-directed gaming and freeplay – align fairly well with my initial definition of videogames, where I claimed that the modes of interaction necessary in videogames were rule and objective gaming or interactive fiction.

We can now also see that the disjunctive aspect of my definition depends on a particular sense of the term *game* where it refers to activities in the mode of chess, where there are predefined goals and prescriptions of legal and illegal moves: the rules of the game. More widely defined, it seems that even an interactive fiction might count as a game, in the same sense that playing in a sandbox, or playing with one's mashed potatoes at dinner, might count as a game. Of course, *playing* and *games* seem to be so varied in meaning – and consequently so ubiquitous in existence – that I doubt they are particularly theoretically meaningful without significant limitations placed on their intended meaning.

With this distinction between a strong and a weak sense of gaming now made, I will narrow my principal focus in this chapter to the strong sense of *objective-driven* games. What are games in this mode, and how do they function? Such goal-directed videogaming is perhaps most easily approached in the case of the *transmedial* games that were noted earlier, given that the theories of games that I will look at here were originally designed to account for these transmedial games in their non-videogame setting. Some videogames, I noted, have migrated into the digital arena, previously having an existence as non-digital games. Games such as chess and *Sudoku*, while retaining the same rules as their non-digital counterparts – and hence counting as tokens of chess and *Sudoku* – become videogames when portrayed in a digital visual setting.

Given that *Sudoku* is a puzzle, it is now also obvious that there is a further distinction to be drawn here: that between games and puzzles. Puzzles are clearly related to games. Though I will not attempt to build a substantive theory of the differences between puzzles and games here – I do not assume that such a distinction can even be unequivocally drawn – I think that the distinction seems to be entailed by the difference between *winning* and *finding a solution*. Games – at least some clear cases of games such as chess and soccer – employ formal rules and objectives to set players in competition with each other to reach a mutually exclusive objective. Puzzles seem to involve reducing the tension or complications within a system so that a stable end state or resolution can be reached. If this really is how the distinction is to be drawn, I think that videogames clearly involve both forms of play. Games like *God of War*, for example, have puzzle sections interspersed through the game so that the player cannot proceed without finding a solution to the puzzles. *Portal* is an interesting case in providing puzzles that involve the fictional traversing of spaces.

There seem to be two crucial parts needed in the explanation of both games and puzzles: the *formal* qualities that the game or puzzle has, and the *behavioral and social situation* in which those formal qualities are put into use by players. The formal aspect concerns the qualities of a particular game or puzzle, its rules, starting configuration, possible moves, objectives, solution, and so on. The latter situational aspects concern the distinctive mode with which such formal artifacts are engaged and how they relate to the rest of the world, such as that they involve group or solitary play, competition or cooperation, player investment in the outcome, and that the events in the games are thought to have only limited consequences for the real world. A great many games, such as soccer, checkers, and *Monopoly*, depend on variations in these dual formal and situational parameters, as do videogames such as *Tetris*, *Donkey Kong*, and *Call of Duty*.

Juul's (2005: 36–43) discussion of gaming promises to be of use in explaining both of these kinds of features. As noted earlier, Juul compares a number of previous theories of gaming, showing them to have a core of shared features. Looming large in this "classic game model," and in Juul's own subsequent definition of gaming, is the role of game *rules*. At the very least, games involve rules, and an objective – what it is to win the game – that is meant to be achieved in terms of those rules. A game rule is a principal formal quality of a game. These rules of a game prescribe legal and illegal moves, but also open up a game space in terms of those rules: they make possible certain progressions of the game. Juul thinks the fact that the rules of a game like chess are both *restrictive* and *productive* is something of a paradox, but it is not surprising at all, and seems to be a pattern shared with other *meaningful* domains. Language, likewise, involves a restricted set of combinatorial relations which opens up a productive realm of meanings (Pinker, 1994). Without restricting what it is to count as meaningful (or within the rules of a game) then one cannot make meaningful utterances (or make a move in a game).

Juul (2005: 61–63) is tempted to characterize the rules and objectives of games in terms of *algorithms*. Using the game of tic-tac-toe as his principal example, he thinks that the game can be described in terms of a series of states, legal state transitions, and terminating states. The rules of a game place restrictions on the types of initial states, state transitions, and objectives that are allowed. Any particular game of tic-tac-toe begins with an opening state (a blank grid of nine squares), a defined set of legal state transitions (players are to alternately place their marker in a free square), and a set of terminating states that define the objective of the game (play continues until all squares are full or a player has connected three adjacent markers, the latter counting as a win). Because of its simplicity, tic-tac-toe has a determinate number of algorithmic profiles, or combinations of state transitions, making the game predictable to the extent that some moves become obligatory (if one wants to win or avoid losing). Though it is much more complicated, chess can be given a description in terms of opening state, state transitions, and terminating states: in this case the state transitions are the various moves ascribed to the particular pieces, and the terminating states are stalemate or checkmate.

In the case of non-videogames, these formal factors – rules about legal and illegal moves, the starting state, the end state or objective – are often encoded in declarative linguistic statements that are known prior to the game, and that can be usefully set out in a rule book. This is to say that the "algorithms" of the game can be set out linguistically, and the "program is run" when players enact those rules and thus give them an interpretation. In the next section I will argue that just how the game states are encoded in videogames is a key difference they have to earlier types of gaming.

Juul is correct that games such as tic-tac-toe and chess (and also the objective-directed gaming seen in videogaming) can be given such an algorithmic analysis. And of course, in the case of videogames, games are quite clearly encoded in a computer algorithm. I am not convinced that the idea *by itself* is of much explanatory use, however: algorithms are much too ubiquitous to be of use in explanation here. Indeed, a great many things that are not games can be seen as algorithms: making a pot of tea, for instance, could be characterized as an interpretation of defined initial state, state transitions, and terminating states, but, of course, this does not make tea-making a game. The algorithmic nature of videogames seems to derive from their nature as deterministic or computable systems that have the features of "substrate neutrality," "underlying mindlessness," and "guaranteed results" (Dennett, 1995: 50–51). Thus the introduction of algorithms alone does not do the work needed of it in telling us exactly what games are and how they function. As such, Juul's discussion is primarily of terminological use, in giving us an alternative way to *describe* games and their rules and objectives.

Characterizing games as an algorithm does allow us to see the incompleteness of a *formal* characterization of gaming, however. What needs to be described is not only the type of algorithm involved in a game, but also the nature of its *interpretation*. Games seem to become games partly in virtue of their accompanying *situational norms.* This is just to say that a game is more than a set of formal rules, it is also an interpretation of those rules in terms of recommended behaviors and practices: that is, how the formal system is used for the purposes of entertainment, competition, or whatever. Indeed, making a pot of tea might become a game if it was situated within a certain behavioral framework: in *The Sims,* such domestic activities have become the topic of gameplay. Similarly, tea-making might become an art form if set in another kind of behavioral framework, as it is in Japanese tea ceremonies.

Fortunately, a number of the earlier definitions detailed by Salen and Zimmerman (2004) in their exhaustive and influential work on videogame design pick out situational factors in addition to formal considerations, referring to a number of earlier theories of gaming. Johan Huizinga (1950) sees gaming as being outside of ordinary life and being unproductive, a thesis which many games theorists have referred to in a general way with Huizinga's rather more specific term, "magic circle." Roger Caillois (1961) characterizes gaming as being voluntarily engaged in, separate from the rest of reality, and unproductive. The separateness referred to in both of these theories seems obvious in many games: in rugby union, for example, the events that happen on the field, which are often quite violent, are ideally held to be somewhat separate from reality: *what happens on the field stays on the field.* A great number of games also seem unproductive: surely, almost all games of checkers are played with no extrinsic goals in mind, but merely with the aim of engaging with and enjoying the activity itself.

Juul's own definition of gaming includes the situational features of "player effort," "player attachment to outcome," and the rather opaque notion of "negotiable consequences" (2005: 36). The latter seems intended to cover something of the apparent separateness and lack of productivity or extrinsic interests seen in the theories of Huizinga and Caillois, but sees these as being negotiable, because of the instances of gaming where games have a significant impact on reality (in a football match, for example) or where games are productive or have extrinsic ends (for example, in gambling). Nevertheless, all of these features illustrate how the formal systems of rules and favored objectives in games are subjected to a range of prescribed behaviors that generate a somewhat distinctive mode of social engagement that is gaming.

This relatively simple theory of games as comprised of a collection of formal possibilities and objectives engaged in with the intention of situating a certain kind of behavioral interaction will provide the explanatory framework as I now explain how videogames – especially the fictively rich variety explored in previous chapters – situate their games. There will be two parts to this explanation: in the next section I discuss how videogames encode the formal qualities of their games, focusing on cases where representationally robust fictions are employed for this function. I then move on to explain the situational aspects of gaming, especially those involving player investment, and competition and cooperation between players, also referring to some unexpected activities, and again making particular reference to how the fictive nature of many games has important consequences for the issue.

Thus, a further note about the scope of my discussion in the following sections is necessary. Gameplay is incredibly diverse, and my discussion here is necessarily limited. My focus in previous parts of this book has been on games with robust virtual or visuospatial fictional worlds, particularly where there is a player-character in those worlds who counts as a fictional proxy. A typical game of this kind is *Grand Theft Auto IV*. Hence, for the most part, I will discuss how the formal and situational features of videogames are encoded in these fictively rich settings. Only a much longer and more specific work could flesh out this theory to be truly general so as to apply to non-fictively robust games such as *Tetris*. Again, my principal purpose here is to tease out the issues in gaming that are most interesting and fruitful for the philosophy of the arts, and these seem to me to be the fictively robust cases. This is not to say that the discussion here has nothing to say about the cases where the fiction of a game is much more minimal, and I hope the reader will be able to see how the general theory can be developed to apply to those cases.

WHAT ARE THE RULES OF THIS GAME?

A game like *Grand Theft Auto IV* depicts the formal features of its game – its initial states, legal state transitions, and terminating states, as Juul would have it – in terms of a fictive scenario. The game is *encoded* in a fiction. *Form* is often contrasted with *content*, so that we might speak of the *sonata form* of a symphonic movement, referring to its conventionally derived structural arrangement; but we can also go on to discuss the melodic, harmonic, and rhythmic content of the movement. The movement is comprised of how the musical content is structured by elements of musical form. Videogames are similar: what I mean by saying that the formal features of videogames are encoded in a fiction is that fictional content – in *Grand Theft Auto*, guns, cars, the streets of a city, various characters – is used to build up a formal arrangement of affordances and objectives apt to support a game.

It will be useful to go through a concrete example that I can refer back to in developing the theory here. A good example, illustrating many of the key aspects of gameplay, is one of the online multiplayer modes in *Grand Theft Auto IV*. As well as the large single-player campaign, *Grand Theft Auto*

IV involves a range of online multiplayer modes in which up to sixteen players can engage in play in the fictional environment of Liberty City. In addition to the multiplayer gameplay staples of deathmatch and team deathmatch – shoot everyone you can within a time limit – and car racing, the game also involves a number of cooperative modes. One, called *Bomb Da Base II*, has the players attempting to shut down a rival computer-controlled smuggling operation. I played the game with a friend, and we were sitting in the same room, so were able to communicate our intentions and so coordinate our actions. All of the following is happening on two televisions hooked up to two Playstation 3s that are connected to the Playstation Network that provides the server for our online activities.

Initially, the game instructs us to steal a guarded security van loaded with explosives and take it back to our base. The game starts, and the player-characters appear as a couple of heavy-set goons. Fortunately, there are two SUVs parked nearby, so the obvious thing to do is to take them and chase down the security truck driving around the other side of Algonquin – the Liberty City version of Manhattan Island – which appears as a blip on the player radar. In our doomed first attempt at the game, we hopped into the same SUV, with me riding shotgun and gunning through the passenger side window. In later attempts, we each took an SUV. After racing through the streets to the security van's position, we were instructed to damage the van enough to make it stop. A couple of guards were inside the back doors of the van and were shooting in our direction, and the van was also guarded by a car full of additional goons. After following the van and shooting at it, it stops, and the guards get out, leading to an on-foot gun fight. With the guards successfully dispensed with by a few well-directed bursts from a machine gun, I got into the security van and drove it to the compound. My partner in crime followed in a car he had carjacked from an innocent passer-by. It is just these kinds of activities that are likely to strike many people as constituting exactly what is immoral about *Grand Theft Auto*; for the moment, though, what is important is how the fictional events contribute to the formal properties of the game.

If either of us has been unlucky enough to have died during the operation – which I have to admit we did – we are *respawned* nearby so that we can quickly rejoin the action. Players have only five lives for the entirety of the mission, however, and the entire mission will be failed if either of the players loses all of their lives before reaching the mission goal. This formal limitation was essentially motivation for us to be more careful in what we were doing, especially given the dynamic of cooperative play, in which the inability of one player to stay alive could prove a failure for both.

After delivery of the security truck to the compound, the second task is to storm a ship – the *Platypus* – and lay charges to sink it. The ship is heavily guarded. Fortunately, our boss has dropped off a helicopter for the task, and so getting to the ship in Broker – modeled on Brooklyn – is made quite easy. In this case I took the pilot's seat of the chopper, my buddy taking the passenger seat. As we approached the ship, we agreed upon a tactic: I would hover the helicopter alongside the ship so that he could take out the enemies on the deck with his submachine gun. We also decided to land directly on the ship, which was made more difficult by the limited space, and led to at least one spectacular helicopter crash, for which I was solidly rebuked. In my defense, I will note that the helicopters are challenging to fly with precision.

On board the ship, the gameplay suddenly becomes a matter of fighting through various galleys, crew quarters, and decks in an attempt to reach the area where the charges need to be placed. The ability to take cover behind a wall and pop out to shoot enemies – one of the control developments in *Grand Theft Auto IV* – makes the whole process quite fun, though I have to admit that I have a habit of charging heedlessly into new areas and attempting to quickly take out enemies with my assault rifle, occasionally getting myself promptly killed – what can I say, I'm fictionally impetuous. After failing one of our mission attempts for just this reason, we came to an informal agreement that I take more care.

After successfully storming the ship, setting the charges, and exiting hastily as a timer counts down, we both jump overboard, and a cut-scene shows the explosion on board the ship signaling our success. A statistics screen displays how many enemies each of us has killed, and how many times we died. All this has taken a little over fifteen sometimes nerve-racking and immensely fun minutes.

A number of formal issues are nicely illustrated in this example. First, in the case of videogames, the *rules* of a game do not necessarily seem to signify rules in a declarative linguistic format that might be written into a rule book. Guiding the action in videogames are often rules of this kind, but also the *affordances* introduced in the previous chapter, and objectives that must be achieved given these affordances. A game might immediately prompt the player with a declarative objective such as "Steal the armored vehicle," but the subsequent game is not played by consulting various declarative rules to see what actions are legal in the game, and what counts as an endgame, but by simply exploring the potential for action in the fictional world. Many games do not even involve declarative prompts of the kind seen in *Grand Theft Auto*, but merely drop the player into a scenario with very minimal guidance as to what the objectives are, relying on their previous experience of gaming, and subtle structural cues, to guide them through the game. Furthermore, though the rules and objectives of a videogame can often be described after the event – one can list in declarative language all the available actions and objectives in *Grand Theft Auto*, as one might find in a game *walk-through* – these descriptions do not have the function of *enabling* gameplay, as the declarative rules of chess or checkers do, but have the function of prompts, clues, or shortcuts to discerning the game's structure. Aaron Smuts (2005b) uses the term "iron parameters" where I have invoked the notion of affordances, to make much the same point about the encoding of videogame rules in fictions. Juul himself argues that the extending of the concept *rule* to the affordances in videogames is appropriate because both things instantiate a particular kind of goal-directed algorithm (2005: 36–43).

In the example above, the starting configuration is the fictional scenario in which the player-characters find themselves: they are heavily armed individuals living in Liberty City, a place that is rich with interactive freedom. Corresponding to the objectives of traditional games is the task that the player is set: to steal the security van and sink the *Platypus*. The rules of the game – the formal features that constrain the activity in the game, defining what is a legal move or valid state transition – are the fictional affordances of that environment: the players are to sink the *Platypus* by *any means possible within the game world*. In the case of *Grand Theft Auto*, these means are comparatively diverse and open: because of the freedom of the fictional world, the players are able to strategize and design quite specific tactics within the game world to surmount its problems. Because we were sitting in the same room, we were able to talk throughout the mission for this purpose; but the game also allows the player to use a headset to talk to other online players. Of course, the game world has obvious limitations, and so some courses of action are obligatory: talking your opponents down is not an option, and conflict resolution in *Grand Theft Auto* usually involves using deadly force. But there are still a number of ways to surmount the problems in the above example, and I expect that through sharing broad similarities, other players tackled the situation in quite different ways. All this is to say that the formal properties of the games in these kinds of fictively rich videogames are instantiated in the fictive scenarios that they depict, and the kind of game activities that arise are determined by the kind of fiction depicted.

Thus, the fiction is not a mere *gloss* on the game, as it may have been in earlier games such as *Pong*, where the fiction is rather basic and even indeterminate (what one sees on the screen in *Pong* could conceivably be a representation of ping pong, tennis, volley ball, or any number of fictional scenarios). Rather, the fiction is essential to the functioning of the game: one simply could not play *Grand Theft Auto* without acknowledging its representational content, because it is this content that makes sense of what is being rendered on the screen (Juul, 2005: 13–15). *Portal* is another interesting example of this point. There the gameplay is characterized by the traversal of fictional test chambers utilizing a portal gun, which is essentially a fictive means to generate new virtual cameras, and hence access new locations in fictional space. But equally, the game is encoded in the fiction: if one does not understand what is fictionally represented in *Portal* – a number of spaces and the portals connecting them – then one simply could not play this game.

As it turns out, the idea that the rules of a game might be encoded in affordances rather than in declarative linguistic rules for interaction is not unprecedented in non-videogames. Though they also have linguistic rules that might find their way into a rule book, much of the gameplay in non-electronic games is encoded in the physical affordances of the physical system to which they pertain. Though rugby union has a set of declarative rules, those rules only make functional sense when set against the physics (*affordances, iron parameters*) of the system to which they apply. The legislated width of the field, the fact that players can only pass backwards, and the number of players are a crucial part of rugby union, but these rules only function against the background of the physics of human movement. If, for example, players were capable of vaulting over each other, then these rules would not be effective in setting up a functioning game, or at the very least it would be a very different game to the one we see.

Similarly, a game like tag, which I remember vividly from primary school, is a clear example of a non-videogame that is encoded partly in real physical affordances. In this case, the game involves making someone *it* by tagging them, thus forcing them into the position to try to make someone else *it*. With this very basic and informal rule set, most of the subsequent gameplay is driven by the physical parameters of the game environment and that of the players. Tag players utilize their physical environment and personal physical capacities to avoid being made *it*, and also target the physical weakness of their opponents. Indeed, the resemblance between tag and modern first-person shooter games is quite striking. *Paintball*, of course, comes closest to being a transmedial form of first-person shooter in a real setting (though even paintball relies on fictional "kills").

We can now see that it is only partly true that videogames differ to traditional games in that the rules in traditional games are comprised of declarative rules and those in videogames are comprised of affordances for interaction. The key difference, of course, is that in videogames the physical worlds and systems used to situate games are also virtual and fictional. This explains why these non-electronic games can be given transmedial rendering in videogaming form: these are formally identical games in depending on much the same formal rule sets, but the physical system is depicted in a virtual fictional setting.

A second important point borne out by the *Grand Theft Auto IV* example is that the rules (affordances) of videogames often are not known in advance and must be discovered through play. It has been known for a long time that a part of the challenge of many videogames involves discovering what the rules and objectives are through trial-and-error inductive reasoning, this being another way in which videogames differ from traditional games where the rules and objectives are known by the players in advance. In one of the earliest academic studies of gaming, Patricia Greenfield makes this observation concerning classic games like *Pac-Man* (1984: 111–117). In modern fictively robust games, the depiction of an initially unknown fictional world allows the videogame to set up games the nature of which can be discovered though fictional exploration or encounters with fictional characters and events, hence guiding a game without the need for explicit declarative rules specified at the outset. This is why player-character epistemology is such an important part of these games. As discussed earlier, the player-character allows the player epistemic access and a behavioral role in the fictional world of the game, relating players to the world, and motivating their play within it.

The further important issue is that a great deal of the interest in these games depends on their *fictive contingency*, and how important that fictive contingency is to the objectives of a given game determines how richly novel the game can be. This is related to "emergent gameplay" – that from simple rules quite complex game interactions can arise (Juul, 2005: 76) – but I concentrate here on the emergence of fictive possibilities in gameplay, given my focus on *games through fiction*. The extent to which the challenges of gameplay are tied to particular game world affordances is called *linearity*. The affordances for action in a videogame are always limited, but often they are very limited indeed, and this can lead to some very artificial game interactions. An extremely linear game is one in which a player must perform a determinate sequence of actions to surmount the problems of gameplay: in some first-person shooter or third-person role-playing games linearity might be comprised by following a linear path through an environment, forcing all players through the same sequence of game world events. Conversely, some sandbox games are extremely non-linear in that a player can take any number of routes to the game's objective. In one of the failed attempts at the mission in *Grand Theft Auto IV* discussed above, my gaming friend stole a fire engine and used its fire hose to overturn an SUV, thus crushing one of the armed enemies: this sort of unexpected fictive contingency adds a great deal of novelty and fun to such games. Realism or representational richness in terms of the fictional worlds of videogames can be an artistic strongpoint in videogames, especially when it is effectively wedded to gameplay. In essence, it provides fictive contingency that can fill a game with unexpected and hence interesting or exciting events, making possible emergent gameplay.

A subsequent point is that the fictional qualities of a videogame are in a large degree determined by the functional qualities that they are intended to encode, and this means that those fictions will often seem less than real. The fiction in *Bomb Da Base II* is not particularly realistic: most obviously, the players each get five lives. Respawning is not available in the real world, unfortunately. In a typical *boss battle* – an end-of-level battle with an especially powerful creature – in a game like *Devil May Cry*, it is not possible to retreat from or avoid the monster, and the player is forced into killing it. If the player does not do so, then the game cannot be played through to its end. The obligatory nature of the boss battle is a *formal channel* or *gameplay chute* that guides the game towards a definite and meaningful objective. But there are lots of more subtle ways in which the fictional situation is manipulated so that it functions as a game. In this, videogaming is like most other games: without the restrictive rules and defined objectives of chess and solitaire, moves in these games would be not only unmotivated, but also impossible. The idea of a move is only coherent in terms of a set of restrictive rules and objectives. When confronted by a new type of game and asked to make a move, new players will typically ask, "What sort of move am I allowed to make?" Linearity is very often a term of criticism, though arguably, all objective-directed games are linear to some extent in virtue of specifying obligatory game-defining objectives. The fictions of videogames always demand the exclusion of possibilities for action that would stifle meaningful gameplay. This is another reason why the fictions of videogames are often limited or unrealistic, as noted in chapter 4.

As well as obligatory aspects, it is also obvious that videogames involve more subtle fictive *nudges* that drive players into certain behaviors so that gameplay can develop. In *Bomb Da Base II*, on the completion of the first part of the mission, a helicopter arrives carrying the boss, nudging the player to use the chopper on the next part of the mission. Using the helicopter is not obligatory – it is not one of the goals of the mission – but without it the players would have to drive all the way to Broker. The initial prominence of the SUVs as the mission begins is another nudge: the fiction has thus been orchestrated to drive the game in a particular direction. Hence, sometimes the fictions of videogames encode their games not in obligatory rules, but in subtle psychological nudges: the fictive content of the game, and its psychological potential for making some decisions more likely than others, is again crucial to the functioning of the game. Richard Thaler and Cass Sunstein (2008) have developed a theory in behavioral economics where such non-intrusive nudges, often taking the form of a "choice architecture," can be used to guide people into making decisions that are better for their economic and social well-being than those they would otherwise make.

Perhaps some of the especially obvious and awkward cases of formal restrictions and nudges are flaws, and game designers should search for more naturalistic or consistent means of representing games. Part of the challenge in games design may be to reconcile the fictional and gaming aspects of videogames, and the solutions that designers discover may be part of what is genuinely artistically interesting about games. To take an interesting example, *Team Fortress 2* is a team-based first-person shooter game that is very fictionally unrealistic: the environments are very small and unnaturally circumscribed, the teams have bases built very close to each other, and death is ever present but rather impermanent. But these facts, ultimately driven by considerations of gameplay, are reconciled with the fiction of *Team Fortress 2* by the very cartoonish and comical style of the game. The unrealistic nature of the fiction sits quite comfortably in this context, just as the very unrealistic events of a *Roadrunner* cartoon fit within its genre location. Ultimately, a lack of realism exists in videogames because the fictions underlying videogames have interests other than total veracity or truthfulness to the real world. Unrealistic fictions are part of the baggage that we must leave at the door when we enter the fictional world to play a game.

A next point that can be seen above is that because the formal aspects of gameplay are encoded in fictions, a part of our response to gameplay becomes a response to its fiction. Surely another reason for the popularity of *Grand Theft Auto* is the exciting nature of its gameplay *content*. In one mission, emerging from a church after a funeral, a number of black cars filled with gangsters suddenly arrived. Fortunately, I was armed with a fully loaded rocket launcher, and the following minute or so played out like an action movie set piece, and indeed, because I was the protagonist in the scene, it was all the more thrilling. The effect was also enhanced by the fact that the explosions in *Grand Theft Auto* are *very* aesthetically pleasing. The gameplay of chess is implicitly aggressive, but in modern videogames, the fictive aggression and violence is worn on its sleeve and often quite skillfully depicted. Likewise, survival-horror games manifest their gameplay in a situation of fear both because of the nature and artistic design of the environments and deadly creatures, and in the situation of desperation encoded in the gameplay of the survival-horror genre. I personally found the first-person horror game *FEAR* at times genuinely scary, even though I am not generally prone to be scared by horror films. Playing *FEAR*, though, I felt as though it was *me* who was in danger (see chapter 7).

Our responses, including our emotional responses, to the fictions of gameplay can even be factored into the decision making and strategy that is crucial to playing videogames. Again, to take *Grand Theft Auto IV* as an example, the aforementioned funeral was for a corrupt cop that I had secretly assassinated. In this episode of the game, the narrative of the game develops to put the player in a dilemma. Niko becomes embroiled in an Irish mobster family filled with the type of tensions and enmities familiar from the gangster genre of film. One brother, Derrick, is a down and out gangster;

the other, Francis, is a corrupt Liberty City cop, and both proposition Niko to kill the other. The moment of choice comes when both are seated at a park bench and Niko has them in the sights of his sniper rifle. In this case, solving the puzzle is driven very much by the player's response to the fictional characters and the potential consequences of killing each brother. I eventually assassinated Francis, the corrupt cop, and mostly I think because I felt more empathy for the down and out brother Derrick, given his lack of control over the situation he found himself in; moreover, Francis was simply a *louse*. Some readers are likely to note that Niko is not given the opportunity to sit the brothers down for a good talk to attempt to get them to change their views, suggesting perhaps that *Grand Theft Auto* reinforces using violence as a means to an end. The *forced move* derives, however, from the mobster genre of *Grand Theft Auto* and the game structure of the fiction.

A further point that can be seen in the discussion piece is that in a game like *Grand Theft Auto*, the gameplay may be defined by a large range of formally quite different challenges: *Grand Theft Auto* is a *meta*-game. The example above involves a driving game, a combat game, and a flying game because all of these can be combined into an unfolding fictional scenario. Furthermore, these games can be hierarchically arranged. On a broad level, gaming involves carrying out *missions* or traversing *levels*: in *Bomb Da Base II* this amounts to shutting down a rival smuggling operation. These missions or levels are further subdivided into tasks that must be achieved to succeed in the larger goal. The tasks in *Bomb Da Base II* are to chase down the security truck, fight its guards, take it back to the compound, storm the ship, and so on. These tasks are also further divided into the employment of skills. Aiming and shooting are skills essential to success in the mission, as are driving cars and flying helicopters. It might be the case that some games – such as *Tetris*, and the puzzle game *Super Bust-A-Move* – are entirely comprised of such fine-grained skills in which what is fictively represented is of negligible significance. *Tetris* involves fitting together differently shaped and colored blocks; *Super Bust-A-Move* involves shooting balls into patterns on the screen so as to rid the screen of balls.

This hierarchical or nested structure is often intricately iterated so that to get to the major goal of gameplay – in *Grand Theft Auto IV*, resolve the problems of Niko's past – a long sequence of smaller transitional goals must be achieved. Thus, gaming often involves the dexterous manipulation of a fictional world at a variety of levels of organization. In the fictively robust games that are the focus here, this means that the player must be able to control the various actions of their character. Because of this many-leveled nature, the fictive practice involved in videogames potentially involves a broader array of our cognitive capacities than is seen in many other cases of fictive engagement.

Finally, because of the interactive nature of videogames, ultimately the game depends on a dexterous manipulation of the fictive prop. This derives from the understanding that in reality the apparent fictional interaction in inter-active fictions depends on a genuine interaction with a fictive prop. At some stage gameplay becomes a matter not of fictionally carrying out actions in a world, but literally carrying out actions on the controls of the game to manipulate the articulated fictive props that underlie gaming fictions. In the case of robustly fictive games like *Grand Theft Auto*, this is control over a character and the weapon or vehicle they happen to be using.

The controller of most modern consoles is a configuration of buttons and thumb control sticks, or perhaps a motion-sensing device. In the default con-troller configuration for many first-person shooters on a personal computer, moving around involves using the arrow keys on the keyboard, and shooting a weapon involves moving the mouse to move the weapon crosshair and clicking on the mouse button to fire. On the Playstation console the same actions can be achieved by manipulating the thumb sticks, and firing using the shoulder triggers. In *Grand Theft Auto IV*, driving a car is achieved by first entering a car by pressing the triangle button. Acceleration is controlled via the lower right shoulder button, braking via lower left shoulder button, and the radio station can be changed by pressing the directional button. Experienced players soon learn that maneuvering the car around the tight streets of Liberty City is easier if the player employs handbrake power slides, which can be achieved via turning into a corner at high speed while acceler-ating and pressing the handbrake button on the upper right shoulder. Doing so in powerful cars requires fine manipulation of the buttons in order to avoid spinning out. Many of these techniques, though originally difficult to employ, soon become natural for the players, as familiarity, and even perhaps *muscle memory*, makes the control surface effectively disappear so that the player can concentrate on their fictional interaction with the world of the game, that is, with meeting the fictional demands of gameplay.

Thus videogames confront players with two classes of formal challenges: those involved in achieving goals in fictional worlds, and those in physically manipulating the gameplay controls. The second class of gameplay can be particularly challenging, and the rewards of gameplay are contingent upon meeting these challenges. It involves the development of physical techniques such as quick tapping enabling the quick firing of a weapon; feathering the analogue controls for fine control of the acceleration of vehicles; learning the buttons that control various aspects of the character actions; becoming familiar with button combinations that have novel effects, such as the com-bination of buttons involved in power sliding; learning shortcut keys; and learning to use the game menus efficiently. As noted elsewhere here, means of controlling games have recently diversified, and include more overtly physical means of control, especially through the motion-sensing controls of the Nintendo Wii. Nevertheless, at some stage in all games, fictionally interacting in a world is a matter of really interacting with a controller.

PLAYING, CHEATING, FRAGGING, AND GRIEFING

The situational features of games constitute how the formal features of the previous section are set within a behavioral framework, thus defining what counts as playing the game and how the game is to be treated with respect to the rest of the world. These factors comprise the *behavioral norms* particular to the social realm of videogaming. The following section is a brief and partial survey of the situational aspects characteristic of videogaming; again, only a much larger work could do justice to the real diversity and richness of gaming practice. I have argued here that a large number of videogames depict their games through fictions: we will see that this also has some quite interesting effects on the situational features of videogaming.

In the games studies literature, an explanation of the behavioral norms of videogames often invokes Huizinga's notion of the "magic circle". Huizinga sought to understand the role of *play* in culture, a role that he thought to be almost ubiquitous. He sums up the qualities of play as

> a free activity standing quite consciously outside "ordinary" life as being "not serious," but at the same time absorbing the player intensely and utterly. It is an activity connected with no material interest, and no profit can be gained by it. It proceeds within its own proper boundaries of time and space according to fixed rules and in an orderly manner. It promotes the formation of social groupings which tend to surround themselves with secrecy and to stress their difference from the common world by disguise or other means. (Huizinga, 1950: 13)

A number of writers about games, in particular Salen and Zimmerman (2004) and Juul (2005), have claimed that the magic circle is crucially involved in the playing of videogames. Indeed, the phrase is pervasive in games studies. Other than in establishing the important role of situational features in enabling games to function, I am just not convinced that the idea of a magic circle adds much to our understanding of videogames that cannot be better achieved by separating out various issues. Like *immersion*, the concept seems to be a loose metaphor that covers a number of issues in a very imprecise way. First, Huizinga's own use of the idea is very limited and is not a general account of play. Huizinga's reference to the magic circle seems mostly concerned with an observation of a mythical game of dice played in the Sanskrit epic the *Mahabharata* (1950: 57). As such it is only one kind of play-space, which includes "the arena, the card-table, the magic circle, the temple, the stage, the screen, the tennis court, the court of justice" (1950: 10). Most of the use that has been made of the idea in game studies, principally by Salen and Zimmerman and those following them, is elaboration or generalization that goes beyond Huizinga's intended meaning. Second, even when built on, the idea of the magic circle remains a metaphor or catchphrase, conflating a number of different ideas, some to be discussed shortly here, which Huizinga himself takes care to separate out (1950: 7–13). Ideally, then, we should attempt to replace the metaphor with something more substantive.

A very basic behavioral fact about games is that players agree to abide by the rules when they play. In playing a game of chess, players agree that their moves are to be constrained within the formal rules of the game, and that these rules are not negotiable: the gamer agrees to be put in a position where they can *lose* the game. Without this risk, gaming is unlikely to draw effort out of the players or their attachment to the outcome of the game. There seems a potential immediate difference in the case of videogames here. Because the rules of videogames are not necessarily in the form of declarative linguistic rules, but rather fictional affordances, this initial agreement might seem obligatory and taken out of the player's control in videogaming: one cannot *not* engage with the rules, if one is to play the game at all. This does seem to be a pretty good observation about very simple games such as *Tetris*: unless the player endeavors to meet the formal requirements of gameplay, games of *Tetris* will not last very long.

On closer scrutiny though, there are possibilities to disengage from a videogame. Videogaming gameplay, even though more obligatory than other forms of gaming, is not entirely so. For example, in first-person shooters, some of the rules are not encoded in the program of the game, but derive from the implicit understandings of the players: players do not have to shoot each other, and it is perfectly possible that they aimlessly run around in circles instead. Indeed, some players do not engage in gameplay, but instead play *against* the rules. I will discuss these possible departures later when I look into breaches of gaming good faith such as *cheating* and *griefing*. But even if non-obligatory, the fictions of videogames do encourage or nudge play in the intended direction. Armed with a large gun in a constrained fictional environment populated by other players, it is almost inevitable that players of *Halo* will spend their time shooting each other. That the score is kept in almost all first-person shooters again nudges the game in this direction.

In concert with the understanding that players are to be bound by the rules, playing is seen as somewhat *non-productive* or *separate* from everyday concerns. The events that occur within the game are thought to have only limited consequences outside of the game. The situational features of separateness and non-productiveness are clearly referred to by Huizinga, and also seen in Caillois' (1961) theory of games. Similarly, as Huizinga also notes, games seem "disinterested" (1950: 9) in a sense related to that used by Immanuel Kant (1790/1951). The idea that gaming really is unproductive or separate from reality is of course subject to counter-examples of gaming having extrinsic uses: poker can be played for large sums of money, and a great many people have an enormous extrinsic investment in the Super Bowl or Soccer World Cup. Videogames have clear extrinsic and productive uses: gaming tournaments are increasingly common and involve big money. It is for these reasons that Juul claims, in something of a fudge, that the consequences of games are "negotiable" (2005: 36). This connects to my definition of gaming, where I claimed that artifacts like games can have a host of *extrinsic* functions, in addition to their basic nature as objects of entertainment. Though originally designed as entertainment, a game like *Counterstrike*, because of its formal fictional nature of pitting player against player, is apt to support other kinds of social engagements, especially formal competition. Juul is probably correct to think that the diverse practice seen in gaming means that it cannot be seen as purely unproductive and separate, even though these descriptions are somewhat appropriate.

Next, it seems quite obvious that *fiction* not only allows the formal encoding of videogames, but it also constitutes an important part of their situational nature. This is also an aspect of Huizinga's theory, where he implies that a game is played somewhere beyond the real world, "within its own proper boundaries of time and space" (Huizinga, 1950: 13). Castronova (2005) calls the world of online games "synthetic worlds" for this reason. There is an obvious behavioral benefit of locating a game in the context of a fiction: fictions have limited costs. Essentially, fiction aids the separateness seen above by placing the action within a hypothetical and imaginary scenario. Fictions allow us to engage with hypothetical worlds without the costs involved in really interacting in those worlds. In traditional as well as videogame fictions, scary, saddening, or violent fictions are inexpensive in that they allow appreciators to have an emotionally rich experience without enduring the negative costs or losses of the situations only fictionally engaged with. Videogame fictions thus allow risky or expensive forms of behavior in a safe environment, and in this sense are a lot like various contact sports, which allow aggressive behavior that is quarantined to some extent from society external to the game, and where the action is carefully regulated to minimize physical injury to the players. First-person shooters, then, can be seen in this context: they allow a form of behavioral interaction – hunting other people – without the costs it would normally have. Of course, some might worry that this lack of costs or consequences is actually quite dangerous, and is a reason for why games can be morally criticized (see chapter 8).

A crucial situational feature of videogames, and becoming more so, is that games involve multiple players. The fictive games we play with videogames are often collaborative affairs in that they involve playing with or against other people. Multiplayer games are especially fun because they add the element of social interaction to the fictive interaction underlying the gameplay: the fiction of the videogame provides a medium for real human interaction. In fact multiplayer videogames are a popular form of social meeting place, contrary to the popular opinion that gaming is a (harmfully) solitary affair. One aspect of the anti-videogame argument is that gaming stunts social interaction or the development of that ability, because of its solitary nature. And yet most gamers themselves will be aware that gaming is typically social, both in the immediate sense that playing is often collaborative, and in the wider sense that it has given rise to a culture of gaming: something given further evidence and argument by Newman (2004).

Because of the often social nature of gaming the interactivity of videogame fictions does not always depend solely on the plasticity of an electronic prop. Like childhood games of pretense, among the most important props in fictive videogames are other players. Most fictions are solitary activities in the sense that our fictive participation does not involve or acknowledge the fictive roles of other appreciators who may be interacting with the same fictional world. In some narrative fictions, even though other audience members are present at the viewing of the fiction, they do not factor into the fictional world that is the object of participation, other than in the very minimal sense that two fictive participants might discuss what they thought or felt about the fiction external to their viewing or reading of the fiction. This is to say that the game worlds of different viewers in most traditional fictions are *discrete*. But with videogames (like some childhood games of pretense, and role-playing games) appreciators might enter the fictional worlds as a group. Furthermore, this group-wise fictive activity opens up the possibility of other fictive activities: the fictional worlds of videogames are often cooperative or, as is more often the case, competitive fictional endeavors.

This is to say that the fictive practice of videogames is enriched by their multiplayer nature: just as there are formal ramifications because of the involvement of fiction in gaming – the content of videogame fictions is often wedded to their nature as games – so there are situational implications deriving from their fictive nature. Multiplayer fictive videogames are *multi-appreciator fictions*: fictions where more than one player-character can step into the fictional world. In terms of the theory of fiction I have been presenting here, we can see that what is occurring in these cases is that multiple appreciators are entering a single fictional world for the purpose of playing a game and hence having a social interaction. Two-player *Pong* achieved this by having each of the rudimentary paddles in the control of each player. In the more representationally sophisticated game worlds of first-person shooters, the players are given graphical representations in the form of characters that form the basis of their fictional interactions. In a sense, the individual player's fictively motivated interaction becomes a prop for the other players. This is very similar to childhood pretense, where children and their minds may become props in the games of make-believe they share with other children.

Competition is the most obvious situational aspect of multiplayer gaming: the formal rules are treated as a system within which players can compete with each other. One of the very first videogames, *Spacewar*, pits player against player, something that is understandable given that generating computer-controlled opponents with the requisite intelligence to provide a real-time challenge was out of the reach of the computer science at the time of its development. A good first-person shooter such as *Timesplitters 2* gains much of its appeal because it allows players to compete within the dimensions of a fictional world. In death match mode the players compete to *frag* each other. But games are also increasingly involving cooperative forms of play, as seen in my discussion of *Grand Theft Auto IV* in the previous section. In cooperative games, players form plans before they enter the fictional world and discuss their intentions while playing the game, and again these are a part of the wider participative fiction external to the interaction with the prop itself. In this regard videogames are like regular fictions in that the fictive activities are not restricted to what is rendered by the prop, but also include how players interact with and talk about the fiction, even when they are not directly dealing with the prop.

Player investment is thus another key situational aspect of gaming: gamers invest effort and significance in the games they play. In a simple game of checkers, this attachment derives from the competition that the formal system of the game creates between players. Of course, it is possible to play a game without much investment: a lot of gaming is *unbalanced*, such as where a parent teaches their child to play a board game and plays badly on purpose. In such cases, to take the game seriously would probably amount to a mean-spirited breach of gaming practice. Indeed, in most gaming player investment needs to be carefully balanced with the *situational separateness* of gaming, otherwise players risk being *bad sports*. For example, taking things overly seriously in a first-person shooter – responding with genuine animosity to being *trash-talked* or losing a game – is commonly seen as poor form. I have personally experienced the investment involved in first-person shooters, which can lead to quite acute emotions of frustration, or on winning a game or having a good run, elation. Incidentally, in videogames, because the games are encoded in robustly detailed fictions, player attachment can take on some very interesting forms. For example, gamers become attached to their player-characters and put a great deal of effort into developing them. The emotions play a clear role in securing player attachment to the outcome of games (see chapter 7).

That there are situational constraints on gamers brings with it the possibility that some players will act in contravention of the accepted norms. Most obviously, cheating – breaking the rules of the game – is a breach of gaming practice. Mia Consalvo (2007) has written about the intricacies of cheating within videogames. Because videogames are encoded in a computer program, a number of the avenues of cheating available in non-electronic games are not available. The player of a videogame form of checkers, for example, cannot take pieces off the board while the other player is not looking; similarly, a videogame version of poker does not allow the player to mark the cards. Because in videogames the game system is encoded in a computer, short of directly hacking the code of the game, the game cannot be manipulated except through the means encoded in its affordances, which, if the designer is careful, are the intended lawful means of playing the game. Because the *encodings* of non-electronic games – hands of cards, the positions of pieces on a board – can easily be manipulated, these games seem to rely to a greater extent on the good will of the players to uphold the rules.

And yet, there are still ways to play outside the spirit of a videogame in a way tantamount to cheating. In computer science, an *exploit* is a use or manipulation of a piece of computer technology that creates an unanticipated effect, usually at odds with its intended use. In gaming, exploits are behaviors performed by gamers that take advantage of the bugs or vulnerabilities in a game, and again which are at odds with the intended use; as such, they form a way in which gamers can breach the norms of gaming practice. A well-known example comes from *Oblivion*, where a *dupe* or duplication bug allows players to duplicate items in their possession, potentially *breaking* the game. Videogames turn out to look quite like sports games, where much of the rules are encoded in the physical constraints of human physiology and the nature of the playing space. And like sports, there do seem to be ways to exploit the games by manipulating the physical systems they are encoded in, or to play outside of the spirit of the game. *Camping* is another form of play in first-person shooters that is widely considered as a form of cheating. In camping, the player finds a spot on the game map where they are hidden and protected from attack, but from which they can snipe or ambush other players who stumble across their position.

In cheating, exploits are used as a means of gaining an unfair advantage in the game, but some exploits are used by players to spoil the game for others. This practice is commonly called *griefing*. In *Team Fortress 2*, players take advantage of the ability to enter spaces in the game's environment that the designers never intended the players to have access to. I have personally seen such *griefers* construct sentry guns underneath the environment's floor that were consequently invisible to players, but which could nevertheless direct their fire upon players in the main game area. *Team Fortress 2* allows players to converse with each other via headsets, leading in the above case to much mirth as players got increasingly angry due to being repeatedly killed for no apparent reason. *Team Fortress 2* griefers also set up teleporters to send other players into other inescapable areas of the game environment, trapping them, and so forcing them to respawn. In a particularly entertaining case of griefing seen on *Youtube*, some gamers learned how to jam the door leading out from the area in which the characters spawn. Effectively blocking spawning players from joining the action, the griefer began asking the trapped players general knowledge questions in exchange for letting them exit the area.

Freeplay, the form of non-rule and objective-based gameplay discussed at the beginning of this chapter, seems to be another way in which players can disengage from the rules of a videogame, thus showing them to be non-obligatory. Not all videogames allow freeplay in any great measure. As noted, attempting to toy with a game like *Tetris* is unlikely to be very successful because the formal system of that game *exhausts* the interactive potential of its affordances. But some games, and increasingly it seems with the rise of the sandbox genre, allow players to diverge from the encoded games and play by their own rules. When I first played *Grand Theft Auto III*, the ability to merely toy with the fictional environment came as something of a revelation. Here was a game that was not forcing me to achieve objectives, but was happy with me merely amusing myself in its rich fictive world. Freeplay can thus be seen as the adoption of a different, more relaxed set of behavioral norms, and it seems to arise where a videogame presents a representation with *intrinsic interest*. In *Grand Theft Auto IV* the player might thus simply ignore the frequent gameplay nudges provided by the mission invitations received via their mobile phone and carry on with their explorative or destructive engagement in the fictional world of Liberty City. To do so is not a breach of the behavioral norms of *Grand Theft Auto*, however, because the formal system of the game – a fictional world – is designed with that very possibility in mind.

Ultimately, as seen in the case of my earlier discussion of *World of Warcraft*, the types of behavior seen in modern videogames have taken on a number of sophisticated, unexpected, and subtle variations, only briefly touched on here. The commercial activity seen there, the malicious virus spreading that occurred in the corrupted blood curse, and even the large-scale faction wars that occur in the game show that many of the social forms of life seen in the real world are now occurring in a fictional way in the worlds of videogames.

CHAPTER SUMMARY

Videogames encode or depict their games not necessarily in declarative rules, but in the possibilities for interaction in a fictional world. *Grand Theft Auto IV*, for example, sets the player a fictive objective, and also provides them a set of fictive means – affordances – to achieve that end. Gameplay is comprised of discovering and employing these means and objectives, often in creative and novel ways. Similarly, the situational qualities of games – their competition, player investment, and separateness from the everyday world – can also be explained in terms of fiction. Videogames are now often multiplayer fictions in which players enter a fictional world to compete and cooperate, or even cheat and grief each other. Games designers have developed subtle means to guide and enhance these games, often by placing constraints on the fictional qualities of game worlds, and so the fictional nature of a gameworld is often determined not by considerations of realism, but of the gaming function of the fictional world.

NEXT CHAPTER

Undeniably, videogames often depict narratives. But for a variety of reasons to be explored, the gaming and the narrative function of videogames can seem in tension. The freedom that players increasingly value in gameplay is partly inconsistent with the close scripting that is needed to portray satisfying narratives. Games designers, aware of these tensions, have designed means to reduce the stresses. Recent games have seen much of the narrative content devolve into gameplay, the personalization of the narrative, and the increasing use of the player's role in the discovery or disclosure of the narrative. The most adventurous response is the attempt to make interactive narratives, where the player becomes in part responsible for the course that the narrative takes.

6

VIDEOGAMES AND NARRATIVE

THE STORIES GAMES TELL

Videogames clearly involve narratives, but in a significant departure from how narratives are depicted in traditional fictions, in videogames the player often adopts a role within the narrative. The nature of videogames as interactive fictions has a significant impact upon the narrative fictions within those games. For the philosopher with an interest in the functioning of narrative, such narrative orientated videogames raise a number of interesting questions. What kinds of narratives do videogames exhibit? What differences do they bear to traditional ways of depicting narratives such as novels and films? In particular, how does their nature as games and interactive fictions have an effect on the ability of videogames to convey narratives? Can game narratives do anything that traditional narratives cannot?

This chapter may sound a little more critical and normative that the previous chapters. This is because, plainly, I am not particularly impressed with the narrative content in almost all of the games that I have played, or with its integration into the gameplay. There may be structural reasons for these difficulties, as discussed in the next section. But a large part of the problem has to be the artistry with which narratives have been introduced into games: they are all too often ham-fisted, clichéd, awfully voice-acted, or simply lacking in interest. There are signs that things are improving: *Grand Theft Auto IV* includes some well-scripted cut-scenes, and involves some genuinely dramatic moments that are integrated into gameplay. *BioShock*, with its themes of control and manipulation, and the moral consequences of our choices, fuses together the story and interactive structure of its fictional world into a coherent and satisfying whole. Still, these are exceptions: gaming has a long way to go if it is to provide narratives that are satisfying to mature art-conscious adults.

The meaning of *narrative* needs to be carefully specified here. Narrative is a concept that recent theorists have used to refer to any number of things, so much so that some uses of the term are now apt to strike many readers as being vacuous (Livingston, 2001). But in a classical sense, narrative – or the near synonym *story* – seems to be some variation of *formal* features of representational artifacts, perhaps how they structure their content into a temporal arrangement providing a point of view – often, but not necessarily, that of a narrator – that motivates and guides an interpretation of that material; or, as I roughly defined it in chapter 2, "a set of events chosen for their contribution to an unfolding plot with a beginning, middle, and an end." This is not always the sense referred to in videogame theory: to fit the action-orientated nature of videogaming within a narrative framework, Poole (2000) envisages a watered-down sense of "kinetic" narratives comprised of a set of unfolding events to which success or defeat can be applied. In this chapter, I have in mind the more robust sense of narrative where the "chosen for their contribution to an unfolding plot" clause is crucial, because it is a focus on this sense that teases out the issues of philosophical interest in gaming narrative.

It is worthwhile introducing some of the very basics of game narrative, pointing out the good and the bad of videogame stories. Recent videogames have involved increasingly sophisticated filmic narratives. One of the better recent narratives to be seen in a game exists in the first-person shooter *Call of Duty: Modern Warfare*, which imparts the striking impression that the gamer is playing a role in a big-budget action blockbuster. *Modern Warfare* employs many of the genre formulas and narrative techniques of modern action films such as *Black Hawk Down* and Tom Clancy-style post-cold war military thrillers. Playing the game through the eyes of a number of combatants, the player-character experiences key events in the narrative, and plays a role in a number of them. Rogue ultranationalist Russian leader Imran Zakhaev, allied with the Middle Eastern leader Khaled Al-Asad, is involved in a civil war in Russia. The game begins with a prologue in which the gamer, playing as SAS member John "Soap" McTavish, assaults a freighter in a stormy Bering Sea, discovering a stolen nuclear weapon on board. After the televised execution of Yasir Al-Fulani, the president of an unnamed Middle Eastern country – a disturbing event that the player experiences first-hand from the point of view of Fulani during the opening credits – Soap's SAS unit is tasked with tracking down Al-Asad and learning where he obtained the nuclear weapon discovered during the game's prologue. Playing as US marine Sergeant Paul Jackson, the player takes part in an American assault directed against Al-Asad's forces, but is eventually killed in a nuclear explosion set off as a last desperate measure by the despot. In a flashback sequence as SAS Captain Price, set in Pripyat, Ukraine, a city abandoned after the Chernobyl disaster, the player makes a failed attempt to carry out an assassination of Imran Zakhaev. In the final climactic scenes of the game, after destroying several nuclear warheads inbound for the Eastern seaboard of the United States, the player finally defeats Imran Zakhaev in person, after the rest of McTavish's squad has been killed by the ultranationalist forces in a final deadly and seemingly hopeless battle. All of this is somewhat clichéd genre narrative, but *Modern Warfare* presents a satisfying experience, and this is surely partly due to the narrative it presents and the role of the player as a character within that narrative.

Many of the narrative elements in videogames are comprised of *cut-scenes* that are interspersed throughout the course of the game, explaining the level the player is engaged in, where they are going, or where they have come from. The cut-scenes in *Grand Theft Auto* typically depict the player-character learning of the nature of their upcoming task, as well as how the mission contributes to the progression of the narrative. Cut-scenes may be specially animated via a high-quality rendering system, or as seems more recently the case given the advances that have been made in in-game graphics, rendered in the same animation system that is utilized to represent the gameplay. Often, these short films are cinematic in intent, and draw their inspiration from the related genre films. *Call of Duty* is a partial exception to this use of cut-scenes to represent game narrative, because much of its narrative is progressed though in-game dialogue and events rather than cut-scenes. *Grand Theft Auto IV* also progresses much of its narrative through the discussions that Niko has with other characters during gameplay. The reasons for these departures from the cut-scene technique should become obvious in what follows.

One interesting development is the use of the virtual camera to simulate camera techniques used in film. The virtual camera can be moved through the representational space of the game in relation to the game's action, allowing the simulation of the cinematographic effects actual cameras are used to achieve, such as panning, close ups, craning, and dollying. In *Call of Duty*, the scene leading to Al-Fulani's execution has an obvious cinematic corollary in the sorts of protracted moving camera sequences used by Martin Scorsese to depict a world busy with detail in such movies as *Goodfellas*, even though in this case the player has partial control over the camera. Cut-scenes also use cinematic editing methods, and as Smuts notes (2005a), even artifacts of the filming process are sometimes simulated to achieve cinematographic effects, such as depth of focus variations or lens glare. Such cinematographic use of the virtual camera can also be employed during gameplay, such as in the *Devil May Cry* series, but such usage is difficult to balance with the interactive contribution of the player and the demands of gameplay, and so the cinematographic portions of games like *Devil May Cry* are often very closely scripted or linear portions of gameplay.

The beginnings of videogames are very often rendered in a cinematic way, and these initial films are sometimes quite brilliantly blended into the game-play proper. This is the case with the atmospheric opening of *Medal of Honor: Frontline*. The game opens with the D-Day landings at Normandy: the player-character is standing in an amphibious Higgins boat observing the bombing of the coast and the enemy aircraft strafing the landing party. As the player is looking around and observing the action, quite suddenly a bomb explodes next to the landing craft, and the player is knocked into the water with the other soldiers, most of whom are not as lucky as the player-character, and are killed. The player-character battles his way to shore, and suddenly is in the thick of gameplay proper with the task of clearing the beach. The transition is seamless and effective because of the high quality (for the time) of the animation that is used in the actual gameplay of *Medal of Honor: Frontline*. *Grand Theft Auto IV* also has a particularly successful cinematic opening to its narrative, establishing the character of the stoic Niko and his drunken but likeable cousin Roman, and their immigrant life in Liberty City.

The quality of the cut-scenes in videogames varies wildly, however. Often, they are successful in furthering the gaming experience by advancing the story and allowing space for interpretation of the game's fictional world. Several of the video sequences in *Grand Theft Auto IV* are excellent in this regard. But more often the film cut-scenes are less appealing. Frequently, though video sequences draw directly from the techniques and themes of movie making, they inevitably draw on clichéd ones. The cut-scenes in the *Metal Gear Solid* series – a critical favorite in gaming circles, mostly I suspect, due to its gameplay – are horribly voice-acted and extremely trite. In a cringe-worthy sequence from *Metal Gear Solid 2*, a demolitions expert reflects on his essential failure in life, and his new-found determination to make a difference. The character dies screaming defiance, in one of the cheesiest scenes ever to grace a videogame. In the middle of an effective bit of gameplay, clichéd material such as this only makes the player cringe or laugh, and adversely affects the dramatic import of the piece. It may be that the genre fictions of video-gaming do not draw on successful dramatic precedents, instead relying on rehashed sequences from action and horror movies. One also suspects that the *auteur* of *Metal Gear Solid*, Hideo Kojima, is prone to frequent lapses of judgment and artistic taste. But even with the better video sequences in the *Metal Gear Solid* series, the very lengthy cut-scenes come with such regularity as to be an annoyance. One of the most recent, *Metal Gear Solid 4*, again has all these faults, and is potentially the most frustrating gaming experience I have had just because of the interruption of badly written cut-scenes during quite sublime gameplay.

Game narratives are also prone to confusing mere sequences of events with narratives. The narratives of many games are comprised of a long list of activities and events, of players going here and there, but with little real emotional or dramatic shape to the events. Worse still are role-playing games filled with caricatured fantasy characters, with long archaic names and titles, and complicated personal histories that become a principal part of the narrative. More than one fantasy role-playing game narrative has left me utterly bewildered as a long cast of players go about odd actions for mostly inscrutable reasons in a way that is utterly bereft of dramatic substance.

This indeed seems to be one of the inherent problems in games design and criticism: the narratives presently just are not very good, with more attention in development being paid to the functionality of the gameplay and the polish of the graphics. Thus, where a game with an overt intention to depict a narrative comes along, unrealistic praise is heaped on it, even though the standard of the narrative is usually akin to that of pulp science fiction or fantasy.

There may be a deeper tension here, however, in that videogames and narratives may make different demands of their fictions which are hard to reconcile into a coherent whole. Despite the similarities to filmic narratives, videogames differ profoundly to films and other narrative forms. Foremost, this difference stems from the nature of videogames as games. Although there is a narrative thread in the game, the vast majority of *Grand Theft Auto IV* is made up of gameplay. The player spends their time fighting through various urban environments, sneaking around and taking sniper shots at enemies, evading the cops by driving recklessly through the streets of Liberty City, and eating hot dogs. Thus, in a particularly significant difference to traditional narrative fictions, games represent their appreciators within the fictional world of the game, and give the player a means by which to change that world. These activities in large part determine the fictive content of the world, and are themselves usually driven by the objectives that the player must meet to proceed in the game, or by the toying with the game world that constitutes freeplay.

The narratives in videogames, however, are mostly non-responsive to the interactive involvement of the player. While the cut-scenes are playing, the player has no control over their character. In essence, the game is temporarily suspended so that the narrative can be presented by means of a short film. Thus the player cannot for the most part change the events of the cut-scene: they are always scripted in advance (even though their rendering can reflect the player's actions, by representing the player with their most recent look). Often, cut-scenes merely serve to break up interactive gameplay with a period in which the player is inert, and so the gaming and narrative aspects of videogames are somewhat disconnected.

At worst, this disconnection between the game and the narrative might imply that videogames are not genuinely narrative in form, with what narrative there is merely being tacked on and incidental to the real substance of the game. Indeed, the narrative in many videogames seems merely an afterthought, something that might be dispensed with without significant impact on the gameplay itself. A player can often safely ignore the narrative aspect in a videogame and still complete the gameplay, or even skip through the narrative sections, as many games thankfully allow. At the very least, the disconnection implies that in videogames the narrative is often inert from the gaming point of view – it is an aspect of the game that does not have the interactive nature typical of gaming fictions.

Given that the narratives in videogames seem subordinate or secondary to their gaming natures, does their ambition to convey narrative amount to anything more than the aping of cinematic clichés? Why are game fictions and narrative fictions in tension with each other? How can videogames most effectively reconcile their narrative and gaming aspects? And interestingly, with their nature as interactive fictions, could videogames be *interactive narratives* in the sense of allowing the player to contribute to the events of the narrative? In the remainder of this chapter I attempt to answer these questions by first explaining why it is that interactive gaming narratives are functionally problematic, and then by exploring the potential for solutions to these problems.

WOULD YOU KINDLY PUT DOWN THAT WRENCH?

There are a number of reasons for the tension between the narrative and gaming aspects of videogames, that is, why the narrative aspect of videogames can often seem to be incidental to their nature as games. Principally, videogames, unlike almost all other narrative forms, are interactive fictions, and for a number of reasons, interactive fictions do not seem entirely apt to present narratives of the kind seen in traditional narrative arts. Furthermore, while videogames do have narratives, their fictions have mixed uses – to present an unfolding story, and to situate a game – and the function as a game seems to be somewhat inconsistent with the function as a narrative. Gaming narratives often implicitly demand that their players momentarily put down what they are doing in the game world, and engage in a quite different mode of activity.

Most clearly, though there are obvious narrators in many games such as *Fallout 3*, the interactive gameplay portions of videogames often do not seem to involve narrators, or even the implied authors that some theorists think exist even when there is no overt narrator in a fiction (Currie, 1990).

In the gameplay portions of videogames at least, gamers often have a "direct" access to the fictional world in virtue of fictionally playing a role there, and if there is a viewpoint expressed in these fictions, it is that of their character proxy. In traditional narratives, the presence of a narrator or implied author allows the reader to assume that the events presented are done so for some reason that would justify a particular interpretation of the sequence of events, even if the narrator is untrustworthy. But because it is the player that chooses many of the events that occur in game worlds, or which events in the world are presented and in which order, the sequences of fictional events that occur in videogames cannot be assumed to have been chosen for their contribution to some overall story. Indeed, many of the events that occur in game worlds are chosen for their contribution to solving a problem of gameplay. Because the reasons for the fictional events in the worlds of videogames are often contingent on the decisions made by the player, they cannot be assumed to be meaningful in terms of the narrative that the game may present in all but the broadest terms specified by criteria that the player must meet to be successful in the mission. For example, a player-character's hesitation in a game world – perhaps in attacking an end-of-level boss – cannot be interpreted as a Hamlet-style reluctance to act, but may simply derive from the fact that the player put down the controller to make a cup of coffee.

Because they are generated by gameplay, the bulk of events that make up the fictional worlds of videogames seem mostly inappropriate for constituting interesting narratives in that they seem uninteresting from a human point of view. The actual sequence of fictional events in a game like the excellent *God of War* may be something like this: climb a ladder, shuffle along a ledge, kill a skeleton (× 5), climb another ladder, kill a medusa, walk across a beam, jump to avoid swinging knives, solve a puzzle, and so on. This sequence of events seems pretty unpromising in terms of its narrative interest, and is hardly the stirring stuff of which epic narrative is made. And, of course, the narrative that does exist in *God of War* is mostly constituted by cut-scenes that a player gets to enjoy once they have cleared a section or level. This also means that for the most part, the *interpretive* involvement of the fiction in *God of War* is not driven by an interest in an unfolding narrative, but by an interest in meeting the challenges of gameplay. Steven Johnson notes that with a game like *The Legend of Zelda*, the type of interpretation appropriate to narrative fictions "will go only so far, because what's important here is not the content of the Zelda world, but the way the world has been organized to tax the problem-solving skills of the player" (2006: 60).

Filmic and literary narratives often involve characterization and character growth, and these things – in the form found in traditional narrative – are almost always lacking in gaming fictions. As argued earlier, characters in videogames are usually functional items that enable gameplay. In *Call of Duty*, for example, Soap McTavish, the principal player-character, is a functional shell, and hence mostly anonymous. Characters can be developed in some videogames, though this development does not amount to the sorts of personality and emotional growth we expect to see in more traditional narrative forms of fiction. Character growth in videogames usually amounts to *leveling up* – the gaining of life points and special abilities, such as magical spells or weapon specialties – rather than personality growth, change, or learning. In *World of Warcraft* the monsters and situations become more challenging as the game progresses, and the only way for the character to succeed against this challenging environment is to become more potent. Attaining a new level is symbolic of attaining more potency in the fictional world. Levels of experience are another feature that videogames have drawn from role-playing games such as *Dungeons and Dragons*. The *Sims* attempts to introduce more humanly interesting content into its game world, but this seems just to replace the tasks of combat, spell casting, and puzzle solving with similarly inconsequential fictional tasks like cooking meals and cleaning the bathroom. Again, hardly promising material on which to build a narrative.

A particular difficulty that videogames face is that they are simply long, and this can have an effect on the ability of the player to sustain their interest in the narrative. Moreover, the length and predominance of the gameplay portions can distract focus from the narrative. *Grand Theft Auto IV*, though presenting one of the most compelling narratives in modern games, took me over 56 hours to complete. Most of this time is spent in gameplay, and as a result, the narrative elements can be overwhelmed by the sheer mass of fictional events. I frequently needed to remind myself of what had occurred earlier in the narrative every time play paused for a cut-scene. Furthermore, the expressive tone conveyed by a particularly successful cut-scene is often quickly extinguished by the quite different responses to the gameplay: the fractured form of the fiction often does not allow the fiction to *sustain* the expressive tone of the game. So, just as excessive narrative may prove an interruption to gameplay, the mass of gameplay can also distract from a narrative.

Some of the fictions presented by games may positively defy reconciliation with the game's ostensible narrative. The actual fictional content of videogames – what happens in the fictional world of the game – sometimes seems to jar with the narratives presented therein: in *Drake's Fortune*, any sympathy one has for the central character would quickly be destroyed if one paused to consider the huge number of people Nathan Drake actually kills during the course of the gameplay. Whereas the death of a character – even a peripheral one – would be considered a significant event in any but the most violent of action films, in videogames these killings are needed to sustain the fictive activities of gameplay. But the narrative of *Drake's Fortune* also calls for sympathy with its protagonist, and as such it is almost as if the player must *quarantine* the gameplay fiction from the narrative fiction, or simply remain insensitive to the potential moral ramifications of Drake's actions. Again, the gameplay and narrative of the videogame seem fractured.

A similar difficulty that the gaming nature of videogame fictions poses for narrative is the lack of finality that player-character death has in a game. Death in videogames almost always plays the function of failure to meet the challenges set by gameplay. Once the player-character dies, the game almost always sets the player back to an earlier stage in the game so that they can retry the section. This formal demand of gameplay introduces elements of repetition and contingency into videogame worlds that makes them unsuitable to presenting sustained narratives (Poole, 2000: 112–114). If the death of the protagonist in a traditional narrative was so easily avoided by merely replaying the scenario, then the events of such fictions would hardly have the emotional impact they do. In *American Beauty*, the finality of the death of the protagonist Lester Burnham, signaled in the opening sequence of the movie, has a significant shape on the course of the narrative, and allows the fiction to have its emotional impact as we discover just how Burnham dies. But in *World of Warcraft*, character death, though of potential annoyance, merely means that the player-character appears in a graveyard as a spirit so that their body can be raised from the dead.

What this contingency and repeatability shows is that the fictional worlds of videogames are quite different to those of traditional narrative fictions. Where the reading or viewing of traditional narrative fictions seems to chart a single world – though one that may be *filled in* by interpretive detail that might differ between appreciators – the fictional worlds of videogames seem to present a *cluster* of fictional worlds in a single playing. The fictional worlds of games branch out as the player explores various fictive means of solving the problems of gameplay; most of these branches terminate in failure, however. In a particular playing of *Call of Duty* – assuming the player-character dies a number of times, as I did – most of the world trajectories terminate when the character dies, leaving the player to return to an earlier fictive period and re-explore the fictive potential of the game in an attempt to clear the level. Furthermore, the game might be replayed, leading to another quite different cluster of trajectories. In terms of the theory of interactive fiction presented earlier, *different worlds might be fictionalized from the same fictive prop*.

The narrative fictions in most games – where the events are chosen for their contribution to an unfolding story – are far more determinate than these gaming fictions, however. The particular narrative represented in *Call of Duty: Modern Warfare* is common to all players and all playings of the game: the narrative in the game progresses in a similar manner irrespective of what the player does in the game, and so might be seen to be a key part of the *work world* of a videogame fiction. For all games, Al-Fulani will be executed, Sgt. Paul Jackson will be killed in a nuclear blast, and the Russian ultranationalists will launch their nuclear attack on America. Such work world *definiteness* is crucial to narrative fictions because it allows the author to guide the audience through a sustained and meaningful set of events; the definiteness derives from the *scripting* of fictional worlds. Scripted props are desirable given the nature of our interpretive interests in narrative fictions. Close control over fictive events aids the ability to sustain narratives that are carefully paced, and develop in a set order. This constancy also allows for the development of subtle meaning and emotional effect. Narrative works can thus give concerted treatments of complex themes. Furthermore, in narrative fictions this linearity seems to give rise to the *normativity* of interpretation: why, unlike the case of the game fiction in *Call of Duty* where many of the player's activities do not even call for interpretation in terms of the narrative, we can inquire into which interpretation of the plot of the game is the *correct* one.

Thus the deep reason for the tension between game fictions and narrative fictions may relate to the role of definite scripting in gaming, compared to its role in narrative fictions. In gaming, definiteness – earlier referred to as *linearity* – is often seen as unduly constraining, as players tend to value their own contribution to the game fiction. But narratives rely on close scripting to have their sustained and meaningful effects: this is to say that the determinateness of the props in narrative fictions lends a particular artistic focus. This means that the definiteness that often seems antithetical to open gameplay is utterly necessary for the depiction of sustained narratives.

It is no surprise, then, that some of the more effective videogames narrative-wise are closely scripted ones. Some of the most evocative sequences in *Call of Duty: Modern Warfare*, such as the stealth mission *All Ghillied Up*, set in Pripyat, are closely directed. In this particular mission, because the player is led through a quite linear environment, the game can carefully control the sequence of the unfolding events. Much of the linearity of *All Ghillied Up* is encoded in the fact that the player-character is part of a two-man team with a superior officer guiding the player's actions. In the middle of the mission, the player enters a building abandoned due the Chernobyl disaster, and the artfully disheveled environment, the lighting, and the subtle use of background music make the sequence particularly evocative. But this is only allowed to occur because the sequence takes place during a lull in the activity of gameplay, and because the player's movement through the area is carefully scripted or, as some critics and gamers have claimed, *on rails*.

The general point here may be that the situational nature of a fictive medium alters the kind of engagement appropriate to it, implying that new forms of fiction will display novel variations when it comes to the ways in which audiences interact with and interpret them. The interactive gaming nature of videogames may thus put them somewhat at odds with the narrative aims of traditional fictions, and the reasons for this should be relatively clear: the events are not "chosen for their contribution to an unfolding plot." Rather, they are chosen by the player, or are chosen by the game designer, for their contribution to a game fiction. This means that the gaming fictions can have features that are disadvantageous to effective narrative: they are non-linear, too long and unfocused, contingent and repetitive, jarring with the tone and content of successful narrative, distasteful, and so on. The challenge in the future of gaming narratives – and it seems to be a challenge that games designers are quite aware of given some of the recent developments in gaming narrative – will be in balancing these seemingly inconsistent demands on the fictional worlds of games.

RECONCILING GAMES AND NARRATIVES

What measures are being taken by games designers to reconcile the gaming and narrative aspects of videogames? I think that we can classify these attempts into two kinds: those measures that can be taken to lessen or disguise the apparent schism between the gaming and narrative aspects of videogames, and those measures that attempt to furnish strongly *interactive narratives.*

Various measures can be taken to hide the joins, as it were, integrating the narratives of videogames with their games. One method – and it is that used by *Call of Duty: Modern Warfare,* and increasingly in games generally, it seems – is in excising cut-scenes altogether and depicting the narrative events within the interactive gameplay portions of the videogame. *Call of Duty* avoids the problem of narrative inertness introduced by cinematic cut-scenes by presenting a lot of the narrative through the game fiction, and so integrated within the interactive portions of the game. The player is party to a number of conversations and events that have a bearing on the narrative. In one instance, after tracking Imran Zakhaev's son to a rooftop in Azerbaijan after a long and intense battle with the ultranationalist forces, McTavish witnesses the younger Zakhaev's suicide within the context of gameplay, a key narrative event that motivates Imran Zakhaev's later actions. It should be noted, however, that the player makes no contribution to the narrative. The conversations and narrative events in *Call of Duty* are scripted, and even though the player can look and move around during the presentation of narrative elements, they cannot change them: the player cannot stop Zakhaev from killing himself. *Half-Life* – a near-future dystopian first-person shooter – is an earlier and notable example of the integration of narrative into gameplay sequences.

Interestingly, in *Call of Duty* and *Half-Life*, both player-characters – Soap McTavish and Gordon Freeman – are silent figures in their respective narratives: neither speaks nor makes an interactive contribution to the dialogue. Indeed, silent player-characters are ubiquitous in videogames. This is not such a bad thing of the narrative in *Call of Duty* – Soap is only a bit player, a member of a squad – but in *Half-Life* this lack of character input seems to me very artificial indeed. The narrative of *Half-Life* has been consistently praised by reviewers and gamers, which is quite astounding given that the protagonist of the narrative does not even speak. Both Soap and Gordon's unlikely inability to speak derives from the combination of gameplay-located narrative and first-person perspective seen in *Call of Duty* and *Half-Life*. Because the narrative is rendered in the interactive portions of the game, having the player-character speak would not be able to avail of a cinematic third-person depiction, but would somehow have to be depicted in the first-person. Not only would it be difficult to make clear to the player that they were speaking, it would also be difficult to coordinate the player-character's actions with their speech. Some first-person games, such as *Battlefield: Bad Company*, abruptly shift to a third-person cinematic scene to depict their player-characters speaking; but the shift of representational perspective in *Bad Company* seems quite awkward, essentially wrenching the player out of their gameplay perspective. Having a first-person character speak may also potentially shatter the impression that the player really is in control of their character, unless the player could be provided with a number of options of what to say, which in itself would make the scripting of the narrative more complicated. Unfortunately, the lack of speech from Gordon Freeman is equally awkward: the protagonist in this game, held in high repute for his deeds throughout the game world, cannot even contribute to conversation, and so is forced into following along as a mostly passive force in the narrative, ordered here and there to perform various tasks.

Perhaps the real difference here is how the structural problem is dealt with in the two cases. *Half-Life*, as an earlier attempt to integrate the narrative within the gameplay, struggles with placing a silent player-character as a coherent figure within the narrative. *Call of Duty*, in demoting the importance of the player-character, and seeing them as part of a much larger narrative in which they are not in control (in fact, in depicting them in several such roles in which they are swept along in events), more successfully integrates its narrative with its gaming fiction. This, again, is an instance of how games designers have over time developed artful responses to the structural features and problems of the medium of videogaming.

Another manner in which gameplay and narrative can be reconciled is by the *personalization* of the narrative. *Oblivion* gives the narrative the illusion of really being about *your* player-character by tailoring the fiction to your character's collection of fictive variations. As noted in chapter 1, this game allows the player a great deal of control over the design of their character, and their design choices are reflected in the narrative. Within the narrative – almost all of which is depicted internal to gameplay – the player-character is referred to by their race, gender, and character class, all things that the player has chosen, so giving the illusion that it is their player-character that is contributing to the narrative events. Immediately after the player has chosen their race and sex, they have a discussion with a fellow prisoner who acknowledges these facts in a taunting exchange; later, in the assassin narrative arc, the player revisits the prisoner, and their identity is acknowledged in the dreadful scene that follows.

Mass Effect, a third-person science fiction role-playing game, goes a step further than *Oblivion* in allowing quite sophisticated personalized dialogue. *Mass Effect* provides a *branching dialogue* in that the dialogue is turned into something of a mini-game. The player chooses a general attitude to a previous sentence from a range of negative or positive responses, which is then concretely verbalized, allowing the player to express their attitude to the events that occur in the game world and narrative, knowing that the response they make may have an impact on the dialogue. As such, the dialogue is further personalized, in giving the impression that it is the *player's attitude* that is being expressed by the character. *Mass Effect* represents its dialogue though cinematic methods and also has all of the dialogue voice-acted, whereas in *Oblivion* the player-character's parts are not voiced but rather represented through text. Being a third-person game, *Mass Effect* is also able to smoothly blend the dialogue portions with the gameplay proper because it does not need to shift representational perspectives to depict dialogue in a cinematic way. A benefit of this is that the game can more effectively show the emotional responses that players have to the dialogue by showing their facial and bodily responses. The dialogue in *Mass Effect* is thus convincing, whereas in many other games, including *Oblivion*, it is entirely flat. The cost of this, of course, is that all the dialogue and exchanges must be voice-acted and choreographed, adding to the representational complexity and cost of the game.

The personalization of role-playing games extends to the ability of players to choose in which order they tackle the quests that make up the narrative of such game worlds. The quest form of narrative seen in videogames owes its existence to pen and paper role-playing games, to the fantasy writing of J. R. R. Tolkien, and through him a number of medieval epic poems, such as *Beowulf*. *Oblivion* arranges a large number of quests or missions that are progressively completed. The player can choose the order in which to tackle quests, and their subsequent contribution to the narrative is stringing a number of such elements together. Given the number of the quests, their sequence for any given game is likely to be unique, and what will certainly be unique is the manner in which they are tackled given the available variations in character type and abilities.

Hence, the quest narratives that are typical of the role-playing genre involve a number of small local narratives strung together into an arc that is unique for a particular player: we might call this *emergent narrative*, drawing a parallel with fictively rich *emergent gameplay*. Though they may share elements of the game fiction with other players, the sequence and combination of their activities is unique to their character, and this constitutes the story arc of their character. For example, one character I played in *Oblivion*, a dark elf mage, was very careful to act for the most part in a moral and upright way for the initial part of the game, playing through the mage narrative in which the player battles to rid Cyrodiil of necromancers. Unfortunately, while sneaking around a dungeon one day, I killed what I thought to be an adversary, but which turned out to be a wandering adventurer much like myself, and so unwittingly committed an act of murder. The Dark Brotherhood – the assassins' guild in the world of *Oblivion* – somehow observed my wicked act, and I was subsequently invited to join their order. Soon I was committing a series of evil assassinations, and so my character experienced a quite significant change in nature. Later, the character became a vampire: about the most disastrous thing that can happen to you in *Oblivion*, forcing you into traveling only at night and causing other characters in the game to recoil in horror as you desperately try to perform the actions needed to rid yourself of vampirism. The narratives in *Oblivion* thus seem to be of a *fictive self*, and are a potentially private and *post hoc* narrative that the player constructs to unify their player-character. Interestingly, the role of such narratives in establishing the real self have been a topic of philosophical and scientific concern for quite some time, and is explored in a study by neuropsychologist Antonio Damasio (1999) on the nature of consciousness. This sense of emergent narrative may thus be a closer cousin to the cognitive narratives that establish self-identity, rather than the narratives traditionally seen in art.

There may be questions over the dramatic effectiveness of such personalized episodic narratives, however. For one thing, though there is a clear beginning to such character narratives, in my experience the narrative ends only when the player loses interest in the character; like many quest and fantasy narratives, they seem rather impotent in the long run. Furthermore, in *Oblivion*, besides getting an achievement on a menu screen, and some equipment or special ability the character may be rewarded, the player-character does not grow to reflect their experience in a given narrative arc. Compare this to episodic TV sitcoms, where the narrative events of an episode are usually forgotten by the next week. *The Simpsons*, of course, has a lot of fun with this feature of episodic narrative, frequently drawing attention to the fictive inconsistencies of its fictive world or *canon*. In quest games, and episodic television, the narrative effectively *bottlenecks* after a given episode so that the changes that occurred in that episode are not preserved into the next. So while allowing for player interactivity, in choosing the order of the narrative they are playing through, such videogames lack the dramatic shape that is offered by self-contained and closely scripted narratives such as *Call of Duty* or *BioShock*.

I think that one of the most effective ways of drawing the player-character into the narrative is where they are made responsible, if not for the content of the narrative, then for the discovery of the content. Videogames often present *narratives of disclosure or discovery*. This is to say that the player-character's epistemic activities (see chapter 4) can be made to play a crucial role in their unearthing of the details of the narrative. In a long list of games such as *BioShock, Condemned, Silent Hill, Resistance*, and *Portal*, though the narrative is scripted, the player has an important role in discovering the facts of the narrative through their interaction. In the science fiction-horror first-person shooter *System Shock 2*, through exploration of initially unknown environments, and by discovering electronic messages traded by the principal characters, the player slowly uncovers the nature of the mysterious events that have befallen the spaceship *Von Braun*. The player is sometimes integrated into the narrative by playing a role referenced in the discovered messages. In essence, the game allows the player to discover facts about the game world, and to reconstruct the narrative on that basis. Because the information sources need searching out, any particular playing can have a more or less complete telling of the game narrative. In this way the interpretation of an interactive game fiction can be made to more closely align with the interpretation of a narrative fiction, as the player effectively takes on the position of the first-person narrators often seen in traditional narrative fictions.

Many such narratives of disclosure employ an interactive twist on *in media res*, with the player waking up amid some unknown situation where many of the key narrative events have already taken place. *BioShock* starts with a plane crash and discovery of a bathysphere that leads to a city under the sea, where it is clear that something horrible has occurred, though the player must struggle to piece the events together. In *Portal*, another narrative of disclosure, the player-character awakes in a baffling test chamber. As such, an important part of many such narratives is the discovery of the player-character's own hidden identity. In *Resistance*, Nathan Hale has been infected by a virus and is being pursued/aided by a shadowy covert ops group that has in mind for him some future use. In *System Shock 2* the player-character is unaware that he is being manipulated to achieve ends other than his own survival.

Sometimes, untrustworthy sources of information are integrated into these narratives of disclosure, further complicating the player's ability to reconstruct a coherent game narrative, and indeed making their contribution to the narrative more robust by allowing them to resist the narrative that is being fed to them. *BioShock* employs an interactive take on the untrustworthy narrator, in that one of the principal sources of information in the game world, and hence the view of the world that is disclosed to the player, is eventually revealed to be a dissemblance. Indeed, the moment of revelation in *BioShock* – when the player-character finally comes to realize the real nature of their role in the game world – is about as effective a narrative event as I have observed in gaming.

All of these methods, I think, provide a genuine sense of *interactive narrative*: a narrative in which the player-character has an interactive role, even if the narrative is closely scripted. In narratives of disclosure especially, even though the player ultimately does not contribute to the narrative content, they are closely entwined in its discovery, interpretation, and reconstruction. In my experience, such narratives of disclosure are artistically satisfying, perhaps indeed, just because the player is swept along in the closely scripted action. They are effective because they retain the scripting that seems necessary for dramatically weighty fiction, but they allow the player-character an interactive role of discovery which engages the player's fear, apprehension, curiosity, and even wonder concerning the events occurring in the game world (see chapter 7).

But perhaps there is a stronger sense of *interactive narrative*, one in which the player has a formative role in the course of the narrative by allowing them to make a contribution to the fictive content depicted in the narrative. In this sense, the player would have some control over just which plot events occur, and how these comprise the events of the story. This is a much more ambitious sense of interactive narrative. The difference to the more minimal sense of interactive narrative discussed above is that not only is the player-character a *protagonist* in the fictional world, the player is also a part-*author* of the fiction. Indeed, it seems that some games designers see this as a desirable objective (Young, 2007). There are two questions we can ask concerning the strong sense of interactive narrative: first, is it possible? Second, is it artistically desirable?

I think that there are two principal ways of generating an amount of genuine authorial control over a narrative for the player. The first is branching narratives of the type also seen in the various branching game books, and increasingly in videogames. In a videogame this usually means that a choice that a player makes during the game leads to different narrative paths comprised of different sets of cinematic cut-scenes, in-game narrative events, or dialogue. Many games now have alternative endings depending on the actions that characters take within the course of the fiction: *BioShock* and *Grand Theft Auto IV* are just two examples from the games already discussed here. In *BioShock* the alternative endings depend on the morally loaded decisions that the player makes in regard to the Little Sisters.

Shadow of Memories – a notable, but not altogether successful Playstation 2 game also released as *Shadow of Destiny* – makes attempts at providing a complex and interactive narrative that is integrated with the gameplay, that is, it cedes some amount of authorial control to the player. Just which narrative fiction emerges from the prop on a particular playing owes to decisions that the gamer makes. *Shadow of Memories* achieves this by allowing for plot branches and thus multiple outcomes in the plot. The game is based on the premise that the player-character can go back in time to change the present in the town that constitutes the fictional world of the game. The town is represented in at least four different time periods, and the player can wander around, noting how the town has developed and grown over time, and the consequences of seemingly simple events that they have observed or contributed to in the past. The objectives of the game are contained in several missions that involve diverting the course of time from arriving at a regrettable state of affairs in the present. The player can move between the various times largely at will, but the possible future-changing decisions are set to be discovered at a particular time and place.

This potential for diverging narratives in which the player has control through their gameplay decisions relates to what was previously said about the encoding of games in fictions (chapter 5). Most game narratives are separate from gameplay. But what is happening in these branching narratives is that the formal structures of gameplay are encoded in the arc of narratives. The objectives of the game are to find a way to reconcile the narrative, and the reconciliation that the player gets is determined by the gameplay choices they make. This also occurs in the assassination mission in *Grand Theft Auto IV*, and what is most interesting about this example is the success with which the game aligns its gameplay with its narrative. The solution to the mission – just which brother the player chooses to kill – also propels the game narrative, and the decision they make seems based in part on the emotional response the player has to the narrative motivating the decision. Thus, *Shadow of Memories*, *BioShock*, and *Grand Theft Auto IV* encode their games at least in part in their narrative fictions.

The problems with *Shadow of Memories* as a game are instructive of the general problems with branching narrative, however. The first problem is that there simply is not enough gameplay in *Shadow of Memories*. The cinematic sequences, and periods in which the player must simply move from one place or time to the next, often impede the player's involvement in *Shadow of Memories*: much of the game is simply too inert from a gameplay point of view. The action that branches the narrative is usually only a single choice by the player, and this means that such interactive narratives provide very little gameplay that is particular to their narratives. In *Grand Theft Auto IV*, of course, the branching narratives are a very small part of gameplay, which for the most part is made up of non-narrative fictive gameplay.

Second, the interactivity of the narrative in *Shadow of Memories* is some-what limited. This is because the path of the narrative branches only at a small number of junctures, and there are only seven possible endings. *Shadow of Memories* thus provides only very superficial authorial control on the part of the player; to provide more would mean the production of many more discrete sequences of video and dialogue to progress the story. To be able to represent extensively branching fictional worlds a videogame would become unwieldy because of the potentially exponential growth of the nar-rative material – cut-scenes, dialogue – needed to sustain a large number of branches (Poole, 2000: 110). But more significantly, even if the game could provide a large number of possible narratives, the narrative would still be scripted: the *definiteness* I have argued to be crucial to narrative success is still evident in these branching narratives; it is just invested in several dif-ferent narrative trajectories. The interactivity of these games is comprised of choosing one potential narrative over another, all of which already exist in the game, scripted by the writers. The player interacts in the narrative events only by choosing the course of a scripted narrative, and not by performing novel fictive behaviors that might lead to novel narrative arcs.

Addressing this last issue – that even branching narratives are fully scripted, and hence not genuinely player-driven – some technologists hold out hope for *procedural narrative* (Young, 2007). We met procedural techniques of creating fictive content in an earlier chapter. The *Euphoria* engine uses procedural techniques to produce novel and hopefully convincing behavior on the part of characters. Rather than cueing a scripted animation or motion capture sequence, the program generates apparent physical and intentional behavior on the fly. This is an attempt to avoid the difficulties of producing non-stereotyped and hence naturalistic content without the combinatorial explosion that would come about if one were to separately animate character behaviors for all the types of situation that a character might meet. Perhaps the same sort of procedural methods could be used in gaming narrative to avoid what are essentially the same problems of com-binatorial explosion seen in branching narratives.

Procedural narrative would amount to an algorithm that through various functional placeholders creates a narrative around the player incorporating their decisions as the narrative develops. This gives the prospect of *strongly* interactive narrative (Lopes, 2001). In essence, such an algorithm would, in conjunction with the player, be a *proxy author*. Games development researcher R. Michael Young (2007) envisages a bipartite nature to this kind of program in the form of an "event generator" and a "discourse generator." The event generator produces the fictive content that is the substance of the narrative, while the discourse generator manages the depiction of these events, and so involves virtual camera movements, editing, and other representational techniques needed to convey the events as a narrative. Though Young does not acknowledge this, the discourse generator also seems to reflect something of the *implied author* function that is seen as key by some of the philosophers of fiction (Currie, 1990). A narrative is not only a sequence of events, but also a perspective on those events.

Will these technologists really be able to design procedural narratives that produce anything other than minor episodic content? Suffice it to say that these problems are far from being solved, and no current games use any degree of procedural narrative. Young's own work is in the testing stage, and it faces severe difficulties. The principal problem is the one discussed in this chapter: situating the player as an active agent within a narrative while retaining the meaning and interest of that narrative. For Young, the problem here is characterized as the tension between the "control" of the player and the "coherence" of the narrative, and he sees this as a major obstacle in the procedural generation of narrative.

I do not really doubt that these technical problems might one day be solved: the technological developments seen in recent gaming are enough to rid me of that kind of pessimism. What seems more worrying are the *artistic* problems. It seems perfectly possible to me that a program could produce a coherent narrative; it is hard to say, though, whether procedural narrative would ever be compelling or artful. What we are really asking for in this case is a *procedural artist* that would, to repeat a passage already quoted, "make it easier for us to weave together a pattern of complex imaginings by laying out a narrative [allowing us to] access to imaginings more complex, inventive and colourful than we could hope to construct for ourselves" (Currie, 1997: 53). This is an ambitious project!

Furthermore, there may be reasons to doubt the motivation of player control over narrative in the first place: is there any reason to think that a player's control over aspects of the narrative is at all desirable? I noted earlier that the close scripting of narratives by authors generates their normativity, in allowing audiences to aim for a correct interpretation. Would player-generated narrative actually offer the ability of normativity of interpretation? What would a procedural narrative be *about* if its key events were chosen by the player? Finally, if games are successful in integrating gameplay with narrative in a seamless and interesting way, as explored earlier, what does it matter that the player has no control over the narrative? There are many interesting issues here, especially concerning issues of performance and authorship in videogames, which I will have to leave aside. For the moment, the narratives that exist in games remain scripted, look likely to remain so, and indeed, owe what success they have as narratives in being so.

CHAPTER SUMMARY

The structural features of gaming and narrative – two of the entertainment functions of videogames – are in tension. Interactive fictions introduce elements of contingency and repeatability that undermine the ability of fictions to convey sustained sequences of events apt to produce emotional and intellectually compelling drama. At worst, narrative leads to player inertness that is at odds with the distinctive interactive nature of videogames, and so the narratives that do exist in games can often seem tacked on, or incidental to the real substance of the game. Games designers, aware of these problems, have attempted to resolve the tensions by more closely integrating the narrative and gaming aspects of videogames, by excising inert cut-scenes, placing the onus on the player to discover the narrative content of the game, and even letting the player in part determine the eventual path that the narrative takes. These solutions are the source of much of the artistic interest in games, allowing designers to produce artful responses to the problems inherent in the medium.

NEXT CHAPTER

Emotions are crucial to our appreciation of fictions. This is no different in videogames, where an emotional involvement in a fictional world adds a great deal of interest and richness to the gaming experience. *BioShock*, for example, has drawn frequent praise for the rich and varied emotional engagement it encourages. Emotions for fictions can be puzzling though, as one soon sees when one reflects on the non-existence of the apparent targets of fictional emotions. The Little Sisters in *BioShock* do not really exist, so what is there to be emotional about? Drawing on the philosophical literature on fictional emotions shows videogames to be very interesting in this regard because in videogames the emotions have an impact on what the player is and is not willing to do in a fictional game world. This allows for some interesting reflection on the role of emotions in videogaming generally.

7

EMOTION IN VIDEOGAMING

HOW CAN WE BE MOVED BY THE FATE OF NIKO BELLIC?

I couldn't bring myself to kill the little girl, even though she had been surgically and genetically manipulated for the purpose of extracting stem cells, and so wasn't really human at all; or so I was told. Still, those big eyes, pigtail, and the pretty frock; I couldn't do it. Instead, I decided to save her, and as I did so, using my own genetically enhanced powers to regain her humanity, an emotion of sympathy and brotherly care swept over me. Later, my actions would revisit me in the most unexpected and emotionally satisfying way. The care that I had shown for the Little Sisters would be reciprocated by their own care for me.

Videogames involve our emotions, and in a number of different ways. *BioShock* is the masterpiece of recent gaming. Genre-wise it is a first-person shooter, survival-horror game with aspects of role-playing – already a complicated mix of gaming forms. What really impresses is its emotional depth, and the way its narrative, set in Rapture, a dystopian city beneath the sea, fits perfectly with its interactive gaming form. The game's narrative is about freewill and morality: how we control our own actions and those of others, and how we resist the control of other people with our own (hopefully, better) judgment. The Little Sisters are the moral locus of *BioShock*. When their first line of defense has been defeated – their chaperones, the ominous, diving-suit wearing Big Daddies – the Little Sisters use our emotions to defend themselves. In one of the taped messages discovered late in the game, the scientist responsible for their genetic design asks why they have to be little girls: to us it should be obvious that the little girls most effectively and sentimentally manipulate our emotions of sympathy and care. Other characters try to manipulate us into destroying the Little Sisters, asserting that they aren't really human at all, but rather genetically designed simulacra.

In *System Shock 2* – developed by some of the same personnel as the later *BioShock* – the overwhelming feelings are those of fear and apprehension. The starship *Von Braun*, isolated in deep space on the other side of the galaxy, is dark, shadowy, and deserted. The few other people encountered in the game world are usually dead, or are screaming and being chased by mutants wielding shotguns, and thus about to become dead. Things have a habit of exploding when approached, startling the player. The personal logs that are found all over the ship are filled with tales of strangeness and terror, as the crew, now mostly deceased, detail their dealings with some unknown menace. In the email logs, crewmembers are about to divulge some secret about what is really occurring, when screams, or explosions, or the sounds of monkeys screeching, cut the recording off mid-sentence. Just what is happening to the monkeys, why are their brains exposed, and why are they so malevolent? The tension builds throughout the game as the player attempts to reach deeper into the ship's decks, urged on by Dr. Polito. Occasionally, when I was getting low on health and ammunition, I got myself into situations when faced by a formidable foe all I could do was panic. My ability to deal with the situation briefly left me, and I hurriedly ran away; I was unable to keep my head straight in order to face the danger. The world of *System Shock 2* is a terrifying and unsettling world. Yet the game is terrific fun because of this.

In *Devil May Cry*, a gothic adventure game in which the hero must defeat multitudes of fiendish monsters and perform difficult challenges such as dodging metal spikes protruding from holes in walls, the experience is often frustrating, even maddening. Yet it is not just the difficulty of the *game* that is frustrating, it seems it is the difficulty of dealing with the monsters and situations that draws the player's rage. Though I enjoyed the game immensely, one thing really annoyed me. This was an enormous and powerful fiery spider that I had to battle. It appeared in a shadowy and pillared room, massive and writhing with power, its armor making it almost impervious to my attacks. Eventually, I discovered that with some difficulty I could leap onto the monster's back and plunge my sword into the unprotected joints between the armor. After seeing it off, I was especially annoyed to see the creature appear a second time. The third time I met it, *it was personal*. When at last I sent the creature to its final doom the elation and relief were visceral. I may have even (really) jumped around the room in triumph. Thus, the other side of the coin of the frustration games cause is the eventual elation that the player can feel on completing a difficult level or game, or defeating a powerful foe.

The role of the emotions in the arts has long been known and theor-ized about, and indeed this emotional involvement is one of the principal reasons why the arts hold the important place in our lives that they do. Our emotions *connect* us to the fictional worlds presented in artworks. Nevertheless, there is a longstanding paradox in the philosophy of the arts concerning our ability to become emotionally engaged with fictions at all (Radford, 1975). How is it that we become emotional for the characters and situations depicted in fictions when we know that they *are* fictions? What is there to be emotional *about*? The paradoxical nature of our responses is strengthened by the *cognitivist* view of the emotions as necessarily involving beliefs: to be afraid is in part to believe that one is in danger (Kenny, 1963). But in the case of a horror movie, we do not believe that the slime slithering toward us actually exists (Walton, 1978). What is there to be afraid of? The so-called "paradox of the fictional emotions" has given rise to a small mountain of literature in the past twenty-five years (Levinson, 1997).

In videogames, as seen in the sympathy for the Little Sisters, the fear for oneself in the world of *System Shock 2*, or the annoyance and personal enmity with the fiery spider in *Devil May Cry*, this paradox comes about in a particularly striking way. Not only do the fictions of videogames arouse our emotions, but these emotions have an impact on what the player is and is not willing to do in a game world. In *BioShock*, how you treat the Little Sisters has an effect on how the narrative finishes, and so that I could see these effects, it became necessary for me play the game again, and to treat the Little Sisters badly so as to harvest their resources: I didn't want to do it, and it made me squirm when I eventually did. This response is not peculiar to me, and it is not as if I am an idiosyncratically overly-sensitive gamer. One gaming friend admitted to me that he couldn't bring himself to kill the Gray Prince character in *Oblivion* – an orc who the player helps to discover his real and shameful nature as part-vampire – because he "felt sorry for him." Another said of the same game that he started the assassin missions, but felt so morally squeamish about committing the actual assassinations that he never finished that narrative arc. Will Wright, creator of the seminal videogames *Simcity* and *The Sims*, admits a similar response when he said: "I felt so bad about beating my creature to death in [the god-game] *Black and White*" (Wright, 2007). I am convinced that many readers will have had similar responses.

But why should I have felt moral compunction when faced with the dilemma of killing the Little Sisters, or fear when confronted by a mutant in the darkened halls of the starship *Von Braun*, or annoyance and anger with that dastardly fiery spider? How can we be moved by the fate of Niko Bellic? I am perfectly aware that these things are only fictional in having no real existence: there really are no Little Sisters, and subsequently, no one is in the least bit harmed when I commit the actions I feel squeamish about. The emotions that are so crucial to the playing of these games might seem at the least atypical, and at worst, thoroughly *irrational* (Radford, 1975). In this chapter I will explore the variety of these gaming emotions, their nature, explanation, and also their role in gaming.

It is here, by the way, that videogames strike me as having the greatest potential to make a distinctive contribution to the arts, in the way they draw audiences into their fictional worlds, reconnecting the fictional emotions with action. Because videogames are interactive fictions, placing players as an epistemic and behavioral agent within a game world, the feelings that those players have can subsequently become an influential part of that fictional world, guiding their actions therein. This also means that the role of the emotions in videogaming is of potentially significant interest within the philosophy of the arts.

MY FEAR OF MUTANTS

How are we best to explain the nature of the emotions that exist in videogames? How are the emotions caused, if not – as is usually the case in emotions (as the cognitivist claims) – by beliefs about the reality of some evocative situation? First, perhaps there are beliefs about things with a real existence that are capable of explaining a gamer's emotional involvement in videogames. The frustration and elation that are aroused in gaming seem to be able to be given such an explanation. When they become frustrated in videogames, it is typically because a gamer believes that they have *failed at a level or task*. Similarly, elation often coincides with the belief of a gamer that they have passed a tricky level or completed a difficult game. These are beliefs about real events, and we can see why they are emotionally relevant ones. Videogames demand a huge amount of effort on the part of the player, as they confront the player with obstacles that are difficult to overcome. Failing at a level for the umpteenth time is bound to be frustrating, enough so that one might throw down the controller in disgust.

Unfortunately, I do not think this explanation is general, for two reasons. First, it surely is the case that many gaming emotions are caused by beliefs about failure or success in a game, but significantly, some are not: the response of sympathy for a Little Sister does not seem to derive from some belief in a state with a real existence, because there does not seem to be some aspect of the *game* (rather than its fiction) to be guilty or morally squeamish about. But secondly, even the emotions of success and defeat that are contingent on games sometimes do not seem entirely amenable to this explanation. Because the games of videogames are encoded in their fictions, understanding just why a gamer is successful or unsuccessful in a game demands that we refer to their fictional activities. What annoyed me when I played *Devil May*

Cry was not merely that the game was so difficult, but that the fiery spider monster was so tenacious. Similarly, in *BioShock*, the Big Daddies are not frightening because they are a formal game obstacle, but because they are *hulking dangerous monsters*. The mere sound they make – a cross between whale song and a plaintive moan – is enough to make my ears prick up and for me to dread the following engagement.

Thus, there is an initial distinction to be made here: some of the emotions caused by games do not have as their apparent object or cause fictional events, but the non-fictive qualities of the game or its playing. Much of the frustration caused by gaming is no doubt caused by the real difficulty of a game. Also, some of the material presented by videogames, particularly of the survival-horror genre, can be genuinely disgusting, and one can be disgusted by the *image*, rather than the fiction it represents. This is especially so when the images presented by videogames are as realistic and visceral as they increasingly are. Similarly, the soundtracks of videogames are frequently emotionally evocative. In regards to the Pripyat mission in *Call of Duty: Modern Warfare* discussed earlier, I noted that the music accompanying one sequence gives it an otherworldly and spooky feel because the music genuinely has that expressive quality. Of course, some of the emotions for the non-fictive aspects of a game are subsequently *integrated* into the fictional game world: the swelling strings that accompany saving a Little Sister *augment* our fictional response of sympathy and care for the Little Sisters, and that is the music's artistic function in the game. But there does seem to be a distinction between fictional and non-fictional emotions – between those directed at what is real of a game, and what is fictional of the world it represents.

It is the game emotions apparently caused by or directed at the fictional events that are of most interest here, because it is no surprise that repeatedly failing a difficult task can be frustrating, or that emotional music can cause emotion – though just how music expresses or causes emotion is a different kind of philosophical problem with its own intrinsic interest (Kivy, 1990). The real difficulty here is how something that is known to be fictional – and subsequently known to have no real existence – can be the *cause* or *object* of the strongly felt emotions evident in gaming.

A second possibility of explaining videogame emotions that seem to be directed at fictions is by claiming that at some level the emotions are caused by *mistaken beliefs* or because of the *suspension of disbelief*. If appreciators somehow mistakenly believed that what was depicted in the videogame was real, then there would be no paradox of the fictional emotions. People clearly become emotional on the basis of mistaken beliefs: an indistinct shape in the shadows might be mistaken for an intruder, prompting a response of genuine fear. Quite similarly, we might think that the emotions arise because gamers intentionally suppress their disbelief in the non-reality of the situations in games (though readers might remember that I rejected this idea in chapter 3, for the reasons to be further developed here). Apart from a proviso to be mentioned shortly about how the emotions involved in fiction are *elicited*, these options are not credible responses to the paradox of the fictional emotions. But reflecting on the problems that such explanations face gives us a vivid additional argument for seeing the playing of videogames as necessarily acknowledging their fictionality, and hence not being *cognitively equivalent* to non-fictive psychology.

A somewhat sadistic thought experiment is in order. Imagine drugging a person and then placing them without their knowledge in a very elaborate and convincing kind of aircraft simulator, perhaps involving actors playing the roles of passengers and flight crew. We could set up the fiction so that the individual is deceived into thinking that the plane will crash unless they are able to land it, perhaps because the flight crew are indisposed, having been poisoned by the in-flight meal. As the deceived participant struggled to land the aircraft, though they were successfully completing the tasks presented by the fictive representations, it would not be the case that they were participating with the fiction *qua* fiction. Instead, it would be that they were mistaking a fiction for the real world. As such, participating with a videogame could conceivably involve a case of cognitive error; this is because, as argued earlier, fiction derives from considerations of pragmatics rather than representational media, and one could simply be misinformed about the pragmatic context of the representations they were interacting with.

But it is clear that *playing* a game could not involve such a mistake. The likely emotional response of the "player" in this thought experiment shows why. In the case that a genuine gamer in such a simulation overshot a runway in their 747 on an attempt to land in bad weather, we might expect them to be excited but ultimately only slightly annoyed at their failure; and they may proceed to reset the game and try again. If our deceived participant similarly ran off the end of the runway, we could expect much screaming and animated shouting of oaths. It is clear, therefore, from the behavior we do observe of videogame participants that fictive practice is not a case of cognitive error – or willing *suspension of disbelief* for that matter – because the types of emotions and behaviors players exhibit are not those of a mistaken participant or of someone who really believes in the reality of the eliciting situation. I think that for this reason we are quite safe in assuming that playing a fictive videogame involves an acknowledgment of the fictive status of the game, and so involves the special cognitive attitude characteristic of fictive practice as a whole.

There is one final kind of belief that might do the job here, however. Perhaps we could say that the beliefs that cause our fictional emotions are beliefs about what is true *in the fiction* (Neill, 1994). Surely we *do* have beliefs about what is fictional in a videogame: unless you believe that in *Grand Theft Auto IV* Niko Bellic is an immigrant and is cousin to Roman, you have failed to understand a key part of the game. Perhaps such beliefs are simply able to cause emotions? I think that this solution merely disguises the real problem, however: just what is it to believe that something occurs "in a fiction"? What it must mean, of course, is that we believe that certain things are imaginary or to be imagined of a fiction. It might be that it is these beliefs about what is imaginary that cause our emotions, but why not then just cut out the beliefs altogether and simply refer to certain things being *imagined* rather than believed, and subsequently conclude that the imagination itself can cause us to become emotional? This, as some should suspect from my earlier account of make-believe, is the explanation I will adopt here. Videogames involve us, guided by digital props, imagining or "make-believing" that certain things are the case, and the perceptual properties of these props and our make-beliefs about what is fictional are emotionally affecting. My emotions for the Little Sisters are possible because what we imagine is often just as capable of causing emotions as what is believed.

The theory presented here, then, is that the perceptual and cognitive states involved in pretense or make-believe elicit affective reactions that we subsequently integrate, as props, as part of a fictional game world (Tavinor, 2005b). Given the nature of our cognitive engagement in episodes of pretense, and what some recent scientific and theoretical studies are telling us about the structure of the emotions and how they relate to higher cognition, there is a lot of internal structure to how this might occur, which I can only hint at in this brief account. First, gamers make-believe in the content of a fiction by imaginatively attending to the fictive prop and, indeed, elaborating on it. So, to adopt a concrete example, in playing a game such as *System Shock 2*, having learnt to tacitly recognize the conventions of fiction, the player understands that the content of the representations within the game is to be treated as fictional. Given that the mutants have taken over the starship *Von Braun* and killed all of the crew, the player make-believedly recognizes that to take back control of the ship they must kill any mutants they see, and that the mutants will unquestionably be hostile.

Next, some aspect of the fictive prop or the imaginary scenario that it represents *elicits* an emotional response. Perceptual or cognitive representations that are prone to causing emotional responses are what Antonio Damasio (1999) calls "emotionally competent stimuli". Emotion theorist Paul Ekman (1980: 84) thinks that in emotional episodes, certain perceptual or cognitive states are detected by an "automatic appraisal mechanism" in the brain that generates a response comprised of stereotyped behavioral and physiological reactions in the body that prepare it for dealing with the eliciting state. For example, a response of fear prepares us to respond to a danger-ous situation by releasing adrenaline, concentrating our attention, raising our heart rate, and tensing our muscles to prepare for a quick getaway. Some of these eliciting responses are *subdoxastic*, in that they are not mediated by higher cognition, lack an inferential nature, and rely on more direct sub-cortical pathways in the brain. An example is the "low road" to the emo-tions detailed by neurophysiologist Joseph Le Doux (1998: 163–165), where simple perceptual phenomena such as a snake, or even a curved stick giving the superficial appearance of a snake, can cause responses of fear in a way that is not mediated through highly cognitive neural pathways.

I think it may be that many of the emotions we have in conjunction with videogames are elicited in such a manner, though ultimately this is an empirical claim to be proved or disproved by scientists rather than a philosopher. Nevertheless, it seems that some of the disgusting or fearful aspects of videogames could be caused through such means, particularly in the survival-horror genre where the images seem primed to trigger the emo-tion of disgust (Rozin, Haidt, and McCauley, 2000). The startle response is another candidate subdoxastic reaction that games designers exploit in videogames, even though it may not technically be an emotion (Robinson, 1995; Griffiths, 1997). As noted, in *System Shock 2* things often unexpectedly explode as you approach them. In this case, it is not the fictive content that drives the response, but the sheer visual and acoustic unexpectedness that the prop generates. Hence, it may often be the case that there is a kind of *mistake* in the causation of the fictive emotions, in that because the star-tle response is reaction-like, it can be provoked by eliciting states that really are not significant at all. Of course, it is not really that the affective *system* is mistaken when it thus elicits an emotional response, but rather that it has looser tolerances in being a "quick and dirty" system that risks false positives (Le Doux, 1998).

It is also widely accepted that highly cognitive states and context-sensitive states can act as elicitors of emotions (Le Doux, 1998: 163–165). Though many affective states are caused by mere perceptual stimuli such as curved sticks, snakes, or smiling faces, there is reason to think that more highly cognitive thoughts, including perhaps those about what is fictional, can also cause emotional responses. Indeed, the abundant evidence that the imagination *can* cause emotions is one reason to doubt a strict cognitivist conception of the emotions where the emotions are always caused by beliefs (Griffiths, 1997: 29). To elaborate on my example of a videogame emotion here, in *System Shock 2*, as a player fictionally rounds the corner of a darkened hall in the starship *Von Braun*, the digital prop coordinates a sudden animation of a mutant appearing out of the gloom. The perceptual experience *and* realization of what is imaginary – that the mutant presents a threat – elicits an emotional response of fear. I suspect that there are a range of elicitors causing fictional emotions that we have in concert with videogames, and so this response of surprise and fear may be augmented by the evocative representations of the fictional world: the grotesque sounds the mutants make, the darkness of the ship's interior, the details of the narrative, the indistinct sound sources, may all contribute to the emotional response.

From the most casual of observations it is clear that these surprising in-game encounters may involve a qualitative component similar to those attending emotions in a "real world" context. The player of *System Shock 2* *feels* their heart race, they may even lurch back from the screen, and their attention becomes concentrated as they attempt to deal with the mutant: the emotion has an effect on the experience of the situation, and can make it very intense. Exactly which physiological responses are being caused is again an empirical question, but I think that it is likely that among the responses to videogames are the physiological effects that are thought to comprise the substance of emotional responses proper: in the case of fear, a "taut stomach, racing heart, high blood pressure, clammy hands and feet, and dry mouth" (Le Doux, 1998: 132–133). Furthermore, on the basis of the physiological disturbances, sensed through bodily feedback mechanisms as a *feeling*, the player of a videogame becomes aware that they are emotional, and this realization can then contribute to the cognitive appraisal of the situation in much the same way as happens in the real world (Damasio, 1999: 52).

How it is that real emotional responses are subjected to highly cognitive "coping methods" has been a topic of much interest in the emotion literature (Ekman, 1980). Depending on the cognitive evaluation of the eliciting situation, an emotional reaction can lead to quite different planned responses on the part of an emotional person. Le Doux claims that while eliciting of the emotions often occurs in a subdoxastic manner, cognition later steps in to *condition* the initial response: the "cortex's job is to prevent the inappropriate response rather than to produce the appropriate one" (Le Doux, 1998: 165). If the curved shape turns out to be a stick, the suitable response might be a nervous chuckle and a sudden realization that one is not in danger. If it really is a snake, however, the reaction-like emotional response has put the agent in a position to best respond to the danger. I think that this means that even if the emotional response to a fiction is caused quite automatically, just how we respond to the emotion can acknowledge the fictionality of its source, and so we can react accordingly for a fiction. With videogames, the fictional consequence-free context of the eliciting state may allow the player to enjoy the emotional states of startle and fear, but also to use these emotions to fashion the nature of their fictional response in the game world. Confronted by the mutant, the player finds that they have run out of ammunition and in the grasp of an exciting emotion of fear, frantically grabs a wrench and begins to bash away at the mutant while trying to avoid its own blows, and hence becomes panicked. The fact that such a scary or frustrating experience can be so much fun seems to be another form of the *paradox of tragedy*, a topic so familiar to philosophers of the arts (Levinson, 1997).

Finally, the player *integrates* this emotional response into their game world by characterizing it in the terms offered by the fictive scenario they are playing in. The player might realize how afraid they were of the mutant, and report this attitude to others. Fictive experiences often do spur players to report that they were afraid of the shotgun-wielding mutants and became panicked when dealing with them, or that they felt guilty about what they did to the Little Sister, even though these things never really happened (really, there were no mutants or Little Sisters). Many people, on learning that I am writing a book about our engagement with videogames, have related their own emotional gaming experiences to me in such an emotionally vivid way.

On my theory, then, such emotional involvement and attribution is largely automatic and unconscious: to say that our emotions are caused by make-belief or pretense is not to say that the emotions are faked or "pretended," as Carroll has proposed as an argument against Walton's quite similar theory (Carroll 1990: 73–74). Rather, emotion arises quite naturally out of an imagined engagement in a hypothetical scenario because of the naturalness of the connection between the imagination and emotion, and is subsequently and unconsciously incorporated into our game world through a self-report or retelling to others because of the familiarity or ease with which we elaborate on our emotions and on our imaginative games. Indeed, it takes a human observer like Shakespeare to spell out the curious nature of our emotional responses to fictions, as the playwright did in *Hamlet* (Act 2, Scene 2). Fictions – which I earlier argued arise out of our designing props to sustain vivid and interesting imaginative episodes – arouse our emotions by exploiting this connection between the imagination and emotion. Artists, moreover, have designed all sorts of novel ways to "press our emotional buttons" by the perceptual and imaginative features they put into the fictive props that comprise their artworks. As we will shortly find, the ability is augmented by the interactive fictions of videogames.

Thus, one of the traditional solutions to the paradox of fictional emotions – Walton's (1990) make-believe account – also serves us well here. Jenefer Robinson (2007) has developed a largely consistent theory in respect to traditional narrative fictions. It is make-believe – both in partially causing our emotions and in conditioning our response to those emotions – that is crucial to explaining how we become *emotionally immersed* in the fictional worlds of videogames. I do not want to give the false impression that there is widespread agreement in the philosophy of the arts that this is the correct solution to the paradox of the fictional emotions; in the space I have here I will not be able to cover all the problems that this solution must still contend with, let alone the competing solutions. What I do think, however, is that the fact that the make-believe solution proves so apt to explaining what is occurring in videogaming emotions itself adds the weight of new evidence that this theory is the correct way to stake out the conceptual ground on this issue.

But this solution also leads to a potentially counter-intuitive conclusion. Walton (1978) is somewhat notorious in philosophical circles for claiming that it is *only fictional* that appreciators of fictions have emotions the intentional object of which is a fictional character or event. We do not really fear the movie slime slithering toward us; rather, it is fictional that we fear the slime. This conclusion seems to me quite credible in the case of many responses to videogames. If asked what caused their startle while playing *System Shock 2*, a videogamer might respond that it was the sudden appearance of a mutant, even though this is not straightforwardly true. The startle was caused by the coordinated representations of the videogame prop, given that no mutants were involved (or, thankfully, hurt) in the incident. It is fictional that the gamer was startled by a mutant. Similarly, it is not straightforwardly true that I felt anger directed at a real fiery spider. Rather, it is fictional that I did so, for just the same reasons it is not straightforwardly true that I was being attacked by a real fiery spider monster. Both kinds of apparent interactions seem equally fictional, the difference being that one is rendered by the digital prop, and one is rendered by a player's cognitive appraisal and self-report of their fictive activities.

Some philosophers have responded to Walton's claim that our emotions for fictions are properly called fictional with the claim that the emotions are real ones, even if directed or caused by thoughts rather than characters or events (Carroll, 1990; Yanal, 1999). Lamarque (1996: 117) notes that "the thought contents derived from fictions do not have to be believed to be feared." I think that Walton's point here is most credibly seen as semantic rather than psychological: that is, a point about what we should say of the semantic status of our utterances about our fictive emotions, rather than about their psychological makeup or how they feel from the inside. Walton in fact agrees that fictions can cause *affective responses* – what he calls, in a much misunderstood turn of phrase, "quasi-emotions" (1990: 245) – though he denies that these are sufficient by themselves to show that one is having an emotion because they lack an intentional object (the slime doesn't exist). Many theorists will not be so reluctant to see affective states as comprising full-blown emotions because they do not think that a cognitive or intentional component is necessary to emotion (Le Doux, 1998). So, in at least one sense, Walton is simply wrong that we do not have emotions for fictions, and his critics are accurate on this point. But he is surely correct that our apparent emotional *relationships* to fictions, evident when we describe ourselves as being in an intentional relationship with a fictional being or situation, are fictional ones. When an appreciator utters that they were "sorry for Anna Karenina" I think we should see this utterance as located within the pragmatic bounds of a game of make-believe, and hence fictional. On this point I side with Walton in thinking that the subsequent descriptions or reports of the emotions offered by participants and observers are no less fictional than the descriptions initially offered by authors in establishing the fictional world. Whereas the descriptions offered by authors detail what is fictional of a work world, participants report what is fictional of their game world (see chapter 3).

Indeed, I think that videogames allow us to grasp the necessity of this semantic point much more easily, because reporting or describing their emotions in a fictional world is only one of a range of things that players *fictionally do*. When attributions of *causal* relationships are framed in reference to fictional people and situations, the semantic problems are again evident, though these cases are less discussed than the apparent emotional attitudes we exhibit toward fictions. After being startled by the mutant, we might ask the player what he did next, to which he might report that he "flailed at it with a wrench, killing it." But, of course, really no such thing happened: the self-report is fictional. This shows that as well as fictional attributions of intentional, emotional, or cognitive attitudes toward fictional worlds, gamers may also make fictional attributions of *causal interactions* with those worlds. The reasons why these causal attributions are discussed less in the philosophy of fiction is that the traditional focus has been on narrative fictions where causal interactions with fictional worlds are not evident. Interactive videogames thus allow us to see how the paradox of fiction is not distinctive to ostensible emotional relationships to fictional worlds but is a more general one concerning our interaction with fictional worlds.

Given that I have argued that videogame fictions are distinctly interactive fictions, what difference does this make to the emotions that we have in their fictive contexts? I think that we have already seen that videogames allow us to have the kind of emotions that traditional narrative fictions usually do not. To see this, we can reflect on the philosopher Alex Neill's characterization of fictive emotions. As noted, *contra* Walton, Neill (1994) thinks that it is straightforwardly true that we believe that things are true *in a fiction*, and the emotions that we have are caused by these beliefs. For Neill, when a reader or viewer of a fiction has an emotion of pity toward a fictional character, it is simply because they believe that in the fiction a character is in a situation worthy of pity, and furthermore, for whatever psychological reasons, beliefs about fictions are emotionally efficacious. However, Neill concludes that this means that we cannot have fictive emotions caused by beliefs that we do not in fact have, and these are those emotions which would demand beliefs about *our* effect on a fictional character or their effects on us. Neill subsequently argues that emotions such as *jealousy* are unavailable to fictive participants because appreciators simply cannot be related to a fictional character in the necessary way. We cannot be jealous of a fictional character because jealousy would involve "a belief that the person of whom I am jealous has, or has designs on, something that is rightfully mine, and a desire to regain or retain whatever that is" (1994: 181). Neill concludes that "the ontological gap between fictional characters and ourselves precludes rivalry with them as well as being threatened by and escaping from them," and that this fits with what we do actually see with the fictional emotions: "how often, after all, do we really want to describe ourselves as feeling jealous of a fictional character?" (1994: 181).

Neill's claims, even if true of traditional fictions, clearly no longer apply in the case of videogames. If not jealousy, gamers certainly experience other emotions that seem to depend on their having an interaction with a fictional world. For example, *pace* Neill, we simply can feel *threatened* by fictional characters: the Big Daddies in *BioShock* are so threatening that the player must steel themselves before an encounter, and the actual encounters – from my experience – are terrifying and frantic occasions. This is because, fictionally, the player-character and the Big Daddy *do* "exist" in the same ontological game world. The entire genre of survival-horror games is built around this kind of emotional response of feeling threatened and helpless in a game world. Similarly, guilt seems to be quite similar to Neill's examples of jealousy and fear for oneself, in necessitating that appreciators exist in the same ontological world as fictional characters, and hence be able to have an effect on a fictional character that it is "rational" to feel guilty for (Davies, 2009). We quite clearly see guilt in videogames: after killing the Little Sisters, I immediately felt guilty for what I had done. Another example I have used in this chapter, that of the frustration and anger I felt while battling the fiery spider monster, was focused on my own apparent role in the world of the fiction: even though the frustration and anger were related to my inability to defeat the game, because the game is encoded in a fiction, they were necessarily focused on my fictional inability to defeat the spider. My growing enmity with the fiery spider is another case of an emotional attitude that bridges the "ontological gap" because of the interactivity of gaming fictions. All of these cases, I think, provide evidence that my account of videogames as interactive fictions is apt to explain many unpredictable and interesting facts about videogames.

THE ROLE OF THE EMOTIONS IN GAMING

What role do the emotions have in the playing of videogames? I can best explain this issue by again relating back to the state of affairs with narrative fictions. Emotions become involved in fictions through the relevance or connections that the representational content involved in fictive practice has for the emotions. In narrative fictions this means that the fictive scenarios that are imagined become the prompt for emotional reactions and attitudes in much the same way as described in the previous section. Readers of novels are acquainted with the premises of the fictional world – learning that Anna Karenina's life is thoroughly wretched, for example – and emote in a manner that is fitting with that content but also how the content is depicted or narrated. Because understanding a fiction can be characterized in part as having *appropriate* emotions toward it, a fully satisfying interpretation of a fiction involves understanding the emotional implications of the fiction. An appreciator does not really understand *Anna Karenina* unless she sees that a sympathetic and sad response is appropriate to that fiction.

Importantly, in almost all traditional narrative fiction, the appreciator is a passive and distanced subject having no effect on the fictional world, and so the emotions that are had are more often than not *relational* in being focused on the characters or situations of the fiction. Philosopher Susan Feagin (1996) has argued that the emotions that we have for narrative fictions are often sympathetic or empathic in form. Only in exceptional and puzzling circumstances are the emotions that audiences of narratives have *self-directed*. A departure from the relational nature of the fictional emotions might be the state of self-directed fear an appreciator of a horror movie has when the fictional blob of slime slithers out of the fictional frame and toward her in the manner of some classic horror movies (Walton, 1978). Nevertheless, in narrative fictions, emotions seem to play an important role in guiding our understanding of those fictions.

With videogames the situation is similar, though in this case the emotions are in the majority self-directed ones, and the emotionally propelled learning is often about the player's own role in the fictional world. I think that it is relatively clear that in videogaming the player's emotions have a role in guiding the player to a successful interaction with the obstacles and situations encoded in the game's fiction. The player of *System Shock 2* is scared and disturbed by the world of that fiction because he is afraid that the mutants will hear *his* footsteps as he explores the ship. As such, he is vigilant and deliberate in his movements, always on the lookout for shapes in the darkness and listening for sounds reverberating through the gloomy halls and corridors. In the car racing game *Gran Turismo*, the frustration the player feels from losing a close race is not only an annoyance, it is a motivation for him to concentrate that bit harder on winning the next race. Players invest a great deal of concentration in winning the races in driving games, motivated mostly by the intense emotions that losing a race can inspire – including the intense emotions that being *trash-talked* by a real human opponent can cause. In *Medal of Honor*, not containing your emotions can cause your actions to go awry. Faced with numerous enemies in an improbable mission, the player sees a panzer tank bust through the wall and fire towards his position. The player panics as his grasp on the situation falters, and he hastily retreats to a position of relative safety. Because the player of videogames has an interactive engagement with these situations, the emotional connection is especially close.

I have argued that a key part of the explanation needed here is that the imagination can elicit real emotion. Emotions are involved in fictive practice because the cognitive and artifactual representations that underlie fictive practice, as well as having their sensory, spatial, and logical significance, have an emotional significance, and act as *emotionally competent stimuli* (Damasio, 1999). The question remains, of course, just why fictional representations act as emotionally competent stimuli: why are imaginary worlds emotionally relevant? An answer is suggested by recent emotion theory, and this answer is suggestive of the role of the emotions in gaming. Damasio (1994, 1999) argues that in general the emotions are involved in representing to an organism the immediate and extended demands of *homeostasis*, allowing them to deal with those demands by giving the organism motivation to change their environment to suit their needs. It is well established that "affect programs" such as joy, fear, and anger clearly have a typical behavioral profile suited to responding to different kinds of environmental situations (Ekman, 1980). But all emotions, claims Damasio, "have some kind of regulatory role to play, leading in one way or another to the creation of circumstances advantageous to the organism exhibiting the phenomena; emotions are *about* the life of an organism, its body to be precise, and their role is to assist the organism in maintaining life" (1999: 51). Emotionally competent stimuli tend to be those parts of the environment that have some bearing on a survival or other homeostatic goal. As such, emotions frame the world as represented, by making salient those parts that deserve our attention.

Faced with a rich *decision space* in which we need to act, emotions not only focus our attention, but also help to bias the choice over options so that efficient decisions can be made. Damasio notes: "What dominates the mind landscape once you are faced with a decision is the rich, broad display of knowledge about the situation that is being generated by its consideration. Images corresponding to myriad options for action and myriad possible outcomes are activated and keep being brought into focus" (1994: 196).

Damasio proposes "a somatic state, negative or positive, caused by the appearance of a given representation, operates not only as a *marker for the value of what is represented, but also as a booster for continued working memory and attention*" (1994: 197–198; emphasis in original). And so "somatic markers" – feedback from the bodily states conditional to affect programs – help to focus attention, to bias among the various representations that are attended to, and to guide the eventual decisions that are made.

Events in fictional worlds – really, thoughts about what is fictional – are among the set of emotionally competent stimuli because of the role of the imagination in planning and forethought. This is to say that the ability of the imagination to cause real affective episodes may exist for good functional reasons. Our imagination is not behaviorally inert, but allows us to conceive of the possible futures that might follow from our current behaviors, and to design our behavior appropriately, perhaps allowing *our hypotheses to die in our stead* (Popper, 1972). But without some connection to emotion, given what Damasio says about the role of the emotions in framing and guiding decisions, such hypothetical scenarios could not have an impact on *present* behavior. The connection of the imagination to the emotions may be necessary for hypothetical thoughts about the future to be motivationally efficacious in the present, and this is why the imagination has an emotional valence.

One of the passages just quoted from Damasio – "What dominates the mind landscape once you are faced with a decision is the rich, broad display of knowledge about the situation that is being generated by its consideration. Images corresponding to myriad options for action and myriad possible outcomes are activated and keep being brought into focus" – could not be a better description of the sorts of cognitive challenges that are represented by videogames. In gaming, the emotions often seem to act to represent to the player the demands of homeostasis *in a fictional world*. Emotions are involved in the *affective framing* of fictional worlds of videogames, making salient the goals and needs of those worlds, so that our interaction in them is motivated and enhanced. The player of a videogame feels angry at their inability to overcome the massive fiery spider, frustrated by the difficulty of completing the platform-jumping task, fearful of possible loss, or elated at defeating the hordes of mutants and crazed chimpanzees. Consequently, the emotions seem to guide participation in the fictional world of the videogame by boosting attention and concentration to deal with these challenges. Indeed, because it is meant to explain how concentration and attention are maintained, this somatic marker hypothesis might provide the basis of an explanation of the *absorption* sense of immersion distinguished earlier (chapter 3). Thus, the emotions we have for videogames may play an important role in immersing us in those fictional worlds.

The emotions not only have a role in directing attention and motivating decisions in game worlds, but they also make those worlds more exciting places to be. I have already noted that one of the situational factors of gaming, *separateness*, reflects the fact that encoding a game in a fiction is *cheap*: we can now see that this has an impact on our emotional experience in gaming. The fictional status of videogames means that our emotional buttons can be pushed in absence of the consequences with which they are usually associated. Fictional worlds seem to allow us a greater access to some kinds of emotionally provocative situations, given that acting in a fictional world lacks the costs of acting in the real world. As seen in my earlier sadistic flight simulator experiment, a player's acknowledgment of the fictionality of a situation can allow them to experience and enjoy a set of circumstances that would in the real world have an altogether different emotional significance. In *System Shock 2* I can feel the thrill of being threatened by a grotesque mutant without the danger of actually being confronted by a mutant. This thrill – like all emotional feelings – is comprised of the inner perception of an emotional disturbance (Damasio, 1999). The technology of fiction – based on the underlying psychology of pretense – allows us to have experiences that lack the consequences they would bear in non-fictive locations, and this is part of the reason why videogames are the delectable fun they are.

Furthermore, because of the plastic and responsive nature of the fictive technology of videogaming, and its modal representational nature, videogames are able to press a wider range of our affective buttons because they allow us to *step into* fictional roles. The different kinds of fictional emotions derive from different kinds of interests in the fictional worlds of videogames. Frustration and elation make us attend more closely to the challenges of a fictional world. As players of videogames, our *fictional fates* hang in the balance. This means that our progress in the game hangs in the balance; if we do not meet the demands of the fictional scenarios that encode gameplay we stand to lose hard-earned progress. The prospect of this loss is bound to give us a much stronger connection with the game, and is likely to make us focus and concentrate all the more.

Interestingly, *restricting* the epistemic access to the fictional worlds of games is often a successful technique in enhancing the player's emotional experience of a videogame. In *System Shock 2* the first-person view, combined with the shadowy nature of the environments aboard the starship *Von Braun*, make for a sense of claustrophobia and anxiety. Partly this is because the first-person view represents a very limited field of vision, in particular lacking peripheral vision, which proves disquieting. Another reason for the sense of claustrophobia is the fictional environment itself. The environments of *System Shock 2* are dark, shadow-filled places. A clear understanding of the immediate environment is a prerequisite for successful interaction in it. When that environment is obscured or confused – as might happen in either visual or auditory modes of perception – then we feel uneasy because this obfuscation threatens to frustrate our ability to survive. This may be a matter of ill-defined or dissonant sound sources presenting a confused "auditory scene analysis" (Bregman, 1990), or of shadows or a lack of peripheral vision leading to an obscure visual environment in which hidden threats might lurk – both things that *System Shock 2* does brilliantly. *Condemned* is another game to make similar effective use of epistemic privation in causing emotions of anxiety and fear. It should come as no surprise that the worlds of videogames are so often dingy, threatening places. Of course, there are also good functional reasons for this feature of game environments – dark corridors and environments shrouded in mist are easy to code, and also allow graphical flaws to be hidden in the murk – but game designers have increasingly made a virtue of this necessity.

The *curiosity* that drives our exploration of fictional worlds also seems to have such an explanation. I have personally spent a huge amount of time exploring the game world of Cyrodiil, and often not with the desire to complete some gameplay mission, but rather for the sheer enjoyment of exploration. What is behind that next hillock, or within the ancient ruin on the near shore? How far can I climb into the mountains? What is the view like from up there? Simple curiosity – a desire to know about our world – is also attuned to the worlds of videogames, and indeed is a powerful force in driving a player's activities toward completion of the narrative: how will this end for me? Videogames are often criticized for the passivity of their players, but really, it is often a sense of curious exploration that primarily interests gamers, and motivates them to explore the potential of a fictional world.

And increasingly, it seems, games encourage our sympathy with their characters, and this is another emotional response that both connects us to their worlds and drives gameplay and narrative forward. Previously, for the most part, characters in videogames have been *game fodder* – things to attack or be attacked by, and obstacles to progression in the games. Increasingly, however, their properties are more in keeping with traditional fictions in being rounded characters with stories, motivations, and roles to play in the narrative and the gameplay. In games like *BioShock*, *Grand Theft Auto*, *Mass Effect*, and *Oblivion*, our emotional responses to such characters become an essential part of gameplay: can I bring myself to kill the Gray Prince in gladiatorial combat? The problem is not that I know he will be a difficult and skilled opponent, but that I may feel sympathy for his plight. It is this sympathy that may bar me from progressing in the game. Thus, the emotions that we have for real people are increasingly being introduced into our imaginative dealings with the worlds of videogames, and impacting on our actions in those worlds. This is to say that our *social emotions* are increasingly being engaged in our fictional interaction with videogames.

BioShock has most fully exploited this ability in the form of our response to the Little Sisters. In the fictional world of Rapture, the Little Sisters have been genetically designed to manipulate our emotions; but in the real world, they are fictive artifacts – articulated digital props – designed to elicit our emotions of sympathy and care. Of course, part of the multilayered irony in *BioShock* derives from the fact that the Little Sisters are *not* really human: they are fictions, part of an imaginary game world with no real existence. Nevertheless, they engage our emotions, sympathy, and ultimately our moral consideration: the sentimental manipulation that allows the Little Sisters to function in the fictional *work world* of Rapture also functions in the *game world* that a player has in that world, in that the emotions make the player pause to consider the appropriate fictional actions. *BioShock* is the brilliant work it is because it so effectively integrates the emotions of its player into the narrative, which, because of the branching structure in *BioShock*, ultimately has an effect on the type of narrative – redemptive or bleak – that the game depicts.

The ability of videogames to engage our social emotions and to use these emotions to fill our gaming actions with additional significance is what I think is truly promising in the future art of videogames. But what this will mean is that games designers will have to become more aware of the aspects of character and motivation that I have argued are for the most part missing from previous videogame characters, and fill out their game characters with human depth. There are signs of such depth appearing: Niko Bellic is arguably the first protagonist in the *Grand Theft Auto* series that acknowledges his moral shortcomings. Niko wants to be a better person, and to control his actions, but inevitably falls into what he – and we gamers – know best: the violent and Machiavellian world where one must use what power or freedom one has in the world to achieve one's goals, even if, in the end, this means that one's emotions are conflicted and there is no easy resolution to Niko's story. As such, *Grand Theft Auto IV* shows admirable cognizance of the balancing act between game and narrative, and our emotional response to both.

CHAPTER SUMMARY

The puzzle of fictional emotions is solved by admitting that imaginative scenarios are as capable as real ones of generating emotional responses. Given what we know about the emotions, it seems that both our thoughts about what is fictional of a game world, and the perceptual features of a fictive prop, can elicit emotional reactions in a player, responses that they subsequently attribute to their interaction in a fictional world. Games designers exploit this emotional potential by designing imaginative and perceptual props that enable rich emotional experiences, in essence pushing our emotional buttons. Furthermore, because videogames are interactive fictions, the types of emotions available to appreciators extend beyond those seen in other fictive media: players are able to feel guilty or threatened because their fictional proxy – the player-character – allows them to have an active role in the fictional world, giving them the opportunity to do things to be guilty for, or to be in a position where it is rational to fictionally feel frightened for oneself. Generalized, this picture of the emotional involvement in interactive fictions implies that emotions guide a player's involvement in a fictional world, allowing them to understand and respond in appropriate and successful ways.

NEXT CHAPTER

Videogames are morally provocative, both in the types of fictions they represent, and in worries about their effects on players, especially young players. Our emotions for videogames can make this moral resonance especially clear: occasionally, while playing videogames, I have felt bad about the way I was acting in the game world. Of course, the sorts of things that my actions would be blamed for in the real world – the consequences – are almost entirely missing in videogames. What then would allow us to say that what happens in videogames is not only fictionally immoral, but also genuinely immoral, as no doubt many people feel? I explore the possibility that there are other consequences of gaming, besides those that are so obviously missing, that might have an impact on our moral judgments about videogames. Finding this consequentialist argument severely wanting, I then consider whether it is the images and ideas that videogames depict – imaginary or not – that make them amenable to moral criticism. Of course, these moral issues have their parallels with other art forms, and so the arguments offered there might also be applied to videogames.

8

THE MORALITY OF VIDEOGAMES

THE PROBLEM WITH CRIME SIMULATORS

The bank robbery was not going well. I had stepped out of the Bank of Liberty City and found it to be surrounded by a number of police cars and armed officers. Realizing that they blocked my escape and that negotiation was not an option, I raised my automatic rifle and started shooting; my criminal pals did likewise. Pretty soon cops were dropping to the ground, mortally wounded, and police cars were exploding from the grenades that I had tossed into the street. The experience was thrilling and intense. Ducking into an alleyway, the world was suddenly quiet. In a moment of reflection, I paused to consider the situation: this was all really horrible! The realization of what I was doing in the game world – killing cops with a high-powered automatic weapon – was suddenly unsettling to me.

Videogames, of course, are not always seen as a positive cultural development. *Grand Theft Auto* has repeatedly been condemned for allowing its players to engage in acts of virtual carjacking, theft, and cop killing. *Manhunt 2* – banned in the United Kingdom in 2007 – has its players perform executions which become ever more elaborate and gruesome through the course of the game. A large proportion of modern games seem to present their players with the ability to perform actions that if existing in the real world would be seen as unequivocally morally abhorrent. I do not think it is totally unfair to call *Grand Theft Auto* a *crime simulator*: just as a game like *Microsoft Flight Simulator* allows the player to fictionally fly various aircraft, *Grand Theft Auto* enables its players to fictionally perform crimes and other immoral acts. It is the same lack of cost that allows *Microsoft Flight Simulator* to provide exciting experiences of fictional flight that also allows players to dip their toes in the waters of immorality. Most pointedly, we might say that *Grand Theft Auto* allows *consequence-free criminality*, and given what we learned in the previous chapter about the emotions, criminality that can be enjoyed.

But the theory of games as interactive fictions developed here means that the events and actions depicted in these games that give rise to the apparent moral qualities are fictional, and thus that the consequences these actions would be blamed for in the real world are altogether missing. *Violent videogame* is a term frequently used in the popular media to condemn games, but a violent videogame no more involves real violence than a zombie movie involves real zombies. The description *violent videogame*, when used as a criticism, seems to tendentiously gloss over this distinction between what is real and what is fictional in order to have its scandalizing effect. If such fictional actions as my cop killing are morally condemnable – as many no doubt feel they are – what are the facts in virtue of which they are so? Can the player be genuinely morally blamed for such fictionally immoral actions? Can the game itself be blamed?

On the basis of the demonstrated fictionality of games, there is an initial response to the moral critics of videogames that can be made here: the moral condemnation of what occurs within gaming may simply confuse what is fictional for what is real. The moral intuitions involved in videogaming can be understood in terms of the discussion of the previous chapter. My response to the fictional cop killings in my robbery of the Bank of Liberty City seems to be of the kind of interactive fictional emotion described there. In the episode, a depiction of fictional violence, toward which I contribute, and replete with striking visual images and sounds made possible by the digital props of videogames, elicits an emotional response that is the basis on which I make a cognitive judgment of moral concern. Some of the examples detailed in the previous chapter also show how such judgments can subsequently have an impact on how a player will or will not act in a fictional world. A result of this theory of videogame emotions is the semantic consequence that our relations *vis-à-vis* the fictional worlds of videogames, no less than those fictional worlds themselves, are properly characterized as fictional. Might it be that though we appear to feel moral abhorrence concerning the fictional acts in *Grand Theft Auto*, our moral response is also properly characterized as fictional? I think it is clearly the case that the player-*character* in this case – Niko Bellic – can be described as morally concerned about some of his actions. But is it the case that *I* was only fictionally morally concerned about my actions in the game? The common moral response to the violence in videogames might in essence depend on a moral illusion: one that arises because the moral critics of videogaming do not take sufficient care in distinguishing the fictional from the real.

I suspect that the above argument – that critics of videogame immorality are confusing what is fictional for what is real – is one that is likely to strike many readers as dubious. Indeed, even though I know that my actions in games are fictional, *my* moral queasiness about the fictional content of some games has been extraordinarily resistant to extinction. I think that we should not be too quick to dismiss the moral intuitions that there are about the content of videogames as *merely* fictional. That artworks can be morally condemned on the basis of their fictions is not unprecedented, and a number of writers within the philosophy of the arts have made such claims (Carroll, 1996; Gaut, 2007).

Interestingly, I find myself in a bit of a no-man's land on this issue given my own potentially contradicted feelings about games, and given that my research bridges the very morally blasé world of gaming, and the philosophy of the arts which seem more morally concerned. Games studies, and gamers themselves, often do not seem to take the real moral potential of gaming very seriously at all. Some games theorists have struck me almost as cheerleaders for gaming, passing off moral worries about gaming as a *moral panic*. Many gamers are also willing to excuse the apparently immoral content seen in videogames as negligible because it is *just a game*. This response is somewhat understandable given some of the frequent unfounded moral hyperbole in the media concerning games, especially in connection to school shootings and other crimes. And yet there is something for games to answer to here: games do depict the player engaged in immoral, albeit fictional behaviors; gamers themselves often have the feeling that what they are doing in games is morally significant. Maybe it really is?

Perhaps the intuitions of those gamers convinced there is nothing wrong with gaming violence might change if we substituted a different set of fictional activities: would gamers be happy to play a game in which it was the player's goal to rape women or commit acts of pedophilia? I suspect that almost all gamers would be reviled at this prospect. Unfortunately, it recently came to popular attention that players of the virtual world *Second Life* seemed to be engaging in acts of virtual pedophilia (Singer, 2007). In the sexualized aspect of what is called *age play* – the role-playing of infants, children, or adolescents – players engaged in virtual sex acts, with one or both of the participants taking on the appearance of a child as their avatar. Though the activities were between consenting adults, and were of a fictional nature, it is clear that much of the popular reaction to these acts was one of moral concern. The properness of a moral response to fictional pedophilia or rape shows, I think, that some game activities cannot be dismissed as being *just a game*, and that the fictional activities of gamers are not entirely negligible in terms of the moral intuitions they arouse. There is the possibility, of course, that the willingness of gamers to reject a moral concern with the murder and violence that occurs in games may simply derive from the fact that their intuitions have been dulled by repeated exposure to that kind of content, and its subsequent normalization, and that they are not yet dulled to the immorality of sex crimes in games.

On the other hand, conservatives – and many philosophers of the arts, I feel safe in predicting – are likely to take an almost diametrically opposed response to the issue: violent and objectionable videogames are a serious moral problem, and the justification that it is just a game reflects the lack of moral maturity that most gamers have. This sort of response is very easy to find: anti-gaming attorney Jack Thompson provides an endless supply of such provocations, frequently terming games "mental masturbation" and blaming them for many of modern society's ills. I have encountered such opinions first-hand on numerous occasions: on hearing that I research videogames, a surprising number of people assume that my studies are about negative effects on players.

The current chapter is an attempt to assess how, or indeed if, the fictional activities of gamers can be the subject of real moral condemnation. I will discuss the morality of games and gaming in the terms set both by the recent psychological studies on gaming, and the literature in philosophical aesthetics on the moral qualities of fictions and art. Berys Gaut (2007) has recently discussed the quite wide range of issues at the intersection of art and morality. Here I want to concentrate on the issues that are distinctive to videogames, and this clearly follows from their fictive interactivity. Can gamers be genuinely blamed for what they *fictionally do*? Are these fictional actions doing me, or any other gamers, moral harm? Here I want to strike a balance between the two kinds of views identified above: game activities are not immune to criticism, as some gamers seem to assume, but neither are they wholly wicked.

ARE GAMES BAD FOR YOU?

The most common moral criticism of videogames comes in a *consequentialist* form: games are criticized because of their apparent effects on the behavior, minds, values, or character of their players. Thus one potential way in which to argue here is that despite the fact that cases of fictional immorality in *Grand Theft Auto* are missing real victims, they do in fact have different kinds of genuine consequences. This is partly the basis of Plato's censure of the representational arts in the *Republic*, where he worries that the feelings we have for fictions might infect how we feel about ourselves (1987: Book 10, §3).

There is a growing psychological literature on the harmful effects of videogames, and a number of studies into the effects of violent videogames on aggression in children do claim a perceived effect, including increased affective arousal, increased behavioral aggression, increased access to aggressive thoughts, and increased delinquency (Anderson and Dill, 2000; Anderson and Bushman, 2001; Gentile, et al., 2004). For example, Craig Anderson and Karen Dill claim that "repeated exposure to graphic scenes of violence is likely to be desensitizing," potentially having long-term effects, meaning that "long-term videogame players can become more aggressive in outlook, perceptual biases, attitudes, beliefs, than they were before the repeated exposure or would have become without such exposure" (2000: 774). Less reservedly, games are morally condemned for "teaching our kids to kill" (Grossman and DeGaetano, 1999), and are routinely blamed for campus shootings: Jack Thompson has repeatedly blamed videogames for such shootings, including, most notoriously, given the facts of the case, in interviews conducted on FOX News and MSNBC immediately following the shootings at Virginia Tech in 2007. If it can be established that these are genuine consequences of gaming, and that they follow from the fictionally immoral activities that are the subject of this chapter, then they might provide a justification of the moral intuitions under scrutiny here.

There are two general problems with a consequentialist account of fictional immorality, however. First, it is not clear that the claimed consequences of gaming are of the significance or extent needed to make a compelling consequentialist case. Second, and more importantly, there are doubts over whether the consequentialist approach is really sufficient to explain the moral intuitions about games, especially given that such intuitions persist in the lack of notable consequences.

First then, the significance of these consequentialist claims seems far from settled (Tavinor, 2007). Though there is at least one meta-study that concludes there is a real and significant effect (Anderson, Gentile, and Buckley, 2007), some researchers are not as convinced that the effects are as important as claimed. Other recent meta-studies suggest the claims of the connection between aggression and violent behavior and videogames may be overstated, and that there is little evidence that videogames adversely influence children to a significant degree (Durkin, 1995; Griffiths, 1999; Freedman, 2002; Kutner and Olsen, 2008). Furthermore, there are methodological problems. A number of the psychological studies into the consequences of videogaming for violent behavior or attitudes can be questioned in terms of what sort of evidence they provide: whether it is *evidence of correlation* or *evidence of cause* (Griffiths, 1999). That gamers with an interest in themes of violence and perhaps with violent dispositions would tend to enjoy and play "violent" videogames more than other kinds of games would be not at all surprising. Some of the studies of the links between videogames and aggression do seem almost entirely correlational, potentially picking out this kind of link, and indeed admit as much (Gentile et al., 2004).

Also, the effects on aggression that there are, often may be attributed to general affective arousal caused by children's gaming activities, rather than to the violent content of the videogames specifically (Freedman, 2002).

Even if the effect of videogames on aggression is statistically significant, this is no guide to whether it is a *morally significant* effect. In a clearly rhetorical ploy, Anderson has compared the significance of the effect of videogames on aggressive behavior to the effect of second-hand smoke on lung cancer (Anderson, Gentile, and Buckley, 2007). But this involves a fudging of the term *significance* between a statistical notion, where these things really are comparable, and a consequentialist notion of significance, where it has not been shown that videogame aggression comes anywhere near to approaching the terrible effects of lung cancer. And there is reason to think the claimed effects are not commensurate: in the studies that do show a perceived effect, Mark Griffiths (1999) notes that it often pertains to young children and to their behavior immediately after the game playing, and the aggression is often *operationalized* and hence measured in terms of attitudes observed in play behavior, or role-playing. All this means that the potential for the application of such studies to the ethics of the gaming activities of adults is uncertain, even though they should have an impact on the quite different issue of whether children should be allowed to play such games.

What might allow these studies to have significance for the moral issues is if they could contribute to a testable theory on how videogame violence might contribute to significant long-term aggressive behaviors or attitudes. But here we are again on uncertain ground. Anderson claims that games may have their effect on aggression by allowing players to "rehearse aggressive scripts that teach and reinforce vigilance for enemies (i.e., hostile perception bias), aggressive action against others, expectation that others will behave aggressively, positive attitudes toward the use of violence, and beliefs that violent solutions are effective and appropriate" and also through "desensitizing" their players to violence (Anderson and Dill, 2000: 774). But all this is still speculative. Griffiths (1999) notes on the contrary that some studies are consistent with games having a *cathartic* effect. Jonathan Freedman (2002) has argued that the notion of desensitization is conceptually suspect. *Desensitizing* implies that one's sensitivity to *images* of violence is weakened by repeated exposure to such content, but is it a necessary consequence of this that one's sensitivity to *real acts* of violence is thus attenuated? Freedman claims that there is little evidence that exposure to images of violent events does desensitize people to violence in the sense of giving them a blasé attitude toward genuine violence.

Surely it is likely that we do learn from fictions, but it cannot be the case in anything but a vanishingly small minority that adult gamers would assume naïvely that their violent actions in the fictional worlds of videogames would be at all applicable in the real world. Similarly, it is undeniable that media can have a profound effect on how people behave; one only has to see the effects that popular movies and music have on fashion to appreciate this. But it is quite a different proposition to think that videogames have a morally significant effect on behaviors that run against the powerful social prescriptions against violence among normal adults. In an article in the *Chronicle of Higher Education*, Bill Blake provides a simple challenge to the idea that videogames could encourage such behaviors: after playing *Grand Theft Auto*, Blake suggests: "Go outside and find a locked car – or go to the back alley where missile launchers hover in a glowing light waiting for you to pick them up, or go drive down the street in your town where all the strippers hang out waiting for you to pick them up – and see if you are tempted" (Blake, 2008). The ridiculousness of this proposition rests on the fact that almost all gamers are surely aware that the situations they are involved in are not real and that the behaviors they are pursuing in those worlds would be utterly inappropriate if adopted in the real world. An exception that proves the rule – illustrating how bizarre it would be to assume that the lessons learned in videogames could be extended to the real world – is the case of the NASCAR driver Carl Edwards, who tried to win a race in 2008 by driving his car into a wall, expecting, on the basis of games like *Gran Turismo*, that the car would bounce off the wall maintaining its momentum! Of course, as he was racing in the real world, Carl merely crashed his car. In videogames, many of the behavioral strategies that are adopted are strategies designed to address the *formal features of a game*, and as such simply have no correlate in a real-world setting because they are unrealistic (see chapter 5). That someone would adopt a violent behavioral script on the basis of what they have seen in a videogame would arguably signal some kind of deeper cognitive or behavioral problems.

Still, even though the effects of games on the attitudes, values, and behaviors external to gaming have not been demonstrated to everyone's satisfaction, there is the clear possibility that games like *Grand Theft Auto* do have real negative behavioral consequences, and that taking this possibility seriously is a moral demand on us given the potential importance of those consequences; gamers and games theorists only undermine their own credibility when they reject out of hand the negative causal potential of games. There is certainly anecdotal evidence linking games to violence; most obviously in the sensationalist reports in the popular media that exploit this moral issue. Furthermore, the lack of compelling evidence of a significant effect may be attributable not to the lack of a phenomenon, but rather to the fact that the necessary research simply has not yet been done. The type of studies that have been carried out in psychology have a very narrow focus on proximate causation. Perhaps if longitudinal studies could be carried out on the effects of gaming on child development, then we might be in a better position to judge the real effect of games.

The most worrying putative effects of gaming are the mass shootings to which they are often anecdotally linked. Though the claimed causal responsibility of videogaming for such crimes is potentially the most emotive reason for the moral condemnation of gaming, it is the most empirically tenuous – far more tenuous, for example, than the empirical studies discussed above. When it comes to evaluating whether videogame immorality really is responsible for the school shootings at Columbine, because our understanding of these events and the long-term effect of videogames on values are so poor, such judgments almost always rely on anecdotal accounts that there actually was a link to videogames in such cases. At the beginning of their study of gaming aggression, Anderson and Dill note: "Harris and Klebold [the shooters in the Columbine massacre] enjoyed playing the bloody, shoot-'em-up videogame *Doom*" (2000: 772). But given the accessibility of videogames to young people, this link by itself establishes almost nothing, and seems to be an attempt to prime the reader's thoughts about the topic.

Even if the responsibility of gaming for a particular shooting could be demonstrated – just what would establish this, beyond an avowal by the shooter that they were provoked into action by a videogame, is unclear – this would still be insufficient for attributing *moral* responsibility for the event to the fictionally violent videogaming that acted as a pretext. In the case of Columbine, it seems undeniable that videogames are one aspect of a nexus of causal features antecedent to the shootings, but to isolate them as morally responsible ignores the fact that the vast majority of gamers who played *Doom* committed no such acts. By any measure, to respond to a videogame as a motivation or incitement to perform mass murder is an extraordinarily *idiosyncratic* response to that game. As the appeals court judge in a prosecution of a media company in relation to an earlier school shooting in Kentucky found:

> Carneal's [the killer] reaction to the games and movies at issue here . . . was simply too idiosyncratic to expect the defendants to have anticipated it. . . . We find that it is simply too far a leap from shooting characters on a video screen (an activity undertaken by millions) to shooting people in a classroom (an activity undertaken by a handful, at most) for Carneal's actions to have been reasonably foreseeable to the manufacturers of the media that Carneal played and viewed. (*James vs. Meow Media, Sixth Circuit US Court of Appeal*)

If we take the dozen or so mass shootings commonly attributed to videogaming as actually stemming from them, this set deals with a vanishingly small proportion of gamers. Even if we could somehow prove gaming did contribute to the crimes, the reasonable conclusion would be that such games were causally significant only in the vanishingly small proportion of players predisposed – for whatever reason – to commit such crimes. These kinds of responses to videogames are *foreseeable*, to put it bluntly, only to the extent that crazy people are apt to do crazy things for crazy reasons. All sorts of diverse stimuli play a role in generating unfortunate effects from idiosyncratic personalities, but in such cases we feel no need to attribute to the *stimulus* moral responsibility for the effect. To take a pertinent example, the shooter in the Virginia Tech killings, Seung-Hui Cho, made numerous references to Jesus and the crucifixion in the video shown on NBC that he made in the hours between the shootings. It would be extraordinarily perverse to blame the Bible for Cho's bizarrely idiosyncratic response to it.

The prevalence of these shooting tragedies is of course worrying, and we do have an interest in understanding their causes so as to attempt to avoid them in future. It would be fortunate if gaming could be proved to be the cause of these events, as it is the type of thing that could be effectively controlled though classification or censorship legislation. Unfortunately, it seems that the real reasons for these events – the social, economic, and psychological problems that societies have always struggled with – are not so easily treated or even identified. Most worryingly, there may even be no prospect of discovering a *generalized* cause of the shootings other than geographical or media generated localization. The historical precedent of campus shootings from University of Texas at Austin, to Virginia Tech, that is transmitted through the electronic media has clearly provided a model for behavior – even though it is debatable just how self-consistent the model of a "school shooter" is – but each of the incidents may have been performed for reasons distinctive to the particular shooter.

I think that the extent of the consequentialist findings in the psychological studies of videogames drastically underdetermines the moral mileage that has been attempted to be made of them. Similarly, in his general defense of the mass arts, Carroll notes:

> It may be argued that since we don't know how to calculate the behavioral consequences of mass art for morality, we should refrain from bluffing about our knowledge of the supposed behavioral consequences of mass art and stop trying to invoke knowledge we do not have to justify our moral evaluations of it. . . . Any group that claims to be able to predict the behavioral consequences of, for example, pornography, it might be said, is simply trying to advance its own sensitivities and moral preferences under the guise of a "theory." (Carroll, 1998a: 301)

The second general problem with the consequentialist approach enters into the debate at this point. Empirical and theoretical doubts about the psychological literature are not the most important problem that this consequentialist evaluation of gaming immorality faces, because even if the empirical findings are largely correct, and even if they could be extended by longitudinal studies and genuine theoretical understanding of the nature of the causes, this would not be sufficient by itself to establish that fictional immorality is also genuinely immoral. Establishing that videogames *sometimes* lead to negative consequences leaves us none the wiser on the issue of whether playing the games in a way that generates fictional immorality can be condemned for *that* reason. In a somewhat parallel case, the use of alcohol certainly leads to some abominable circumstances, and we have a pretty good understanding of why this occurs, but this in no way establishes the immorality of my (relatively) consequence-free drinking of a glass or two of pinot noir. To the best of my knowledge, my cop killing in *Grand Theft Auto* has not actually impacted on my disposition toward violence external to the game.

And yet some moral critics would probably be prepared to say that even though a gamer's fictional deeds have not generated any negative consequences in their particular case, they are nevertheless morally culpable when they act in a fictionally immoral way. I suspect that some people would think that if the simulated murder (pedophilia, rape) *never* led to negative consequences, that it would still constitute a moral wrong. If the immorality of fictional actions is attributed purely to the negative consequences of videogames, this will not be sufficient to explain intuitions about the immorality of game activities. This might lead us to think that videogame violence must be morally wrong, if indeed it is, for different reasons.

ON BEING OFFENSIVE

If the consequences of player behavior cannot be used to establish the immorality of their fictional actions, then what can? Arguably, it is the sheer content of the fictions in itself that is morally condemnable. I think we can refer to this position as *cognitive moralism* because it finds the mere *content* of a representation to be the kind of thing that is rightfully amenable to moral criticism. We can approach this issue through a discussion of the *content, attitudes,* and in particular, the *actions* involved in the fictive practice particular to videogames. In each case there are potentially legitimate moral worries to be raised. Furthermore, it may be that videogames, in virtue of this kind of content, express an objectionable viewpoint for which they might be morally condemned. A related issue often treated under the rubric of *moralism* claims that the moral qualities of an artwork can also have an impact on its aesthetic qualities (Carroll, 1996). I will not be directly addressing this aspect of the debate here, though no doubt it is an interesting one in the case of videogames.

First then, even though the apparent violent and criminal actions of gamers are fictional, these things are represented through genuine content and images, and it is these representations that are the proper target of moral condemnation. In the philosophy of fiction, the other functions that language and representations play often can be over-shadowed by the concern with the lack of reference of the apparently referring singular terms within fictions. For example, Sherlock Holmes may not exist, but the sentences being used to portray the fictive content of the novels in which he fictionally plays a role certainly do. Though the representations in fiction lack the reference they would bear in a factual connection, they nevertheless continue to hold those of their psychological associations and logical consequences that are independent of that particular reference. It is almost always the case, of course, that to depict a character *fictionally swearing*, an actor really uses a swear word (unless it occurs in a bowdlerized made-for-television drama where a script might substitute nonsense words). Swearing in a fiction is no less offensive – to some people, at least – for that fact. Furthermore, even though the particular situations depicted in a fiction may not exist, the general terms of the representations still pick out real kinds of things. The concepts in fictive representations are real concepts, and so when murder is portrayed in a fiction it is not merely fictional that the idea of murder is the concern of the fiction, even though there is literally no murder involved. These facts mean that, despite their lack of reference to real actions and events, fictive representations are cognitively and emotionally significant, and this significance can have moral consequences.

A fiction that portrays senseless violence, that portrays the idea that violence is a sensible and useful way to deal with certain situations, expresses this content even if it is asserted of a fictional world, and because it does so, such a fiction could be criticized from a moral standpoint. A lot of the moral offense caused by videogames, no doubt, derives from the concepts, images, and emotions associated with or aroused by the fictive representations. This criticism becomes all the more pressing when it is noted that the representational means of videogames include 3D graphical environments which, with the incredible recent developments of the technology, are quickly approaching photo-realism. The realistic representation of violence and gore is an important feature of many games, and one that players take great enjoyment in. Players also enjoy horror elements, and the more effectively and realistically these are represented, it seems, the better for some players. A game like the very stylish *God of War* on the Playstation 2, for example, is an exceedingly graphic affair, with torrents of blood filling almost every minute of the game. *Fallout 3*, setting new levels for the stylish depiction of gore, involves numerous slow-motion shots of exploding corpses and decapitations. These representations, though of fictional situations, are genuinely disturbing or offensive, and so might seem prone to moral evaluation for this reason. Some games are sensitive to this moral effect, and allow the player to turn off the blood and gore.

That the mere content of fictions and imaginings can be the subject of moral censure is a commonplace understanding. There is a long history of the moral criticism of fictions, stretching from Plato's observations in the *Republic*, to the rather more recent and widespread moralism about the violence and sex in Hollywood movies. The idea is needed to explain why it is that classification and censorship apply equally to fiction and non-fiction. The moral relevance of imagined content is also borne out by our moral response to people who fantasize about criminal and immoral acts: it is hardly a morally neutral act to fantasize about acts of rape, pedophilia, cannibalism, or murder. Some might worry, of course, that videogames provide a minimal objectification of sadistic fantasies that some people do in fact have, by representing them in the robust and interactive graphical medium of the videogame. This, essentially, may be the source of the moral worry about the age-play seen in *Second Life*.

Next, the interpretive attitudes that players adopt in their playing of videogames and other fictions can also be the proper topic of moral criticism. Carroll is a philosopher who thinks that interpreting some fictions may require us to adopt systems of beliefs or affective attitudes from which we can learn, and that these attitudes might occasionally be of a morally questionable nature (Carroll, 1998a, 1998b). He suggests that what makes narrative artworks the proper object of moral assessment is that they allow their appreciators to refine, rehearse, and clarify their moral knowledge and sensitivities. He claims that narratives "provide us with opportunities to, among other things, exercise our moral powers, because the very process of understanding a narrative is itself, to a significant degree, generally an exercise of our moral powers" (Carroll, 1998b: 141). Insofar as narratives call on us to adopt a questionable moral viewpoint, they might be seen as immoral (Carroll, 1996). Furthermore, it is implied that a willingness to so engage with such a fiction might show a moral fault in the appreciator.

Though Carroll's target is traditional narrative fictions such as Bret Easton Ellis's *American Psycho*, without too much effort we can apply it to videogames. In responding to the gameplay scenarios presented in videogames, the player must draw on his stock of everyday knowledge to make sense of what is happening. He must also deploy his moral emotions in placing the material in a moral context. Yet, we might judge that videogames are all too often lacking in a reflective component that would make the moral context obvious to the player. Furthermore, far from being disturbed by the content of the fictional worlds of videogames – the response that we would expect if one were to encounter the violence of *Grand Theft Auto* in the real world – the prevalent response of gamers is one of amusement or even hilarity, a fact I can personally vouch for: I have never laughed more than I did while playing *Grand Theft Auto IV*.

This criticism is a variation on a theme seen in much of the recent philosophical literature on art. The theme maintains that art narratives enable readers and viewers to learn moral lessons (Nussbaum, 1986, 1990; Davies, 1997; Levinson, 1998), that great art explores the topics that a "morally serious" person would naturally find interest in (Miller, 1998), and that by reflecting on the warrant of our emotional responses to fictions we stand to learn something about the moral situation and our response to it (Feagin, 1994). Because they allow us to mull over complex moral situations in the comfort and safety of our armchairs, perhaps by allowing us to project ourselves into the role of fictional characters and to identify with them (Currie, 1997), fictions are seen as a source, if not of explicit statements of novel moral facts, then at the least of experiences that can enhance the reader's or viewer's understanding, clarification, or emotional appreciation of morally charged situations.

We can guess the response that this moralist theory would have when confronted with the immoral joys of *Grand Theft Auto*. Videogames, it might be said, pervert moral understanding by allowing the player to wallow in a sordid and unreflective fictional involvement. Players of videogames are not afforded moral learning because they are unreflective; if they did pause to reflect, they would quickly learn that their fictive involvement is degenerate. Videogaming, on this view, can be condemned for its moral viciousness. Though I will not do so here, this line of argument might be developed in tandem with some form of *virtue ethics*, perhaps further strengthening the moral case against fictional immorality.

Thus, even though it is merely fictional that a player of *Grand Theft Auto* might enjoy an act of murder (really, there was no murder to enjoy), it is nonrestrictedly true that they enjoyed a game of which the topic was murder. It is not what players are fictionally doing that is morally condemnable, but what they are really doing: enjoying a fiction that is about something considered immoral, and hence having what might be considered as an inappropriate moral response to a fiction. Again, the mere content of a fiction can be the proper subject of moral criticism. Our intuitions tell us that what we willingly imagine, and what we imagine and feel about it, are not morally neutral things.

Also, the actions performed in videogames – the fictional ones, not the non-fictive actions such as mashing buttons and control sticks, which mostly seem to be morally neutral – can be the topic of criticism, even if fictional.

The moralist arguments above can be elaborated and perhaps strengthened in the case of videogames, because in this case the fiction not only calls on the player to respond with an appreciative attitude, it asks that they respond with fictional actions in the world of the game. Technically, this amounts to using the gaming machinery to render fictional representations of violence, as detailed in the earlier part of this book. If someone plays a videogame in a violent manner, even though the violence is only fictional, we still might pause to consider the genuine moral significance of the content they have had a part in generating. The fact that this content originates with the player seems to make the player much more complicit in the fictional immorality represented on the screen. And so if fictional immorality really does amount to genuine immorality, the interactive nature of videogames gives us a stronger reason to blame not just the author of the fiction, but the player as well, because of the player's active role in generating the fictionally violent and immoral content.

It does seem as though pretended actions – like fictive content and attitudes – are things that we routinely think of as morally blameworthy. We scold children if they play *certain games* of pretense. We would also be especially worried about a person if they got a kick out of pretended sexual violence. Again, the fact that a representation is a fiction is no immediate reason to think it is morally negligible *as a representation*, and this is as much the case for player-generated representations of fictional actions as it is for the author-generated representations found in fictions such as novels and movies.

Finally, there are the ideas that are expressed through a game. A videogame may contain individual representations that are objectionable, but it may also express a point of view that is so. The point of view expressed by an artwork can be characterized in terms of pragmatics, a concept I employed earlier (chapter 3). Just as a sentence might have a meaning obvious in its words and their combination *and* an implied meaning, so artworks have these dual levels of meaning. This, indeed, is the source of much of the interest in art; in a movie like *Forrest Gump*, the fictional occurrences are plain to see, but they also prompt audiences to ask the further question: what is this movie *really* about? In the case of *Forrest Gump*, we might wonder if the movie is a call for a return to conservative values, about the basic contingency of life, or merely a simple story with no significant intended meaning. Furthermore, we can question the moral qualities of a work's intended meaning. Perhaps the most famous example of a morally deficient viewpoint in an artwork is Leni Riefenstahl's *Triumph of the Will*, a film documenting the 1934 Nazi Party Congress in Nuremberg. Many see this film as morally objectionable, in spite of its clear aesthetic qualities and artistic achievements, because of the admiration it expresses about the Nazis.

Unsurprisingly, there is a long history of criticism of videogames as expressing objectionable viewpoints about violence, women, and minorities. *Manhunt*, a game that depicts the filming of snuff movies, might seem to imply or express the view that such things are properly seen as entertaining. *Grand Theft Auto* seems to some people to express objectionable views about minorities and women; and these criticisms were certainly again aired with the release of *Grand Theft Auto IV*. These criticisms hold even given the fictional nature of these games (that really, no people were in the least bit harmed because none of the depicted events occurred). And furthermore, because the player contributes to the content of the game, they might be held complicit in the immoral views expressed. Videogames can therefore be blamed because they do express morally deficient viewpoints.

STICKING UP FOR VIDEOGAMES

There is, then, a genuine reason for the events and actions depicted in games to be morally criticized, even if fictional: representations in themselves are amenable to moral criticism, especially where they express an objectionable viewpoint. However, I also think that a range of considerations can be raised that deflate something of the moralist criticisms of the previous section. In the final section of this chapter, I want to attempt to situate the moral intuitions that have been the topic of this chapter in a better informed context. Indeed, I think that it is a *lack* of a good contextual understanding that all too often leads to the moral criticism of games, because their critics assume videogames to be something they are not. The contextualization I offer here, drawing on the theory developed throughout this book, is another potential contribution this present study can make to the understanding of videogames.

I claimed in the previous section, developing a position called *cognitive moralism*, that the content alone of games might be the basis on which fictive immorality can be criticized. Ultimately, though, the context in which content is expressed can have important effects on the intuitions it provokes and hence on its moral significance. By itself, content may be offensive, but that is not enough to establish that it is also immoral. For example, no one would think of offering a moral criticism of the contents of criminal court proceedings, even though the actions being referred to there may be the subject of serious moral condemnation: the descriptions of the events – as harrowing as some no doubt are – are themselves morally neutral or perhaps even praiseworthy given that they serve an important legal function. It is the context in which content is presented in addition to the content itself that is of genuine moral significance, and this is also something captured by the final line of argument in the last section: it is the viewpoint that a work expresses, rather than the content it contains, that often seems most morally pertinent.

This fits with our intuitions about other forms of fiction. It is not violent or offensive fictions *simpliciter* that strike most reasonable people as morally condemnable. Rather, it is fictions for which there is no redeeming or mitigating context which strike us as expressing an objectionable viewpoint on the content they depict. A movie such as *Saving Private Ryan*, even though its graphical depictions of violence are far worse than *Commando* or *American Ninja*, is less morally objectionable than the latter movies, even though its content is far more disturbing. It is so because it has an artistic and moral standing that contextualizes the content so that the attitude fostered toward it is one of reflection. The latter movies, conversely, seem to express a glorification of violence, seeing it as a thrilling and sensible way to solve one's problems, and also passing lightly over its consequences.

It can be noted, by the way, that such mitigating contextual factors are also commonly invoked in classification legislation, such as in the New Zealand case where "merit, value, or importance that the publication has in relation to literary, artistic, social, cultural, educational, scientific, or other matters" are all to be taken into account in judgments on the restriction of objectionable publications (New Zealand Ministry of Internal Affairs, 1993). An amendment to this piece of legislation to take into account digital publications allows videogames to be treated the same as other publications in New Zealand, which has led to *Grand Theft Auto IV* being rated R18 – restricted in sale to those over 18 years of age – and a wholesale ban for the game *Manhunt*.

The question now becomes whether videogames do, at least on occasion, provide contextual factors – matters of "literary, artistic, social, cultural, educational, scientific" significance, perhaps – that alter the attitude appropriate toward their content in a way that insulates them from moral criticism. Also, do they express morally laudable viewpoints on their undoubtedly disturbing content? It is my contention that on both counts they do, and for much the same reasons as traditional artworks often do.

First, that the content in videogames makes up the formal qualities of a game does seem to have a contextual effect on the content. Foremost, *Grand Theft Auto* is a game, and much of the immorality of the fiction derives from the sorts of fictions that are needed to sustain gameplay: in the bank robbery incident, the cops act as an impediment to finishing the mission. In a first-person shooter, other characters are obstacles, and how those obstacles are tackled is typically by fictionally killing them. Note also that on just who the violence is perpetrated in many videogames – Nazis, aliens, monsters, zombies, genetically manipulated mutants – extracts some of the moral bite from the content of the fiction in that these things are seen as somewhat outside the purview of regular morality. This *moral bracketing* allows these characters to more effectively function as *game fodder*. Indeed, when realistic or morally significant characters are used as formal game obstacles – the Little Sisters in *BioShock*, the Liberty City cops in *Grand Theft Auto* – the game often takes on a different moral tenor. This provides something of a contextualization of the killings in violent videogames: it is not that the act of fictional killing is valued in itself, and that it is the killing activity that drives the player's involvement in the games because they enjoy fictionally killing things, but rather that the gaming activity relies on the fictional killings for substance.

Is this just a more sophisticated version of the *just a game* defense? Some might think this to be a bit of a glib response, and that it displays the real problem with the content of games: that games designers too often rely on violent fictions to depict their games, and that this shows that surely gamers do enjoy fictionally killing things over other alternative activities. Surely there are other actions that could be used to sustain gameplay? *The Sims* substitutes domestic activities for the killings of first-person shooters (though even in *The Sims* players often work out ways of being sadistic to their Sims, such as walling them off without food or social contact). Why do games designers so often fall back on shooting and combat? Just why violence and death is so common in videogames is in itself an interesting topic, though I cannot say much about it here. I will say, however, that videogames are not distinctive in this regard. Steven Pinker notes that fiction and drama tend to explore universal human themes: "There are a small number of plots in the world's fiction and drama. . . . More than 80 percent are defined by adversaries (often murderous), by tragedies of kinship and love, or both. In the real world, our life stories are largely stories of conflict: the hurts, guilts, and rivalries inflicted by parents, siblings, children, spouses, lovers, friends, and competitors" (1997: 427). Videogames are brimming with murderous adversaries; moreover, opportunities to murder your adversaries. Our persisting interests in violence in the arts may be natural, though this is not to morally justify those interests, of course.

Understanding the inherent sociality of videogames also allows us to contextualize their fictions. The parable of Harris and Klebold, loners who would eventually take out their frustrations and anger on peers from whom they felt alienated, no doubt drives many people's conception of what gamers are really like. Another popular image of gamers is of friendless nerds tied up in their digital fantasies, an image depicted quite brilliantly in the *Make Love Not Warcraft* episode of *South Park* where the boys become obsessed with defeating a high-level character in *World of Warcraft*, only to turn into housebound, obese, spotty geeks. This image of gamers is *largely* a caricature – though having played *World of Warcraft* in the preparation of this book, I am perfectly aware of the transcendent levels of geekery that exist in that game world. Videogames are very social experiences, and with the rise of online gaming, are becoming more so. Indeed, videogames are beginning to give rise to communities and a subsequent access to social behavior that was previously impossible for some people. Lawrence Kutner and Cheryl Olsen (2008) have also written about the surprisingly social nature of games, and of the potential benefits for children in this sociality. Some of the very things that the *South Park* episode lampoons – especially the planning and coordination of group action that the boys use in defeating their nemesis – could be genuine social learning experiences for children. Furthermore, understanding the sociality of fictional violence and death in videogames gives us a quite different view of those things. In multiplayer *Grand Theft Auto* deathmatches, one inevitably gets killed a lot by other players, but the experience is not an unpleasant or anti-social one. Though one might try to take revenge on a player who has just shot you, the real feeling is one of fun and community with fellow players. The reason why I find multiplayer *Grand Theft Auto* deathmatches so enjoyable is not because I am a sociopath who revels in the death of other players, but because I enjoy the good social fun of the game.

Next, consider that black humor and sardonic social comment frequently contextualize fictive content so as to modify our moral response. The Todd Solondz film *Happiness*, a film including depictions of pedophilia, is on the face of it an incredibly offensive work – that is to say, I would never want my mum to watch it – but this content is presented in a deeply satirical context. The same content presented in a more prurient framework would be not only offensive, but also, I think, unethical. *Grand Theft Auto* is itself a case where such contextual factors mitigate some of the moral criticism that might be offered of the game. As I noted in chapter 1, the *Grand Theft Auto* series of games are really interactive black comedies, and understanding this can change their superficial appearance as adolescent crime fantasies, into the more accurate image as intelligent and subversive humor. It helps that *Grand Theft Auto*, though being a deep portrait of modern America, is largely produced in Britain, and the humor in the game probably owes a lot to the external perspective on American culture.

Gaming and gamers are a lot more reflective than they are often given credit for, and the comically dark moral world of *Grand Theft Auto* is attractive to players in part because of its edginess in allowing the player to break accepted taboos and moral strictures through their fictional actions. The game has a mischievous moral tone, with players enjoying the dubious content they are engaged in, in part because they understand the moral dimensions of the interactive fiction. After all, it is often the especially immoral content of videogames that draws the biggest laughs, suggesting that such responses acknowledge the moral significance of the material. To have a morally mischievous response to *Grand Theft Auto* is to frame that response *as* fictionally immoral: the game seems self-consciously immoral.

Similarly, cartoon abstractness and humor can also modify or contextualize violence. The classic Warner Brothers cartoon *Roadrunner* is a horribly violent affair, and yet reasonable people should agree that to criticize the cartoon morally would be absurd. The videogame *Timesplitters*, filled with cartoon violence, could be given a similar defense. In one level of the game, the player is challenged to punch off a set number of zombie heads in a short period of time. Though the topic of decapitation is far from polite conversation material, the comical way the heads pop off when they are punched modifies the content so that an attitude of humor and not moral offense is genuinely appropriate. This sort of grotesque humor is found throughout gaming, and while not to everyone's taste, it is not clear that it is immoral for that fact.

Increasingly, videogames hope to express a morally serious point of view. *Fallout 3* and *BioShock* both attempt to provide a morally serious narrative, and are morally reflexive in a way fitting with the arguments of cognitive moralism. *Fallout 3*, in particular, is resoundingly bleak in tone and it is hard not to think seriously about nuclear annihilation given the vividness with which it presents a post-apocalypse Washington, DC. *Fallout 3* presents a Hobbesian view of post-apocalyptic society as a war of all against all, where slavery is once again widely practised, and where the player has to make a sequence of morally difficult decisions about how to survive in the wasteland. The point of view expressed in these games, though they are undoubtedly filled with violence and other objectionable material, is not what it might seem to the outsider.

It is also possible to turn this contextual defense on its head: we might say that rather than being an undesirable aspect properly dispensed with, videogames need the potential to be morally disturbing and provocative if they are to be art. As I will argue in the final chapter, one of the important aspects of art is that it is *challenging*. Perhaps the moral contentiousness of gaming is a condition of its artistic potential, and that prohibiting its possibility for moral transgression would be to prevent its potential as genuine art. There are parallels in the issue of children's art. Much literature and film made for children strikes me as an attempt to provide an anodyne vision of reality where good is good and bad is bad, and where there is never any possibility for confusing the two – recent Disney movies in particular spring to mind as cases of this heavy-handed moralism. The more interesting and artful film and literature for children is not so prudish, and actively engages in moral difficulties and ambiguities. The Brothers Grimm fairytales and Roald Dahl's stories and books are often not sanitized, and frequently confront the brutal facts of life and fantasy in an uncompromising way, and they are all the better as art for doing so. Thus, we might think that the potential for moral transgression in videogaming goes hand in hand with its aspirations as art. Videogames are extremely new, and it is only recently that games designers have really taken up these moral and aesthetic issues, albeit in what is sometimes a rather crude manner. Perhaps we can attribute the moral callousness in much gaming to its infancy, and take the abundant signs of maturation – found in games like *Grand Theft Auto IV*, *BioShock*, *Fallout 3*, and *Fable 2* – as genuinely promising a morally serious age of gaming.

Having sympathy and taking time to understand games on their own terms – which has been my general approach in this book – may be the best way to defuse this moral issue. Videogames may not have the moral depth that some traditional narrative works do, but neither are they altogether oblivious to their moral dimensions. Videogaming is already morally aware in a way that some critics might not be aware of. To claim that gaming is always an unthinking pursuit in which players are oblivious of the moral significance of the fictions they are engaged in is often to underestimate the sophistication of videogames and their players. This act of underestimation is understandable given the popular image of games as a juvenile and geeky pursuit.

If the basis of my defense here really is accurate, and videogames are more contextually reflexive than they are commonly given credit for, then we are left with at least two explanations of when the fictional immorality of videogaming is indeed worrying. First, games in which there is no mitigating context should be the subject of moral criticism. The conditional nature of my defense rests on the ability to find a redeeming contextual treatment in a videogame. The cases that are worrying from a moral standpoint are those where there are no redeeming factors or where there is little of the contextual sophistication that is needed for a response to a fiction that is cognizant of the moral implications of the fictive content. A gratuitously violent and shallow game might not have access to a moral defense of the type formulated above for *BioShock* and *Grand Theft Auto*. This, perhaps, is the worry with the apparent fictional pedophilia in *Second Life*, which seems altogether divorced from a mitigating artistic or social context, seeming closer to mere fantasy in a very primitive and prurient sense.

Second, my defense of videogames depends on players being able to appreciate the contextual features of videogames, and it is clear that not everyone is capable of such an engagement. Children, in particular, are not always able to appreciate the contextual significance of fictions, often leading them to misjudge the significance of a given fiction. This, alongside the psychological literature discussed earlier, is an important reason for why children should not have access to the games that have been the topic of this chapter. I think censorship legislation is very sensible in this case. It is also important for parents to understand exactly what can be found in videogames these days. These exceptions to my limited defense, I believe, allow us a principled way to justify the partial censorship and classification of videogames, thus assuaging those who do continue to have moral qualms about videogaming.

What about informed and consenting adults, though? Should they be free to play games that are morally objectionable? Say I really feel like playing the next ultra-violent game to hit the shelves; should I be free to do so? Perhaps in the cases where it is not clear that anyone is harmed, we simply should defer to principles of personal freedom. Where there is no danger to society, people should be allowed to pursue the activities they want to, even if a significant proportion of their society regards them as morally dubious. Moreover, in almost all cases, it should not be forgotten that it *is* just a game. Even if games express morally dubious viewpoints, and may be distasteful, compared to other moral issues, such things as laughing over the bloody, slow-motion decapitation of a zombie in *Fallout 3* is pretty small beer. It may be the prompt for personal doubts about one's own level of moral decorum and maturity, but that seems to be an entirely personal issue. Perhaps, indeed, these moral issues are most pressing in the personal case, and this is what is so interesting about my moral response to the bank robbery I carried out in Liberty City: a videogame can provoke my moral assessment of what I am fictionally doing in a game world.

Ultimately, my moral defense of gaming would find its strongest support from an argument that videogames are art, given the precedents for this issue to be found in the arts. Certainly, my defense of videogame immorality is less compelling for videogames than such a defense is for some traditional artworks. This may be because games are in their infancy, and are only recently beginning to display the representational means necessary to engage with serious ideas and to do so in an artistically interesting way. Some readers may simply not agree with my judgments about the artistic merit or contextual sophistication of *Grand Theft Auto* or *World of Warcraft*. But, at the very least, the potential for this kind of artistic appraisal of games must be acknowledged.

Are videogames really art? In the final chapter, I turn my attention squarely to this issue.

CHAPTER SUMMARY

Videogames are clearly morally worrying to a great many people, including many gamers. The most common attempt to explain the justification of this moral worry – a consequential survey of the negative effects that videogames have on players and wider society – cannot be used to establish that games or gaming are immoral activities. There are worries with the consequentialist claims, but more importantly with their application to the moral issue. Even if true, they would not be sufficient to support the intuitions that videogaming is morally suspect, because some people might still want to claim that videogames are morally dubious even in the majority of cases where there are no obvious morally significant consequences. To meet these intuitions, we can direct our attention to the genuinely offensive content and images depicted in very many videogames: even if fictional, these things are clearly offensive to some people. But this opens up a partial moral defense of gaming: the possibility for moral transgression can be excused in the case that games also have significant artistic merit. Indeed, such moral transgression might be a precondition of videogames becoming serious – and hence potentially challenging – art.

NEXT CHAPTER

Many people have the intuition that videogames are art; equally, others are not so sure that the appellation is appropriate. Settling this issue will be a matter of considering whether videogames sit under the criteria specified by philosophical theories of art. In particular, I will employ a cluster theory of art that claims that art can be identified or even defined by its ownership of a significant proportion of art-typical features, such as representation, direct pleasure in perceptual features, emotional saturation, style, and imaginative involvement. To a significant extent videogames meet these criteria, many of which have been discussed through the course of this work, and so should be classified as art. But there is a necessary proviso to this claim: videogames also involve at least one feature atypical of art, in the form of the competitive aspect of gameplay that is so crucial to their functioning.

9
VIDEOGAMES AS ART

ARE VIDEOGAMES ART?

In a book titled *The Art of Videogames* the reader is safe to expect some argument that videogames are indeed a form of art. I have left my discussion of this issue to last so that I can best reflect on what the rest of the book has shown about the nature of videogames, and how this nature sits in relation to the arts. I also hope that the reader is now sympathetic to the case to be made here, having seen something of the potential for artistic sophistication in gaming. Drawing on the material of the previous chapters, and on recent definitions of art, I will query whether videogames do sit naturally within the category of art. I judge that though they have their own non-artistic historical and conceptual precedents, videogames sit in an appropriate conceptual relationship to uncontested artworks and count as art. In particular, videogames count as art when viewed under a number of recent *cluster* theories of art in virtue of their display of a core of characteristic properties. At the same time, videogames have their own distinctive features, meaning that as a form of art they should be treated on their own terms and not simply seen as derivative forms of pre-existing types.

There are a number of preliminary issues and clarifications to cover here. First, we can distinguish the various arts to be found practised within the making of videogames, and the idea that games are art in themselves. *Art direction* is a common aspect of games, and a great number of the people involved in designing games are described as artists. Those people involved in the artistic and aesthetic design of worlds, cultures, creatures, levels, characters, and items found within videogames practise a craft similar to those involved in producing such aspects in film and other works of art. Furthermore, we can also refer to what these people produce as being the art of a given videogame. Nic Kelman (2005) has collected an impressive range of the art design featured in videogames. A book produced for the limited edition release of *Grand Theft Auto IV* includes a discussion and various illustrations of the aspects of art and design to be found in the game. The involved art is quite impressive, ranging from the architecture of the city, the commercial design of shops, advertisements, and goods, and character design, to technical aspects such as lighting effects. The latter are extraordinary, especially in the way the light changes during the course of the day from the watery green light of early morning, to the late afternoon, burgundy glow of a setting sun. Sometimes I start up *Grand Theft Auto* just so that I can fly around Downtown Algonquin to see how the light changes the city scene.

The question here, though, is whether the objects that these people ultimately play a hand in producing are artworks. It seems the case that the production of some non-artworks also involves such art and design aspects. A television talk show or cooking show might have an art department, in which someone with training in the arts and design is vested with designing sets, wardrobe, make-up, props, on-screen graphics, and coordinating these into a coherent art direction, but we would not necessarily say that the television show produced was subsequently art. This is just to say that there can be an art of producing some object or event without that thing necessarily becoming an artwork for that fact.

I also need to distinguish the question of whether videogames are art from the issue of *videogame art*. A genre of art has recently adopted the visual lexicon and often the technological means of videogaming for artistic purposes. Such artworks are not games, principally because they are not played, having few of the formal and situational features described in this book, but rather engaging audiences in the appreciative and interpretive behaviors associated with the traditional visual arts. Similarly, *machinima*, the genre of film where existing game engines or virtual worlds are used to produce filmic narratives, is a case of an artifact clearly related to videogames, and one that may be considered art in its own terms; but these things are not really games, but rather traditional narratives produced using the technology originally developed for producing games. This is something quite different to what is at stake here. I am not concerned with whether the traditional arts can assimilate or adopt the visual and thematic concerns of videogames, or whether the technological means of videogames can be used to produce artworks – on both scores it seems clear enough that they can – but whether videogames themselves are art. Is *BioShock* art?

Next, there is clearly an honorific use of the classification *art*, where the designation exists as little more than a term of praise, or perhaps a spurious comparison. The usage of the term *art* over recent times has clearly expanded in its apparent extension, with almost anything enfranchised as an art, or any profession described as that of an artist – mostly, one suspects, to flatter those involved. It remains possibile that videogames are art only in this honorific sense of the term – that *Grand Theft Auto* is a "work of art" in the same way as a particularly good Beef Wellington might be so. Such a claim might not have any real bearing on whether videogames really should be classified alongside uncontested artworks. The worry with this blasé commendatory use of the term *art* is, of course, that if everything is art, then nothing is. Surely the question of whether something really is art does make sense and that more hinges on it than a thing merely being an exemplary instance of its kind. The question that is of principal interest to me is whether videogames are art in something like the way that the exemplars of a more traditional conception of art – Shakespeare's *Hamlet*, Mahler's Ninth Symphony, Van Eyck's *The Arnolfini Marriage*, Joyce's *Ulysses* – are art.

Superficially, videogames are like the uncontested artworks just mentioned. Videogames are representational artifacts in the way that many other forms of art are, and though differing to traditional artworks in certain respects, they do have perceptual and formal structures that are the object of an aesthetic and interpretive engagement in much the same way as other artworks. Games are created by talented individuals and groups who can garner a reputation for their creative exploits, and who we are in many cases tempted to call artists. Videogames are also the target of critical activities, somewhat like those that attend the traditional arts. There is a growing amount of connoisseurship within the gaming community, with people displaying an interest in a level of detail that many casual gamers – not to mention non-gamers – would be unaware of. Games also display a concern with style, with many games being particularly notable for their pervasive sense of aesthetic continuity and coherence. In each of these ways, games share traits somewhat indicative of artworks generally.

However, games are also importantly different to the arts. Arguably, *gameplay* is the participative focus of games; it is certainly predominant in the criticism of games, where representational beauty is often seen as of secondary importance to gameplay. That games are active pursuits and gamers have an interest in their outcome – one can win or lose a game, and be in competition with other players – might seem in tension with a nature as art. Games have not typically been a major part of the Western conception of the arts. Does this act as a barrier to including their gaming nature within a discussion of the aesthetics of videogames as I have proceeded here? Does it exclude videogames from being art?

I also suspect that there will be a lot of resistance to the idea that videogames are art, not on the basis of their being games, but rather because they are *popular entertainment.* Some will believe that on the comparison of videogames with the uncontested artworks just mentioned, videogames come off very poorly indeed. Art involves something more than *mere entertainment or amusement,* and some might think that it is that extra something that videogames lack. It may also be argued that videogames are immature, derivative, mass produced, distasteful, and do not afford the sorts of perceptual and cognitive pleasures that proper artworks do. Of course, in the past such arguments have been leveled at other forms of popular art, such as film, fiction, and music. In his defense of popular art against these kinds of charges, Carroll (1998a) argues that we have no principled reason to deny some of the products of popular culture the appellation *art.* Carroll deals with arguments that were prevalent throughout the twentieth century against the mass or popular arts, including the arguments of Collingwood, Horkheimer, and Adorno, claiming that the majority of such arguments fail to hit their targets. The criticisms that have been leveled against popular artworks – that they are crude, formulaic, appeal to prurient interests, encourage passivity, are mass produced, and so on – both fail to apply to all popular artworks, and to apply only to popular artworks.

My case is made a great deal easier by ceding to some of these criticisms, however, and admitting that not all games are art, and furthermore, even when they are so, the standard is not always high when compared to traditional art forms. I argued in chapter 1 that the artistic sophistication of games is increasing. I stand by this claim, and I think that it is the case that almost all of the serious candidates for being art among videogames are the recent games that have been the focus of this book. My argument will have to show, then, that even though videogames started out as something quite different – for the most part, simple games played on a computer – they have subsequently developed into a form capable of producing at least some instances of genuine art.

A CLUSTER THEORY OF ART

How are we to answer the question of whether the videogames I have sought to explain in this book really are a form of art? What can be said beyond the similarities just noted? One of the few other philosophers of the arts to seriously consider videogames as a topic of study is Aaron Smuts. Indeed, Smuts (2005a) claims that the primary question that the philosophy of the arts should ask when concerning itself with videogames is whether or not they are art. He concludes that the best way to solve the problem is to consider videogames in relation to previous definitions of art, arguing that the comparison is ultimately favorable and that "by any major definition of art many modern videogames should be considered art." Smuts' working out of this thesis is occasionally problematic; for example, he does not distinguish between videogames and videogame art such as machinima, thinking that establishing the latter as art is sufficient to show that the former are also art. Some of his conceptual connections between videogames and art are also rather loose: just because "self-defense, protection of others, dread of the 'undead,' fighting against overwhelming odds" are themes shared by videogames and traditional art says very little, given that the themes may also be shared with non-art such as role-playing and board games, diaries, folk stories, or traditional histories. In general, I think Smuts could have done more to show exactly how videogames fit within the criteria proposed by previous definitions of art. His observations are merely suggestive rather than logically compelling.

Despite these quibbles with the details of the argument, my response here will follow on from Smuts: I will compare videogames to extant theories of art, asking if and how they fit the criteria proposed there. Videogames will count as art if they fit within an appropriate theoretical understanding of art. This raises the inevitable question of just which theory or definition of art is the best bet. Remembering the discussion of the technical difficulties with the nature of definition (chapter 2), the reader may be unsurprised that the definition of art debate is far from settled. In fact, there are a number of theories still in play, ranging from definitions that seek to secure art status in the institutions involved in the *Artworld* (Dickie, 1974), to those that specify the aesthetic function of art as its defining component (Zangwill, 2001). Drawing from twentieth-century skepticism about the definitional project (Weitz, 1956), some philosophers still doubt that art can be given a satisfactory definition (Gaut, 2000). Needless to say, I cannot settle this issue here, and even rehearsing the state of the debate would take this book far from its intended topic. But I do need to propose a suitable theoretical prototype of art, and to give the reader some idea why I think it is appropriate.

I take as my specific chosen model the *cluster* theory of art. This is because I find such theories quite plausible concerning art itself, and because I think that they can be used to make a very strong case for the art status of videogames. Cluster theories of art derive from the claim that many concepts function, not by specifying sets of necessary and sufficient conditions that any item sitting under the concept must have, but by specifying a potentially fuzzy set of criteria or "family resemblances" that an object might meet in any number of ways (Wittgenstein, 1968). The concept of *cup*, for example, may work not by specifying definitive conditions of all and only things that are cups, but by picking out a collection of properties inhering in a range of typical cups. Identifying a cup is a matter of judgment about how closely the object in question aligns with the cluster conception of typical cups. There are well-known difficulties with this theory of concepts, especially concerning its dependence on the problematic notion of *similarity* (Goodman, 1972), and the fit with how children actually acquire concepts (Keil, 1981). I cannot pursue these difficulties in the limited space I have here.

Cluster theories of art claim that art can be characterized by a set of conditions which an object might meet in any number of ways. Furthermore, different types of art might include differing typical collections of the characteristic conditions. E. J. Bond (1975), Berys Gaut (2000), and Julius Moravcsik (1993) have all advocated forms of cluster theory. Some philosophers think that a cluster theory of art, suitably formalized as a disjunctive definition of the type discussed in chapter 2, can also provide a definition of art (Davies, 2004; Dutton, 2006). Gaut stops short of thinking that art can be defined as such, aligning his view with anti-essentialism about art. Of his form of cluster theory, Gaut claims that the following are

> properties the presence of which ordinary judgment counts toward something's being a work of art, and the absence of which counts against its being art: (1) possessing positive aesthetic properties, such as being beautiful, graceful, or elegant (properties which ground a capacity to give sensuous pleasure); (2) being expressive of emotion; (3) being intellectually challenging (i.e., questioning received views and modes of thought); (4) being formally complex and coherent; (5) having a capacity to convey complex meanings; (6) exhibiting an individual point of view; (7) being an exercise of creative imagination (being original); (8) being an artifact or performance which is the product of a high degree of skill; (9) belonging to an established artistic form (music, painting, film, etc.); and (10) being the product of an intention to make a work of art. (Gaut, 2000: 28)

These, for Gaut, are *the kind of conditions* that will eventually make up the successful cluster account of art, given that he is rather more interested in arguing for the cluster form itself. As such, Gaut thinks that the list might be revised to account for new or recalcitrant artworks.

Dutton's (2006) list of characteristic features shows a substantial overlap with Gaut's, by including direct pleasure, the display of skill or virtuosity, style novelty and creativity, criticism, representation, "special" focus, expressive individuality, emotional saturation, intellectual challenge, traditions and institutions, and imaginative experience. Though some artworks may lack one or more of these conditions, we could not imagine an artwork lacking a significant number of them. Furthermore, that a newly discovered object has the majority of these criteria would tempt us to see the object as an artwork. Dutton also takes a distinctly naturalized spin on the cluster theory of art, claiming that the conditions stem from the evolved psychological, behavioral, and social dispositions of our species, and hence are universal among all human cultures. This is the case *even if* the culture in question fails to have a cognate of the Western concept art in its native language (Dutton, 2000). That is, Dutton has a theory about just *why* this cluster exists: art is a part of our evolved and universal human nature (Dutton, 2009).

Why am I adopting this cluster approach? First, in its disjunctive form, I think this theory has potential in solving the definitional disputes about art. There may simply be more than one way for something to be art, and so if an object lacks one of the characteristic features of art, it may nevertheless be art if it has a sufficient number of the other typical features. My own definition of videogames employed this same virtue of disjunctive definition, and I see no reason why the same tactic might not be appropriate in the case of art.

Second, a cluster theory of art allows us to recognize people in dislocated cultures – artists and patrons in a New York City art gallery, Maori carvers in New Zealand, and even Paleolithic cave painters – as engaged in the same kinds of practices, and producing and appreciating the same kinds of objects. This is especially important when many of these examples of diverse cultural activities seem problematic in terms of popular institutional (Dickie, 1974) or historical theories of art (Levinson, 1979). George Dickie has famously argued that it is the approval of the *Artworld* that confers the status of artworks, allowing us to see how some very atypical objects – readymades such as the urinal that comprises Duchamp's *Fountain* – are properly art. But even though there is no evidence that Paleolithic cave painters had anything like the cultural institutions that surround Western art – indeed, the idea verges on the silly – it is extraordinarily tempting to see these people as creating art somewhat of the kind seen in the Western tradition. Historical theories of art claim that it is in virtue of historical links between various artworks, and their modes of production and appreciation, that art status is defined. However, the historical connections between dislocated peoples such as modern New Yorkers and pre-colonization Maori seem too insubstantial to explain the depth of similarity in the items they produce and appreciate – and the fact that Maori artifacts so easily make their way into the New York Metropolitan Museum of Art *as art*. In essence, a cluster theory may be less *chauvinistic* than previous theories that credit art with arising out of an actual culture, institution, or history, allowing us to see the cultural products of other societies as art, often on a par with that of our own tradition.

Third, especially in the form of Dutton's (2006, 2009) naturalist definition of art, cluster theory also allows a role for naturalism in art theory, connecting art to the idea of universal human traits (Brown, 1991; Dutton, 2001). Dutton argues that art theory has for too long been orientated around the art of the *avant-garde*, with examples like Duchamp's notorious

Fountain taking a role in the debate that far outweighs their real significance. The definition of art debate is *anomaly fixated,* and to the detriment of the theories it has produced (the institutional theory of art, in particular, seems couched in a way to account for the art status of avant-garde works like *Fountain*). A cluster theory, based on naturalist and cross-cultural principles – thus focused on the regularities across human cultures, rather than idiosyncratic objects found within one culture – may allow us a better understanding of art in general.

In an oblique way, the question of whether videogames are art *is* a cross-cultural issue. Modern culture seems increasingly splintered and compartmentalized. Though this is largely a result of the sheer number of people who are now able to take part in culture due to increasing levels of affluence, it is surely also because of the technological globalization of culture and the increasing ease with which cultural niches are able to communicate and connect their interests through modern means. The Internet, to take the most prominent reason for cultural compartmentalization, allows geographically dislocated groups to sustain their cultural interests in rich ways unavailable to previous ages, when information flow was rather more restricted and localized. Fan fiction, alt-rock, fantasy role-playing, conspiracy theories, and cosplay all seem to be the effect of this specialization of cultural diversity; largely invisible in the "real world," each has a rich subterranean existence. Equally, videogames feel the effects of this specialization. Though videogames are also obvious in the mainstream media, for many, games are very much a mysterious world because gaming culture is most lively in less prominent cultural spaces such as Internet review sites and forums. Once one actually discovers these cultural spaces, the amount of subject-specific information, shared understandings, language, and numerous shibboleths can make gaming culture almost impenetrable to the outsider.

Comparing games to previous forms of art really is a cross-cultural endeavor, but the comparison is not with the culture of a newly discovered geographically isolated way of life, but with an *interstitial culture* to which many people are oblivious. There are intersections between cultural worlds – of course, videogames are informed by mainstream film – but much of what happens in games and gaming is generated by their own distinctive and semi-isolated cultural history. This is an important reason why we should approach videogames on their own terms, and not always judge them by more familiar forms of culture that philosophers of the arts and other theorists have typically dealt with.

Thus, a subsequent strength of this disjunctive "cross-cultural" approach is that it may allow us to abstract away from the superficial differences that videogames have to Western-paradigm art, and especially *high art,* and that may generate skepticism that videogames are indeed art. Potentially, a lot of the resistance to the idea that games are art will derive from unfairly treating games as an art form they are not. If we look to videogames for sophisticated meaning or moral seriousness of the kind associated with great literature, we will more often than not be disappointed, but because of this focus, we may also miss the genuine art that exists in their dynamic and interactive representations of a fictional world. This mistake has also been difficult for me to avoid, given my own philosophical and artistic inclinations. I think games designers commit the same error when they ape the conventions of other artworks to the detriment of the real nature of their artistic medium. In order to come to a fair evaluation of whether videogames are art, we need to appreciate the lessons of the previous chapters about their real nature.

THE ART IN VIDEOGAMES

It is worthwhile to fit videogames into this cluster approach, aware that there are likely to be both surface differences and deeper continuities. I will do so clause by clause, using those conditions picked out by Dutton and Gaut in their analyses.

Dutton and Gaut both pick our direct pleasure in aesthetic qualities as being characteristic of art. Aesthetic properties and pleasures are much discussed in the philosophy of art. In a classic paper, Frank Sibley (1959) argues for a strong distinction between aesthetic properties such as beauty or grace and non-aesthetic ones such as brightness or angularity. I do not mean to take a position on the distinctive existence of aesthetic properties or the putative faculty of taste, but I think it is clear enough that we do have an aesthetic *vocabulary* that is employed when describing the properties and experiences afforded both by artworks and natural scenes. Gamers also employ much of the same aesthetic vocabulary, and games do seem to afford a great deal of pleasure through their capacity for beauty. The glistening and verdant jungles in *Drake's Fortune*, the rich cityscapes in *Grand Theft Auto IV*, the graceful movements of the characters in *Heavenly Sword* – all seem to engage our aesthetic sensibilities. These things are not only accurate and technically excellent representations, but *beautiful*. Thus, gamers do seem to have aesthetic interests somewhat comparable with those of traditional art appreciators. That gamers are particularly concerned with the aesthetic qualities of the graphics and sound of games is shown by the expense to which many go in setting up their gaming hardware with pricey visual and audio displays, and state of the art consoles or graphics cards. The reader will be in the best position to judge for themselves, of course, by experiencing first-hand the aesthetic qualities of the games that have been discussed here, but the inclusion of aesthetic pleasures is surely one of the key reasons why we are tempted to situate videogames within the category of art.

Though it is clear that many games do have aesthetic qualities comparable with those of other artworks, in other respects there are differences in the aesthetic qualities experienced in videogames to those found in traditional artworks. Some of the aesthetic terms applied to games seem to refer to their interactive qualities, and many of the pleasures provided by games are *kinesthetic pleasures* in that they involve the qualities of the physical interaction with the gaming device and the physical world it depicts. A significant proportion of the aesthetic qualities gamers and critics refer to in games have this kinesthetic quality – gameplay might be described as *flowing, fluid, jerky*, and so forth – and these terms refer to the interactive, moreover *physically* interactive, structure of one's involvement in a game world. As such, *frantic*, when applied to a game, refers to the character of the gameplay, particularly that the challenges it offers are presented in a hurried succession and that the player is always at the risk of being overwhelmed or becoming panicked by the difficulties. Though this might sound strange to a non-gamer, the cars in *Grand Theft Auto IV* have a satisfying physical *heft* and there is much pleasure to be taken in simply driving around Liberty City for this reason. To be applied to videogames, aesthetic theory would seem to need to adapt itself to the interactive and kinesthetic form of those games to explain exactly what generates the direct pleasure in games, perhaps drawing from the theory of kinesthetic arts such as dance.

The existence of aesthetic features in videogames leads to an interesting question: when did games first take on this aesthetic dimension? I do not think that videogames have always been art. The games spanning the earlier years of gaming, indeed up to the early 1990s, strike me as much less artful than recent games. This is because the aesthetic qualities that characterize recent games are mostly missing in earlier games, which were far more orientated around gameplay. *Pac-Man* has a distinctive look and design, but I think it would be a stretch to say that one might take pleasure in its visual design. Poole claims of *Spacewar* that it is "serene, austere, a thing of alien beauty" (2000: 30), but I am unconvinced. Poole's claim seems to me a rather subjective judgment that would not have made any sense to the designers of the game: to me, there is no evidence that *Spacewar* was designed as anything other than a game, and what minimal aspects of design it does have are wedded to this intention and the basic fiction it depicts. If *Spacewar* is beautiful – which I personally do not see in the object – it is accidentally so and not as a function of its being art.

Beside the focus on producing games, I think that the graphical limitations on early games restricted their aesthetic and artistic potential. The basic bitmapping used to represent early games did not allow early designers much aesthetic scope. Only with increased computing power did aesthetic considerations begin to loom larger in game design. *Myst*, released in 1993, seems to be an important development in the aesthetic qualities of gaming. *Myst* is an explorative adventure game quite unlike contemporary games of the early 1990s in that aesthetics are at the forefront – and potentially to the detriment of the gameplay, as noted earlier. *Myst* presents the player with an opportunity to explore a mysterious fictional world. *Myst* is not a 3D game, however, and the world is mostly static, rendered through a sequence of computer-generated stills depicting different locations. As such, structurally *Myst* is very similar to earlier text-based adventure games like *Colossal Cave Adventure* and *Hunt the Wumpus*, differing in the graphically rich depiction of the fictional world and its greater scope. All of this makes the game a little inert, and means that the actual gameplay in *Myst* is limited to a small number of decisions about which areas to explore and the actions to perform in those areas: in Juul's terms, it is a classic game of "progression" (2005: 67–75). But what *Myst* did do is make obvious the aesthetic potential of exploring a fictional world.

It is also obvious that games involve the element of *representation* that Dutton and many others – including Plato's disparaging remarks in the *Republic* and Aristotle's rather more positive assessment in his *Poetics* – have claimed to be an important condition of the arts. The development of the representational abilities of videogames, which was the focus of chapter 4, is another of the most artistically significant things about the cultural form. The ability of videogames to construct visual representations of a fictional world that can be appreciated as a character within that world is another principal reason why videogames should be seen as art. When the kind of aesthetic experience seen in *Myst* was wedded with the contemporary representational developments in 3D game worlds being made by Id Software in their archetypal first-person shooters *Wolfenstein 3D* and *Doom*, a new form of game arose that would quickly come to dominate videogaming. If one looks at more recent game releases, a large proportion of them, and typically the ones that are most commercially and aesthetically successful, are in part world-exploring games. *Oblivion, Portal, Grand Theft Auto, BioShock, Crysis, Call of Duty 4, Halo 3, Assassin's Creed, World of Warcraft, Prince of Persia, LittleBigPlanet, Fallout 3*, and even racing games like *Gran Turismo* and *Grid: Race Driver* all involve the aesthetic exploration of an environment, though the gameplay may ultimately involve shooting zombies, casting spells, jumping pits filled with snapping alligators, or racing cars. Indeed, it is just these games that have been my main focus here, and have made this book on the art of videogaming a plausible endeavor. Videogames have developed the ability to represent interactive fictional worlds with such a depth and vivacity that the player really can become *immersed* in these worlds – and in all of the senses identified earlier: an obsessive, absorbed, fictional player-character.

Liberty City, the setting of *Grand Theft Auto IV*, is a high-water mark of aesthetic representation in gaming. Here is a city, rich with detail and character, with living inhabitants, that changes to reflect the time of day and the changing weather, is simmering with economic and ethnic politics, has great architecture, and is everywhere making comments on our real world, so that through the lens of Liberty City we are able to see the absurdities and contradictions of contemporary city life. There are certain developments in art that open up new realms of representational and artistic possibility: in Ancient Greece, the discovery of lost-wax bronze casting allowed sculptors to create dynamic self-supported figures, so that soon the lifelike master-pieces *Discobolos* and *Doryphoros* were produced. The discovery of the three-dimensional surface of paintings by Cézanne led to the fracturing of representational form seen in Cubism. The development of the stream of consciousness technique by literary Modernists such as Joyce led to the new psychological depth of their depiction of human life, so that we could witness the equanimity, humor, and intelligence of Leopold Bloom and the complexities of his daily life. How could the real-time depiction of a virtual city, with the appreciator placed within that city in an epistemic and behavioral role, not be a stunning development in the *possibilities* of art?

Equally obvious from these observations and from the theory developed in this book, is that the imaginative experience Dutton thinks to be a criterion of art is also present in videogames. A great many artworks seek to prompt their audiences into flights of imagination, guided and enriched by a prop that the artist has themselves invested with detail through the employment of their own imaginative talents (see chapter 3). This is among the clearest of connections between videogames and the arts. I have argued throughout this book that a principal feature of recent videogames, par-ticularly those that do strike us as art-like, is that they seek to deliver us into an imaginative world with all sorts of engrossing particularities. I think that it has long been an unanalyzed assumption that videogames (and other popular electronic media) are distinctly lacking in imagination, and that the viewer is simply enthralled by the game, and hence cognitively passive. There may be a half-truth in this bias: if we restrict the imagination to the ability to *visualize* rich fictional scenes, then visually rich recent videogames do demand less of the imagination than less representationally robust written forms of fiction. But once we move beyond this limited conception of the imagination, and realize that the fictional nature of videogames calls on the ability to imagine what is not real, both on the part of producer and consumer, we will come to a more realistic conclusion about the central role of the imagination in gaming. One aspect of immersion, I argued in chapter 3, is the ability to submerse oneself, through make-believe, in a fictional world. Furthermore, though I have not spent any great time discussing it here, it is clear that videogames also involve their players *elaborating* on imaginative scenarios, reasoning their hidden structures, so as to formulate effective means of meeting the demands of gameplay (Greenfield, 1984). By this measure, videogames are extraordinarily imaginative.

Both Dutton and Gaut also see skill and virtuosity as being a criterion of art. Art often displays a high degree of skill on the part of its creators and performers: *artist*, of course is often used as a term of praise, picking out those individuals capable of employing a skill to an excellent degree. Much skill and virtuosity can be seen within game design, especially within their graphical design. In large part such artistry is enabled by the technological advances in computer graphics, but games are valued as an aggregation of skilled *performances* from designers, artists, and writers working within the technological medium of gaming. For many people, recent art in traditional forms such as painting and sculpture has lost its connection with skill and virtuosity: putting a dead shark in a box of formaldehyde is not an act that takes any *artistic* skill at all, it would seem. What is important in much recent art is not the expertise that went into constructing the artwork, but the ideas that it supposedly expresses, which can often really only be discerned when one acknowledges the title of a given work. It is subsequently almost proverbial to hear in response to a new work of modern art the refrain: "I/a child/a monkey could have done that." There are reasons for these developments, of course, a popular one being that mechanical forms of representation such as photography have displaced the visual arts from their traditional depictive roles. But in videogaming the artistry is plain to see, perhaps because the technological form of 3D graphics has reinvigorated the role of the artist in the process of rendering realistic but stylistically distinctive visual representations. The technology that has developed so quickly over the past twenty years has made possible new kinds of virtuoso artistic achievements.

Thus, leading into the next criteria of the cluster theories under discussion here, videogames certainly involve the style, novelty, and creativity critical to Dutton's definition, and also the related creative originality referred to in Gaut's theory. Though it is common for gaming critics or theorists (Smuts, 2005a) to attribute "photo-realism" to recent games – indeed, as I have here – it is really a falsehood that the graphical depictions of videogames are *principally* concerned with photo-realism. Instead, almost all games seem to attempt to *enhance* the graphical appearance of their fictional worlds, usually presenting them with a distinctive or novel style. Arguably, a realistic car racing game like *Grid: Race Driver*, compared to reality, provides a *superior* graphical depiction of car racing in that the designers are able to more carefully control the aesthetic qualities of the racing experience. Such games do not look realistic at all: they look *super-realistic*. Equally, *Team Fortress 2* depicts its team-based first-person shooter – a genre often approached with a sense of seriousness, as in its forebear, *Counterstrike* – with a very stylish comic sensibility. The game is essentially a large cartoon, and this fits quite naturally with the over-the-top gameplay. Whatever else might be said of *Metal Gear Solid 4*, it is an incredibly stylish game: sometimes to the extent that its style overwhelms its gaming aspects. *Portal*, too, adopts a creative style. Here the environments are unexpectedly stripped down: there is not an attempt to present a richly dynamic environment so as best to show off the graphical capabilities of the game engine – as so often games are guilty of doing – but a spare graphical style that fits with the test chamber narrative and simple puzzle-directed gameplay. The dry and ironic dialogue of *Portal*, the many incidental oddities and jokes, and the final unexpected and eccentric song, also provide a compelling sense of style. The very length of the game – it can be completed in four or five hours, where many recent games stretch to ten times that length – is also a stylistic decision that I personally wish more games would follow. The length allows the game to present a more concise vision, rather than the bloated Behemoth that so many recent games have become, where one leaves the world not with a sense of artistic completion, but with frustration, confusion, or boredom.

Of course, in gaming there is a very large amount of less than creative work: very many games are merely *cookie cutter* or formulaic games. But the severe criticism that these games often receive only strengthens the claim that in gaming novelty, style, and creativity are genuinely valued. This is a repetition of the claim I made earlier in this chapter. Perhaps not all game types really are art, or that a great many games are simply bad art, with only a few aspiring to real artistic significance. But this is equally true when we look at the great majority of art forms. *The Da Vinci Code* rather than *Ulysses* is the norm in written fiction; most films do not take their cue from *Citizen Kane*, but rather from *Star Wars*.

Gaming also increasingly involves criticism, another criterion of Dutton's definition. The principal outlets for gaming criticism are games magazines, criticism in the print media, and online games review sites. Often, however, games criticism is merely a part of marketing: the main consoles have official magazines and the gaming reviews one finds in these are often little more than advertisements. Online sources are potentially more impartial, but they face another difficulty: much of the criticism is just not very good. One reason for this is that much criticism is written by *fanboys*. These are people with an overbearing emotional investment in the videogames or consoles they write about – consumers who have bought in to the ever-present hype surrounding modern media entertainment and technology.

Another problem such reviewers have is a lack of art literacy, and the subsequent difficulty of linking games to other art forms. A failure to understand what is possible in film or graphical art can undermine the judgments that are made in videogaming criticism. This lack of perspective has had a disastrous result for much gaming criticism. I am always suspicious to hear that a game has a compelling narrative, because I know, partly because of the problems discussed in this book, that the narratives presented by games are currently a poor shadow of their cousins in filmed and written fiction. The *Metal Gear Solid* series of games, created by the game auteur Hideo Kojima, are frequently praised in games writing for having engrossing narratives. As I noted earlier, for me, these games are an exercise in frustration. The tone of the games is wildly erratic, with vulgar jokes placed alongside very stylish sequences intended to convey seriousness. The level of human drama in the *Metal Gear* series is soporific and frequently juvenile. Most disastrously, the balance between narrative and gameplay in these games is terrible, as the game involves *very long* stretches of non-interactive cut-scenes and scripted dialogue between portions of gameplay. Encouraging the player to watch twenty minutes (or in many cases, much more) of asinine narrative seems to me to be a gross misunderstanding of the art form. And though the player can *click through* the cut-scenes this only serves to emphasize their basic redundancy. One of the important themes in Poole's book on videogames, and one that is effectively argued, is that films and videogames have differing artistic or aesthetic functions, and that when videogames imitate films they are inevitably bad games (2000: 78–124). For many games, I have to agree. That the gameplay in *Metal Gear Solid* is frequently brilliant and deep has no doubt distracted many critics and players from its flaws – or provided a means of excusing them – but one suspects that many critics are either so completely sold on the game before they play it, perhaps having an emotional attachment caused by their enjoyment of earlier games in the series, or unaware or uninterested in the real potential of narrative, that they are not in a position to come to a fair judgment of the artistic qualities of the game.

The biggest development needed in gaming criticism is for the form to move beyond the *game review* and into a level of discussion that is capable of situating videogames within a wider understanding of culture and the arts. A theoretical understanding of the place of games within the arts seems to be necessary here. Indeed, while not wanting to sound too self-important, I hope the present book can make a contribution in this regard. A philosophical work on the art-theoretical significance of videogames could itself be a critical signal that videogames are taking a confirmed place within the arts.

Is there evidence of what Dutton calls "special focus" in videogaming culture? In itself this condition strikes me as a little intangible. What is it that is special? How special? What kind of focus? Dutton characterizes this *specialness* in terms of art being "bracketed off from ordinary life, made a separate and dramatic focus of experience" (2006: 371). If special focus is thusly taken to pick out the various *situational* features of art – that it is separate from ordinary life or unproductive – then this aligns with what I said in chapter 5 about the situational nature of gaming. Whether we use the ideas of the *magic circle, separateness and non-productiveness,* or *immersion* to refer to this quality, it is of little consequence: videogames do seem set aside from everyday life, though this frequently leads to videogames being labeled as *pointless* because of a lack of sympathy and understanding of gaming, and just why gamers take it as seriously as they often do.

Furthermore, if we take special focus to refer to the cultural significance of an artifact, the esteem and seriousness with which it is regarded by its community of appreciators, then there is reason to think that this kind of thing does attend videogames. The release of *Grand Theft Auto IV* in 2008 was treated as an incredibly special event in the gaming community. There was a great deal of anticipation for the game – more cynically, *hype* – and from my own personal experience, picking up and playing the game was a memorable event. Many people pre-ordered the game, not that there was really anything tangible to be gained in doing so, but because of the importance they invested in the game. And even though I was sitting alone in a darkened room, exploring the fictional world by myself, I felt connected to other players. Discussion forums on the Internet were fixated on the game, and many of the more articulate players blogged on and critiqued the game in huge depth. I had long and involved discussions with friends both about what I had done in Liberty City – retelling my personal narrative in the game world – but also about the game's significance, how it would impact on the rest of gaming, and indeed on the rest of culture.

Both Dutton's and Gaut's theories also take art to characteristically involve expressive individuality. In much art, the author, painter, sculptor, or composer becomes a focal point of the art experience, and their works are seen as an expression of their distinctive personality and individual point of view on the world. *Ulysses,* for example, is a clear work of expressive individuality: it is the work of a genius attempting to frame his vision of the world and of the art form that he is using to do so. Joyce is justly a celebrity for his achievement. Compared to the previous cluster criteria of art, I am less convinced that this aspect of art really is present in gaming, or, if it is, that it is involved in anything more than an incipient and debatable form. The videogame *auteur* is somewhat evident in gaming – Hideo Kojima (*Metal Gear*), Will Wright (*Simcity, The Sims, Spore*), the brothers Sam and Dan

Houser (*Grand Theft Auto*), Kazunori Yamauchi (*Gran Turismo*), Shigeru Miyamoto (*The Legend of Zelda*), Ken Levine (*System Shock 2, BioShock*), and Sid Meier (*Civilization*) all to some extent are seen as auteurs particularly associated with the genre or game they helped to create. However, like film, videogames are now productions of sometimes vast teams of people. Though a principal producer, writer, or designer might have a significant say, what we eventually get is a collaborative effort, and not the expression of a single individual. Nevertheless, given the diverse functions of videogames as games, narratives, and graphical worlds, and the divestment of their design into specialized groups responsible for each aspect, some amount of creative control at the head of the chain can be exerted in terms of *selection*, even if a great deal of the actual design is aggregated from a large number of artists.

Even if the auteur theory is unrealistically applied to videogame production, videogames have something of the studio set up that characterized the golden era of Hollywood, with certain studios being identified – rightly or wrongly – as creators of premium content. Thus, if it is unrealistic to say that a videogame is an expressive effort of an individual person, we might say this individuality is so of a studio. Even if gamers do not know who Sam and Dan Houser are, they are almost certainly aware of Rockstar as a creative force. Rockstar have traded on an image of creating fairly edgy, subversive, and adult games. Still, studios are fairly intangible things, with actual artists and designers migrating here and there. *BioShock* was billed as a "spiritual successor" to the widely praised *System Shock* series, not merely because it came from the same studio as *System Shock 2*, but because a number of key personnel, including Ken Levine, were shared between the games, and *BioShock* took up the rather rich role-playing content of its progenitors. Blizzard, the studio responsible for the *Warcraft*, *StarCraft*, and *Diablo* series of games, also generates widespread recognition, expectation, and loyalty on the part of players.

Art and its experience seem characteristically emotional, and this criterion is expressed in both Dutton's and Gaut's version of the cluster theory. I think this is among the clearest of the connections of gaming to uncontested art. I spent all of chapter 7 explaining just how the playing of videogames can be an emotionally concentrated experience, even though the emotions experienced may be somewhat different to other art forms, in that they are not the second-hand relational emotions typical of narrative fictions, but first-hand emotions derived from one's role in a game world. *System Shock 2* – the game that really convinced me of the ability of videogames to be emotionally compelling – made me incredibly anxious and fearful, so much so that I look back very fondly on playing that game. Furthermore, not only do games arouse these emotions, but the games themselves are expressive of the emotions. Ultimately, *BioShock* – depending on the ending you get – is enormously uplifting or unremittingly bleak; but the emotional palette of the game ranges from surreal wonder, crushing peril, and moral angst, to tenderness.

Again, both Dutton and Gaut pick out intellectual challenge as characteristic of art. Dutton thinks that "works of art tend to be designed to utilize a combined variety of human perceptual and intellectual capacities to a full extent; indeed, the best works stretch them beyond their ordinary limits" (2006: 372). Do videogames involve such intellectual challenge? If this book prompts any non-gamer readers to attempt playing games, then one thing they will very quickly discover is how hard games can be. The difficulty is not just with physical control of the gamepad – even though I expect this to be a severe impediment for many potential gamers – it is also intellectual. If the reader has played the puzzle game *Lemmings*, they will surely be aware of the potential of gaming for intellectual challenge, but also, like the emotions involved in gaming, the type of intellectual challenge involved in gaming may be quite different to that involved in other uncontested forms of art. The intellectual challenge is often not to an issue outside of gaming – a challenge to "received views and modes of thought" as Gaut puts it (2000: 29) – but a direct challenge to the intellectual capacity of the player to solve problems.

Portal is a good example of the intellectual potential of videogames. One key source of the challenge of games is interpreting their game structure, which is partly encoded in the structure of their fictional world, and hence calls on the player to hypothesize and reason about the nature of the game world and what must be done to surmount its problems. The initial impression of many games can be one of total bewilderment. In *Portal* the player is introduced into the first level *in medias res*. Unaware of the nature of their environment, and immediately prodded by a spatial discontinuity that seems utterly mind-bending, the player can see their character from two points of view, one from the perspective of their fictional proxy, and one through a spatial portal in front of them. To proceed in the game, the player must move through spatial areas employing the portals, and along the way they are *nudged* by the game into learning behaviors that are crucial to clearing the levels. A level might be initially perplexing, but by applying what the player has learned about the physical nature of the world they are in through the previous levels, and their affordances for actions within it, they are eventually able to puzzle out the conclusion, often feeling a *eureka!* moment as the level clicks into organization or as they successfully string together the actions needed to solve the puzzle. *Portal* is essentially a learning experience, and I think that its intellectual challenges are not so different from those in traditional arts. Many narrative fictions also involve puzzles. In a film like Paul Thomas Anderson's *Magnolia*, the plot is incredibly complicated, and it is not initially clear just how the many characters or events stand in relation to each other. Interpreting *Magnolia* is – in a way similar to *Portal* – a matter of understanding the nature of its world, and placing the various parts of the world into a coherent scheme so that the individual parts make sense. Indeed, *Magnolia* has such a surfeit of content that the audience can watch the movie repeatedly and continue to make new and informative connections. This kind of intellectual puzzling activity exists in fictions ranging from the television show *Lost* to David Foster Wallace's *Infinite Jest*. The difference between these fictions and videogames is that in gaming the player is in a position to act on their understanding because of their interactive involvement in the game world.

Dutton's disjunctive theory of art takes institutions and tradition to be crucial to art. As noted, institutional theories of art such as that proposed by George Dickie (1974) are a significant theoretical model, allowing us to account for the art status of some works that seem extraordinarily atypical, especially those of the avant-garde. The institutionalization of art, particularly in terms of art shows, museums, and art theory – the Artworld – allows artists to produce quite unprecedented works, and to move in directions only understood in terms of those institutional factors. Do videogames have this institutional aspect? Smuts (2005a) thinks that there is "clearly a burgeoning art world for videogames." As evidence for this, he notes that there are awards shows for games, that games are increasingly reviewed in mainstream publications, and that some games have even made their way into art museums. All of this is certainly true. However, I am not convinced that it is all that significant in terms of whether the institutionalization of gaming can be used to establish its art status. The claim about museums is particularly weak. Given the recent non-art uses that modern museums have taken on, I think that videogames have made their way into museums not as art, but as popular culture, and furthermore that this is an act of *appropriation* on the part of museums, rather than something that has arisen naturally out of gaming culture. (In my opinion, the last thing that videogames need, given their present vitality and creativity, is academic entombment in a museum.) Videogames clearly have growing institutional respect in the form of a growing literature, the institutional study of games, games awards, and so on. It is just not clear to me that there is any reason to call this an *Artworld* rather than a *Gameworld*; indeed, settling on the former seems to me to merely beg the question. Given the ubiquity of institutions and traditions throughout human culture, I am not convinced how much can be made of the existence of institutions and traditions in the case of videogames *vis-à-vis* art.

NEW ART FROM OLD BOTTLES

I claimed that videogames would be art if they fitted comfortably within an appropriate theory of art. How do videogames stand in relation to the criteria set out above? Both Dutton and Gaut think that if an artifact has a certain proportion of these characteristics then it is sufficient to make it art, though exactly just how many conditions are needed, and which collections of conditions are sufficient for art status, is not entirely clear. Nevertheless, I think that the argument of the previous section makes a pretty compelling case that videogames are art. As a category of artifacts, videogames exhibit, in some form, nearly all of the conditions picked out by this cluster conception of art, even though in some cases just how they meet the criteria is distinctive in the case of videogames.

What is equally obvious, however, is that when we approach games *individually*, we will often *not* find this collection of features. Given that videogames have only recently begun to display some of these criteria – in particular, direct pleasure and aesthetic qualities, emotional saturation or expression, skill and virtuosity, style – it may be that not all videogames really are artworks. Previously, videogames may have sat more squarely in the category of games, and only as their representational, aesthetic, and social aspects evolved have they grown into a form capable of producing instances of art. *Pong*, for example, lacks direct pleasure in aesthetic qualities, skill and virtuosity, style, the potential for critical evaluation, expressive individuality, emotional saturation, and intellectual (rather than sensory-motor) challenge, in anything other than a near-vacuous sense of these criteria. Other, more recent, games have a greater proportion of these characteristics, but still lack some of them. A number of very recent games may have nearly all of the criteria. So where *Grand Theft Auto IV* may well count as art under this theory, it is not clear some classic games will. I suspect that some gamers might not like this judgment, especially those with a strong interest in *retro* gaming. But it is not intended as a critical judgment – earlier videogames such as *Frogger*, *Donkey Kong*, and *Pac-Man* are surely engrossing and fantastic *as games*. But that these earlier games are art seems to me a more difficult proposition. I simply do not think that they display enough of the core of art-making properties discussed above to really count as art in anything other than the honorific sense distinguished earlier.

There is an important complication here that might temper the above conclusion. Videogames also seem to involve conditions that sit squarely *outside* of this conception of the arts – most importantly, the formal and situational features of gaming, such as rules, objectives, and competition.

The disjunctive theories considered here claim only that a certain proportion of conditions are sufficient for something to be art. What they do not specify is whether there are any conditions that might count *against* an artifact being within the category of art. *Competition* might be just such a quality: competitive activities, even those with aesthetic qualities, are more often characterized as *games* or *sports*. Smuts (2005a) notes that some instances of uncontested artworks such as Greek tragedy do involve competition. But in this case the competition seems to be an external fact about the artworks, rather than a fact about their intrinsic nature or how they are appreciated. Greek tragedies were a product of a competition, whereas videogames are far more like sport in that competition is a part of the thing produced and how it is interacted with. One could be oblivious to the fact that Greek tragedies were produced for competitions, but still understand and be moved by the work, whereas if one was oblivious to the fact that multiplayer *Call of Duty* involved competition, one would not even be able to play the game. To head off this complaint, Smuts notes that in fictions such as *National Velvet* or *The Karate Kid*, we might "root for one side of a competition" and hence the appreciation of narrative fictions might involve intrinsic competition of a kind. But this is unconvincing: having sympathy for a person involved in a competition is not sufficient to be a part of that competition itself. Surely being in a competition implies that one must be able to act in a way so as to influence the outcome of the competition and so to compete.

For this reason, I think some might be tempted to conclude that, though there is a substantial overlap between videogaming and art, videogames are also somewhat distinctive in having qualities not traditionally seen as crucial to art. Videogames are not alone in this *partial overlap*. Gaut and Dutton both note that a number of other behavioral types map onto much of the same conceptual territory of art, but also have clear differences. Gaut states "what makes something an artwork is a matter of its possessing a range of properties that are shared with other human domains" (2000: 41). Dutton observes that sport involves expressive individuality, traditions and institutions, criticism, special focus, and the display of skill or virtuosity in at least some sense of these terms (2006: 376). Craft also maps onto much of the same territory as art, differing, perhaps, in its lack of individual expression and style. The question will now be, is this overlap between videogames and art significant enough to consider extending the concept of art to the case of videogames?

Is there really a way to choose between situating videogames in the familiar category, or leaving them out, perhaps locating them in their own distinctive category that though related to art in having an overlap of shared characteristics, is not quite identical? This problem may really owe to the cluster account itself, in that it must contend with the difficulty of specifying just which clusters are sufficient to make something art. In the case that the category was closed and we had enumerated all the categorical instances, we could potentially definitively settle the art-relevant clusters. In open-ended categories, however, the features that we choose to include in our cluster analysis will be included so as to meet our intuitions about the cases we have thus far encountered and counterfactual intuitions based on these. It may be that when something new comes along, we have the opportunity to revise these conceptual intuitions, perhaps discovering a new art form. Videogames may be art, but at the very least they are *distinctive art*, in particular with their own distinctive modes of appreciation, including competition.

Gaut's cluster account in particular gives this plastic appearance. Confronted with an artifact that bears a substantial categorial overlap with the category art, but which includes atypical features, one suspects that Gaut might have to say this event counts as a *discovery* that there is yet another way for something to be art. Videogames may count as the discovery that competitive games can sometimes be art. But this discovery may itself serve to *shift* our intuitions about art so that in the future we may be tempted to include works that from a previous standpoint would seem quite alien to the category. As such, some readers may suspect that the cluster account is cheating us, and that really it threatens to provide us with a theory of art that is protean and expanding, perhaps indefinitely so.

But how else could it be? In the case of videogames, the artistic potential of the form is contingent on unpredictable technological developments that make possible robustly represented virtual fictions that can depict not only richly aesthetic worlds, but also worlds that can situate social interactions such as gaming. Like the revolution that occurred in Classical Greek sculpture with the advent of lost-wax casting, the revolution of digital interactive fictions has led to the ability of artists to explore and develop new and largely unprecedented areas of artistic possibility, in this case, *artistically rich games*. These problems with pinning down art echo the inductive problems that the gathering of knowledge about the world always contends with. Videogames are a cultural platypus, connecting categories – art and gaming – once thought discrete. Like non-metaphorical platypuses, their discovery should prompt the subtle revision of our classificatory schemes.

This is not the first time such revision has been appropriate, of course. We can profitably compare videogames to the early days of cinema. The artistic form of films – narratives comprised of moving pictures – is clearly related to earlier forms of art such as theatre, sharing many of their representational techniques, but differing in its technologically derived medium. Looking back on the early days of film from our perspective over a hundred years later, early movies are apt to strike us as crude and naïve. Georges Méliès' films, such as *A Trip to the Moon* – important works no doubt – are nevertheless comprised of quite rudimentary combinations of scenes that only roughly depict a narrative. One suspects that in these early films it is the basic novelty of the medium that is valued; and so in *A Trip to the Moon* we find the medium used to make simple visual jokes. But the technological medium of film, even if initially used for novelty purposes, quickly attracted people with altogether different aims. Only over a considerable period of experiment, and as they explored the unique nature of the medium, would film makers develop the representational and artistic techniques we are now familiar with and in which we see the artistic virtues of film. Inevitably, there was a great deal of skepticism that films were a genuine form of art, or that they had the potential to be any good as art, and many culture theorists saw film, as a mass produced thing, as a debasement of art (Carroll, 1998a). But no one should any longer doubt that film has the potential for producing art, even though many films do not achieve any great level of artistic merit, rather remaining simple entertainments. In fact, film has developed into a medium capable of sophisticated and moving art, and has produced its own master-pieces. As a result, our usage of the term *art* has expanded to encompass a medium with quite different artistic means and aims to those seen in earlier forms to which the term originally referred.

The parallels with videogames are clear. Games originally started out as novelties, and many certainly remain so, but it is also clear that artists have now engaged with the medium. In the last fifteen years, especially, where the rapid improvements in digital technology have made possible the realistic and aesthetically rich game worlds seen in *Grand Theft Auto IV* and *Fallout 3*, games designers have been exploring the potential of the medium – and its problems – and have slowly developed a representational and artistic tool kit that allows them to make works that exploit the unique aesthetic potential of the medium. We have met a number of these developments in this book: texture-mapped polygonal models, the virtual camera, rendering techniques, player-characters as an epistemic and behavioral proxy, narratives of discovery and disclosure, and emotionally provocative game choices, are all developments that have further explored and refined the artistic potential of videogames. We are still at a stage where there is much doubt about the art status of videogames; even gamers themselves often voice these doubts. But increasingly, I think, the games that are being produced should make us more confident about the art status of games. Perhaps in the future, as in the case with film, no one will seriously doubt the potential for the medium of videogaming to produce sophisticated and moving art, and our use of the term *art* will have once again expanded to encompass a new type.

The lesson here is that we must use our *judgment* rather than a set of clear logical conditions to decide whether and indeed when videogames are art. Furthermore, that judgment should be informed by our understanding of art, and it is for this purpose that I have chosen cluster theory, particularly of a naturalized form. Because of this theoretical prototype – which is driven by the truly general features of human art, rather than those displayed in the rather more narrow field of Western high art, and still less by the avant-garde strand of that art – perhaps a stronger conclusion is warranted here. In some ways, videogames seem to align better with the arts widely conceived than do many of the examples that most concern many philosophers and art theorists. Videogames seem to share more of the cluster of properties characterizing artworks – such as representations, aesthetic properties, expression of emotion, and stylistic and obvious virtuosic achievements – than do some instances of modern avant-garde art that seem bereft of such qualities. When we compare videogames to earlier forms of art – which were often popular works, or called for a practical engagement, as with religious music and literature, and were valued for their obvious representational beauty – or to art in different cultures, then videogames might sit more naturally within the category of art than do many recent efforts of Western high art.

As noted, many videogames are still in the realm of novelty and entertainment, and despite the rapid growth in sophistication of videogames, even the best seem to retain something of their unrefined past. I have argued that recent games engage the moral sensibilities of their players, but the level of moral drama is still rather blunt. Will videogames ever be a serious art form, approaching the sorts of issues that a literary novel can? This is not a work of futurology, and I cannot predict whether gaming will develop into serious art; this is of course contingent on many unpredictable factors. But even so, I think I have done enough to show here that games are, in their best instances, beginning to share the concerns and forms of the traditional arts. I'm optimistic about the artistic future of games. Watching the development of videogames over the past twenty years, I have constantly been surprised by what artists have achieved in the medium. This new realm of artistic activity calls for an understanding of how the topics of traditional interest to philosophers of the arts – fiction, graphical representation, narrative, emotion, morality, and so on – play out in this new media setting. Videogames, as I hope to have shown in this book, are fascinating in this regard, and deserve further thought.

CHAPTER SUMMARY

Videogames – at least, some of them – show considerable overlap with the conditions that are taken by cluster theories of the arts to identify or define artworks. In their new digital setting, videogames achieve many of the goals and functions we associate with art, historically and cross-culturally, such as aesthetic pleasure, stylistic richness, emotional saturation, imaginative involvement, criticism, virtuosity, representation, and even special focus and institutional aspects. Yet, in each of these cases, the way that videogames meet the given criteria bears significant differences to previous forms of art. As well as continuities with art, videogames bear connections with the largely independent cultural form of gaming. Because of this, videogames have a property that is frequently not associated with art: competitive gameplay. Thus we may need to temper our conclusion about the art status of videogames and say that though they significantly align with art, videogames may count as a new and distinctive kind of art.

GLOSSARY

absorption: A state of mental concentration where one loses awareness of features of the immediate environment incidental to the task at hand.

aesthetic property: A perceptual property that produces an agreeable or pleasing response, examples being beauty, grace, litheness, and vibrancy.

aesthetics: That sub-discipline in philosophy that deals with the aesthetic aspects of artworks and nature, their appreciation, and in the case of artworks, their creation and evaluation. The philosophy of arts is potentially broader in scope than aesthetics, dealing with issues such as cognitive and emotional responses to the arts, art and morality, and the definition of art.

affordance: A part of a game that allows the player an aspect of control and therefore some means by which to cause a change in the formal system of the game. In fictionally rich videogames an affordance can very often be characterized as a fictional action, such as shooting a gun, jumping a fiery pit, or casting a spell.

algorithm: A process made up of discrete steps that has the features of substrate neutrality, underlying mindlessness, and guaranteed results, and hence which is a computable function. Crucial to computer programs, and Juul argues, games.

arcade game: A videogame built for use in an arcade, often housed in an upright cabinet, and typified by immediate and uncomplicated gameplay. In a wider sense, a game on any platform that has these gameplay characteristics.

articulated fictive prop: A prop in a fictive game that is designed to be flexible so that its manipulation easily generates new fictional content. Sackboy in *LittleBigPlanet*, for example, is based on a graphical model that can be controlled so as to generate a detailed fiction of a character moving through a fictional world and responding to it.

artificial intelligence (AI): That part of the program of a game that assures that the non-player-characters or other intelligent agents in a game world appear to act in an intelligent or, at the very least, predictable fashion.

auteur: A film director – and potentially a game designer – who holds particular sway over many aspects of production and who is able to produce works with a distinctive style and/or themes.

behavioral norm: A set of often tacitly prescribed rules in a given domain that regulate behavior in that domain. Among the norms in gaming are separateness from everyday concerns, non-productiveness, and player investment.

bitmap: An array of pixels with defined color values that forms a picture or pattern used in the animation of some videogames. Bitmap graphics is also called Raster graphics. Bitmapping or rasterization is also employed in rendering 3D graphics into a form suitable for display on a 2D screen.

boss-battle: An end-of-level set-piece involving a boss-monster that must be defeated before progress can be made in the game. A boss is usually a monster many times larger and more potent that the creatures in the rest of the level, and which often can only be defeated by adopting a specific set of tactics that may take several unsuccessful attempts to discover.

bot: A non-player-character that is controlled by the computer, usually in first-person shooters, real-time strategy games, or driving games. Bots allow single players to play multiplayer levels by adding in computer-controlled opponents.

branching narrative: A game narrative that branches at various points, usually contingent on a decision made by the player, so that the player has some input into the eventual shape that a narrative takes. Also seen in game books, branching narratives are now making their way into sophisticated games like *BioShock* and *Grand Theft Auto IV*.

camping: In multiplayer first-person shooters, the practice of hiding in a secluded spot to snipe at opponents, or surprise them as they come across the encampment. Often seen as bad form, hence a breach of the behavioral norms of first-person shooters.

cluster theory: A theory of some concept that sees the application of the concept as relying not on a clearly specified single set of conditions that each and only the items under the concept has, but through the overlay, perhaps partial, of the concept on a cluster of properties.

cognitive: Concerning thought.

cognitive moralism: Here defined as the claim that thoughts and attitudes are amenable to moral criticism in virtue of being offensive or expressing immoral viewpoints.

collision detection: That part of a videogame's physics software that ensures that objects in the fictional world of a game observe some basic physical necessities, such as colliding with each other rather than passing through the same space. When a car fictively hits the wall in *Gran Turismo*, it is collision detection that ensures that it bounces off the wall, rather than passes through it.

condition: In a definition or theory, the property picked out that is intended to have a bearing on the application of a concept. A conditional statement is an *if then* statement, and so claiming that entertainment is a condition of videogaming means that *if* an object is a videogame, *then* it will have the property of being intended as entertainment.

consequentialism: A form of moral theory that claims that the moral properties of an action are defined in terms of some specified subset of its consequences. Utilitarianism is a form of consequentialism that defines the relevant consequences as the greatest happiness of those affected.

console: A dedicated game device such as a Nintendo Wii, Sony Playstation, or Microsoft X-Box that supports software in a proprietary format.

contingent: Accidental and not necessary; conditioned by or dependant on some further event or thing.

controller: Any kind of device used for controlling the action in a videogame. In the case of console and PC games, often a peripheral device like a gamepad, steering wheel, keyboard, or joystick; but often, as in arcade and handheld games, a control stick and buttons integrated into the hardware. The range of peripheral controllers now extends to microphones, replica guitars and drum kits for music games, and motion-sensing controllers.

cut-scene: Video sequences that are used to introduce the game or to progress the narrative where the game has a storyline. Players often lack the interactive input in cut-scenes that they have in gameplay proper.

death-match: A popular game type often found in first-person shooters, but also in other genres such as real-time strategy games, where the objective is to eliminate all opponents as quickly as possible. Team death-match, such as the online form in *Grand Theft Auto IV*, allows teams of players to battle.

declarative: Set forth or made known explicitly or formally.

definition by necessary and sufficient conditions: A definition that specifies a set of conditions such that if an item is to fit within the defined concept, the item must have, and that if obtaining in an object, guarantee the item as an instance of the defined kind. Often abbreviated as *iff*.

desensitization: The idea that repeated exposure to a stimulus extinguishes its affective valence; in the case of violent media, making people less concerned about the existence or significance of real violence.

diegetic: Existing internal to a fictional world, as opposed to at the level of the fiction's representation.

disjunction: An either/or statement. A disjunctive definition claims that there may be more than one way to meet the conditions of a concept, and so involves a disjunctive either/or clause among its conditions.

emergent gameplay: Gameplay that arises from the unexpected combination of simple formal elements or affordances in a game system. From the limited rules and play space of chess, for example, any number of creative or interesting chess games might emerge.

emergent narrative: Analogous with emergent gameplay, a narrative that emerges from the combination of a number of simple elements such as quests, missions, or unscripted events in a game world.

emotion: A mental and physiological response involved in the motivation of action in the organism, also involving characteristic feelings and thoughts. The cognitivist theory of the emotions classifies and explains emotions in terms of their intentional objects. Fear, for example, is a response to a situation in which one is perceived to be in danger. Other non-cognitive theories see emotions as akin to neurophysiological programs that allow an organism to best respond to the demands of its environment, and that occur in a relatively automatic manner when elicited by a relevant stimulus.

epistemology: The philosophical theory of knowledge. *Epistemic* refers to the properties of knowledge or knowledge seeking.

essence: The features of a thing that are essential, permanent, and real of that thing, as opposed to its merely contingent properties. Classical definitions are aimed at specifying the essence of a thing.

exploit: An employment of a piece of digital technology that is at odds with its intended use, in the case of videogaming, often to gain an unfair advantage over the game system or other players.

extrinsic: External to a thing, and not owing to its nature but to its contingent relations to other things.

fanboy: A person (not necessarily male) with an obsessive relationship to or emotional investment in a given popular culture phenomenon, often with an unrealistic attitude toward the genuine artistic or cultural significance of the phenomenon.

fiction: A representation of an object or event, intended to be understood as having an imagined existence only. A work of fiction is a representational prop that specifies such a fictional scenario in some detail, often for artistic purposes.

fictional world: A fictional place that is substantive enough to give a world-like impression, often, but not necessarily, formalized by being referred to by name. Such worlds may involve interfictional carry-over, in being referred to in more that one work of fiction. Fictional worlds may also be based, with more or less realism, on real-world locations, as in *Grand Theft Auto*'s Liberty City, a fictionalized analogue of New York City.

first-person shooter: A genre of videogame involving the representation of a fictional world from the first-person view of the player-character. The objective of these games is often to kill as many of the other occupants of the fictional world as possible, though many have significant role-playing, adventure, or narrative elements.

flow: A concentrated engagement in an activity such as videogaming involving both an exceptional degree of interactive felicity and obliviousness to one's surroundings. Related to the psychological concept of *absorption*.

formal property: Relating to the structure or arrangement of a thing, in contrast to its content.

fragging: Killing an opponent in a first-person shooter. Derived from the practice in the Vietnam War of the killing of a fellow soldier, usually a superior officer, with a fragmentation grenade, a frag is also used to denote a single kill in terms of a score.

frame-rate: The number of frames of animation per second (usually hypothetical) a piece of gaming hardware or game runs during play. Higher frame-rates give rise to more fluid animations. Frame-rate and its enemy, slow down or frame-rate stutter, are common dimensions of videogame criticism.

freeplay: Gameplay lacking authorized or defined objectives, where the player may instead explore or toy with the possibilities of a game system or fictional world.

game-engine: A software program, often proprietary and shared between different games, that combines the representational and functional features of a videogame into a coherent platform that becomes the technical basis of a performance and creation of a videogame.

gameplay: The activity of playing a game, usually defined so as to exclude the other artistic functions of a game, such as narrative and the aesthetic enjoyment of visual representations.

game studies: The interdisciplinary study of videogames and interactive entertainment, encompassing new media studies, psychology, social science, and computer science.

god-gaming: A genre of games related to strategy gaming, in which the player controls tribes, armies, or entire civilizations. Rather than necessarily adopting the fictional role of a god in such games, the name comes from the player's god-like abilities to manipulate the game world.

gold-farming: The commercial collection of game world resources that are on-sold to players through third-party sites, so that players can advance without the investment of time necessary to do so through legitimate play. Gold-farming techniques often involve *grinding*, but also other more sophisticated methods such as the guiding of players through dangerous areas to retrieve rare items.

griefing: A breach of the behavioral norms of gaming, where players annoy, disrupt, or generally make nuisances of themselves to other players.

grinding: Engaging in the extremely repetitive gameplay needed to advance in levels in role-playing games such as *World of Warcraft*; often involving activities like repeatedly killing the same kind of monster or obtaining the same resource to gather the experience points.

handheld game: Portable games consoles such as the Nintendo DS and Playstation Portable (PSP).

haptic: Those representational elements of videogames, such as rumble controllers, that appeal to the sense of touch.

head-up display (HUD): The 2D elements in a videogame display that are used to depict game information such as player health, ammunition levels, and mini-maps. Sometimes diegetic or internal to the fictional game world (for example, in a modern combat flight simulator) but also often clearly not to be thought of as fictional of the game world.

homeostasis: The tendency towards equilibrium in a complex system. A homeostatic mechanism, such as emotion, is one aimed at maintaining homeostasis in an organism.

hypothetical thinking: The cognitive ability to conceive of things as they might be rather than as the way they are, crucial to make-believe and fiction, but not exclusive to these; also involved in planning, conceiving of counterfactuals, and understanding others' mental states.

imagination: The cognitive act of forming mental images or concepts of things not present to the senses, or without any existence in fact.

in media res: A narrative technique where the story begins with major plot events already underway. Often used to establish an impression of mystery or action. From Latin, *into the middle of things*.

intentionality: The *aboutness* of a mental state, or its potential for external reference.

intrinsic: Of the very nature of a thing.

intuition: A direct non-inferential judgment about a given domain such as logic, linguistics, or morality. Unlike the case with most empirical studies, in moral philosophy intuitions are usually accepted as a key part of the evidential basis which moral theories must align with or explain. That a moral theory produces a consequence that is counter-intuitive – suggesting, for example, that eating babies is sometimes morally acceptable – may be counted as a mark against a theory.

isometric game: A quasi-three dimensional form of graphical representation where the game action is represented in one or more fixed or scrolling isometric perspectives; for example in *Simcity*. Unlike 2D representation, isometric representation gives some impression of game world depth without allowing for the movement into the picture plane that is possible in true 3D graphics.

level: A subsection of a game with discrete goals – in a most basic form, to reach the other end of a fictional space avoiding obstacles along the way. Seen in 2D platform games, where the player might almost literally trace a single level from left to right, to more sophisticated 3D first-person shooters where the level might be comprised of a geographical area, set of city streets, or building interior. Levels are also commonly interspersed with loading sections, and so act as an important functional unit of game design.

leveling up: The process where the player, by accruing experience points or some other functionally equivalent unit, advances in potency and strength in the game world, allowing access to new equipment and abilities. Often found in role-playing games, and also found in their pen and paper forms. Some games also level the encountered monsters and game scenarios to the player's level, so as to maintain a consistent gameplay difficulty.

linearity: A term used to describe a game where traversing a level involves tracing a linear path through an environment that is common to all playings of the game. Other less literal forms of linearity arise where the player is required to perform a particular series of tasks to complete a level. Linearity is frequently seen as a critical failing of videogames, though something like linearity seems to be involved in the close scripting of narratives.

ludic: Relating to play or playfulness.

ludology: The study of play or games.

machinima: Film-making, often low budget and hobbyist in nature, that employs the graphical means of virtual worlds and videogames technology.

magic circle: Huizinga's term for a ritual referred to in the *Mahabharata* that invests a space with a magical significance somewhat separate to the rest of reality. Expanded by some games theorists to refer to the virtual, fictional, or behavioral situation in which videogames are played.

make-believe: The cognitive attitude, parallel to belief but differing in pragmatic context, in which propositions are not taken to refer to reality, but to situations with an imagined existence only.

massively multiplayer online role playing game (MMORPG): A role-playing game, such as *World of Warcraft*, where many players inhabit an online persistent world; often involving rich social behaviors such as trading, clans, and global game world events.

menu: A textual or pictorial arrangement of information and affordances that plays a key role in enabling gameplay. The functions performed by the menu may relate either to the fictional content of the game – as in selecting spells or tuning car performance – or its mechanical aspects – as in changing the speed of a game, its difficulty, or its graphical or audio qualities.

mission: A discrete section of a game often comprised by a task or a sequence of tasks that may be achieved independently of the other sections of the game. In *Grand Theft Auto* the player accepts missions from other characters in the game, and has a great deal of freedom over the order in which they carry out the missions.

modal: Relating to the manner or mode of a thing, especially given its appearance to the primary forms of sensation, such as vision, hearing, touch, etc.

moral panic: A phenomenon whereby media or society at large become concerned – potentially disproportionately – about something that seems to present a threat to prevailing cultural values.

motion-sensing controller: A type of controller, used most significantly by the Nintendo Wii, but also the Playstation 3, where the game tracks the player's movement through physical space and maps that into the representational space of the game world.

narrative: A representation of sets of events chosen for their contribution to an unfolding plot with a beginning, middle, and an end, often but not necessarily involving a narrator.

narrative of disclosure or discovery: A gaming narrative in which the player is encouraged to search out the narrative-relevant facts, and hence in which the progress or extent of the narrative depends on the player's own activities in the game world.

narratology: The study of narratives.

nominal definition: Nominal means *in name only*, and so a nominal definition is one that specifies how a term is conventionally used.

nudge: A term introduced into behavioral economics by Cass Sunstein and Richard Thaler to describe a means of influencing social and economic behaviors at a level below explicit coercion, often in the form of careful design of a *choice architecture*. In videogames similar techniques are used to guide gameplay while sustaining the impression of player freedom.

occlusion: The feature of graphical programs that allows parts of three-dimensional models to be obscured so that the impression of solidity is given.

on rails: Gameplay that is closely guided; in its most literal form, guided through a defined path in virtual space. Early 3D games involved on-rails gameplay because depicting the action from a defined path through representational space is representationally and computationally less demanding than open-world 3D representation. An extended sense of the term refers to genuine 3D games that nevertheless carefully script gameplay events.

ontology: The philosophical study of existence or being. *An ontology* might refer to what it is one takes to really exist.

paradox of fictional emotions: The Big Daddies that the player is afraid of in *BioShock* do not really exist. Because emotions for fictional circumstances thus seem to lack intentional objects, under the cognitivist theory where emotions are seen to be in part comprised of such intentional objects, fictional emotions appear paradoxical; there seems to be nothing to be afraid *of*.

physics: That part of the software of a computer game that represents the virtual physics of a fictional world. An early instance of game physics is the simple *inverse r squared* formula that represents the gravity of a central star in *Spacewar*. Modern physics engines are more sophisticated than this by many degrees.

platform: The hardware basis of a videogame, whether a console, personal computer, or arcade game.

platform game: A form of game particularly popular from the mid-1980s to the early 1990s in which the character and environment are depicted in two dimensions, and the environment consists of levels that must be traversed by avoiding obstacles and monsters, climbing ladders, and jumping from platform to platform. *LittleBigPlanet* is a recent example of the genre that depicts its action in the form of a quasi-3D world with sophisticated physics.

player-character (or avatar): A term, derived from role-playing games such as *Dungeons and Dragons*, which denotes the character that acts as the player's fictional proxy in the game world.

polygon: An animated enclosed two-dimensional figure with three or more sides, employed in the representation of modern videogames. Multiple polygons are joined together to form the wire-frame skeletons of three-dimensional objects, which may then be *texture-mapped*.

pragmatics: Pertaining to the use to which a linguistic item like a sentence may be put, rather than its syntactic or referential properties.

procedural: In videogames, aspects of a representation that are not previously scripted or animated during the game's design by an artist, but that are generated on the fly by some algorithmic routine of the computer program.

prop: A representational device used in a fiction or game of make-believe that augments the imaginative scenario by supplying additional content.

raster graphics: Graphics that employ bitmapping as a principal means of representation and animation, and not just in the rendering stage, because the pictorial content is encoded in a bitmap rather than in geometric functions, as in vector graphics.

real definition: A definition that is descriptive or empirical, and so complies with scientific investigation of the referent of a concept.

realism: In philosophical parlance, a commitment to some thing having a mind-independent existence in the external world. In artistic terms, the extent to which a representation gives a lifelike or veridical appearance of the thing represented.

real-time game: A game in which the action does not pause when control inputs are made, thus allowing competing players (human or computer controlled) to make simultaneous inputs.

rendering: The step in the process of digital animation where the final image is produced as a bitmap array suitable for depiction on a 2D screen.

representation: The process whereby a character, term, symbol, image, or suchlike is taken to express, designate, or symbolize some real or imaginary thing; an instance of such.

respawning: Where a player-character, non-player-character, or monster is regenerated after having died. For player-characters, respawning often serves as a default save-game, allowing the player to return to an earlier point in the game so that they can replay the level or mission in which they died. Sometimes respawning is given a fictional gloss, as in *BioShock*'s "vita-chambers" where the player reappears after being killed. Killed monsters are often allowed to respawn so that a previously cleared level can continue to supply combat opportunities if revisited.

role-playing game: A game in which the identity of player-characters and their ability to be customized or changed over the course of a game is prominent. Such games are one of the strongest links between pen and paper gaming such as *Dungeons and Dragons* and videogaming, a link explained by their historical convergence.

sandbox game: A game such as *Grand Theft Auto IV* or *Fallout 3* that presents a large open fictional world that players can explore largely on their own terms, taking up missions at will.

semantics: Relating to meaning or the study of meaning.

shader: Part of the so-called *graphics pipeline* of the latter stages of computer graphics where aspects like texture, coloration, and volumetric detail can be applied to the geometric shapes and pixels during the rendering process.

side-scrolling: A two-dimensional environment common in *platform games* in which the environment scrolls from one side of the screen to the other as the player makes progress through the environment.

simulation: A representational prop that accomplishes the goals of investigation or learning by depicting a virtual model of the target of study. In videogames the term has a wider sense in referring to such items with an entertainment function.

somatic marker: The felt feedback from a physiological reaction such as an emotion that causes the subject to attend to the stimulus that caused or contributed to the reaction.

strategy game: A game such as *Civilization* in which the decision-making and organizational skills of the player, rather than their physical abilities or

chance events in the game system, are crucial to achieving the objectives of the game. Chess is the strategy game *par excellence*.

studio: The principal commercial and organizational grouping responsible
for modern games development. The early history of gaming often
involved individuals or small groups producing games. Given the com-
mercialization and changes in the nature of videogames, most modern
games are produced by studios somewhat modeled on movie studios.

subdoxastic: *Doxastic* refers to beliefs, and so subdoxastic states are those
mental states that are lacking in cognitive content, lacking in conscious
awareness, or that are predominantly physiological.

survival-horror game: A game such as *Silent Hill* with horror and mystery
elements and often where the player is placed in a weakened state
relative to adversaries, encouraging a pervasive feeling of threat, and
cautious gameplay.

syntactic: Concerning the combinatorial properties of language.

text-based game: A game is text-based if its representation is primarily in
the form of text. The text-based game has non-digital variants, such
as the *Choose Your Own Adventure* game books and *Dungeons and
Dragons* role-playing games.

text tree: An arrangement of prewritten particles of text that contains
instructions whereby one may explore a *branching* path through the
text. Very close in form to some basic programming languages, text trees
were also employed in early text-based computer games and game books.

texture-mapping: The applying of colored or textured surfaces to the facets
of 3D graphics models.

three dimensional (3D) graphics: Three dimensional graphics allow the
objects or perspective of a representation to be manipulated in three
dimensions. Changing perspective on objects involves suitable algorithmic
transformations of size, shape, occlusion and so forth. The development
of vector graphics led to modern 3D graphics, which now involve
additional effects like texture mapping, lighting, particle effects, and
physics.

transmedial game: A game type such as chess or tic-tac-toe, which might
find instances in various media and which can thus shift between different media.

trash-talking: The practice of talking up oneself or abusing other players
prior to, during, or after a multiplayer videogame. Trash-talking often
involves the liberal use of obscenity and creative abuse.

turn-based: Almost all board games are turn-based, in that the players take
alternating turns to make moves. Turn-based videogames – contrasted
with *real-time* games – pause the action to allow the player to make a
move, to be followed by the opponent's move (be it player or computer controlled). Turn-based combat involves each player (human or
computer controlled) taking a turn to perform an attack.

two dimensional (2D) graphics: Two dimensional graphics allow represented objects to be manipulated through only two dimensions of the picture plane. The visual perspective in 2D graphics is fixed in reference to the horizontal and vertical picture plane, though it may be allowed to scroll along one or both of these vertices. Many classic platform games such as *Pac-Man* are represented in 2D graphics and often employ bitmapping. A 2D game might nevertheless suggest that the fictional *world* it represents is fully dimensional, as in the platform game *Abe's Oddysee*, where cut-scenes indicate the dimensionality of the game world.

vector graphics: A system of graphical representation that employs geometrical simples to represent picture elements. Because of their definition in terms of vectors, these elements can be algorithmically transformed in a variety of manners while retaining elements of their original spatial configuration, thus allowing manipulations like rotation and enlargement.

virtual: Being in effect or practically; for example, a virtual computer is a process that is apt to be treated as a real computer. A virtual representation is one that reproduces structural elements of its target, allowing the representation to be treated, for some purposes at least, as the thing it symbolically represents.

virtual camera: A virtual representational point of view that is employed in three-dimensional graphics for the purpose of specifying the player-character's spatial location, a cinematic view on that location, the view of a fictional camera, or as in *Portal* where virtual cameras are iteratively nested, a visual conduit to another spatial location in the fictional world.

visuospatial fiction: A fictive work in which the primary mode of depiction is vision, especially those that allow movement through visual space.

walk-through: A document produced to give hints or guide a player through a game by describing in some detail the environment, events, and objectives of a game; sometimes involving strategy guides, control layouts, secrets, and cheats.

wire-frame: The three-dimensional skeleton formed by connecting animated polygons together. Some early 3D games included basic wire-frame models as the final rendered representation.

REFERENCES

Aarseth, E. 1997. *Cybertext: Perspectives on Ergodic Literature*. Baltimore: Johns Hopkins University Press.

Aarseth, E. 2004. "Genre Trouble: Narrativism and the Art of Simulation," in P. Harrigan and N. Wardrip-Fruin eds., *First-person*. Cambridge, MA: MIT Press.

Aarseth, E. 2005. "Doors and Perception: Fiction vs. Simulation in Games," conference paper presented at the Digital Arts and Culture Conference, Copenhagen.

Anderson, C. A. and Bushman, B. J. 2001. "Effects of Violent Games on Aggressive Behavior, Aggressive Cognition, Aggressive Affect, Physiological Arousal, and Prosocial Behavior: A Meta-analytic Review of the Scientific Literature," *Psychological Science*, 12: 353–359.

Anderson, C. A. and Dill, D. E. 2000. "Video Games and Aggressive Thoughts, Feelings, and Behavior in Laboratory and Real Life," *Journal of Personality and Social Psychology*, 78(4).

Anderson, C. A., Gentile, D. A., and Buckley, K. E. 2007. *Violent Video Game Effects on Children and Adolescents: Theory, Research, and Public Policy*. Oxford: Oxford University Press.

Aristotle 1987. *Poetics*, trans. S. Halliwell. Chapel Hill: University of North Carolina Press.

Balicer, R. 2007. "Modeling Infectious Diseases Dissemination Through Online Role-Playing Games, *Epidemiology*, 18(2): 260–261.

Barboza, D. 2005. "Ogre to Slay? Outsource it to Chinese," *New York Times*, Technology Section, 9 December.

Blake, B. 2008. "Go Ahead, Steal My Car," *Chronicle Review*, 54(42): B6.

Blizzard 2007. Press release. Archived at www.blizzard.com/press/070111.shtml.

Bond, E. J. 1975. "The Essential Nature of Art," *American Philosophical Quarterly*, 12: 177–183.

Brand, J. E. 2007. *Interactive Australia 2007: Facts about the Australian Computer and Videogames Industry*. Eveleigh, NSW: Interactive Entertainment Association of Australia. Archived at www.ieaa.com.au/5.research/Interactive%20Australia%202007.pdf.

Bregman, A. S. 1990. *Auditory Scene Analysis: The Perceptual Organization of Sound*. Cambridge, MA: MIT Press.

Brown, D. E. 1991. *Human Universals.* New York: McGraw-Hill.

Caillois, R. 1961. *Man, Play, and Games.* New York: Schocken Books.

Carroll, N. 1990. *The Philosophy of Horror or Paradoxes of the Heart.* New York: Routledge.

Carroll, N. 1996. "Moderate Moralism," *British Journal of Aesthetics,* 36: 223–238.

Carroll, N. 1998a. *A Philosophy of Mass Art.* Oxford: Clarendon Press.

Carroll, N. 1998b. "Art, Narrative, and Moral Understanding," in Jerrold Levinson ed., *Aesthetics and Ethics: Essays at the Intersection.* Cambridge: Cambridge University Press.

Carroll, N. ed. 2000. *Theories of Art Today.* Madison: University of Wisconsin Press.

Castronova, E. 2005. *Synthetic Worlds: The Business and Culture of Online Games.* Chicago: Chicago University Press.

Consalvo, M. 2007. *Cheating: Gaining Advantage in Videogames.* Boston: MIT Press.

Csikszentmihalyi, M. 1990. *Flow: The Psychology of Optimal Experience.* New York: Harper Perennial.

Currie, G. 1990. *The Nature of Fiction.* Cambridge: Cambridge University Press.

Currie, G. 1995. "Imagination and Simulation: Aesthetics Meets Cognitive Science," in A. Stone and M. Davies, eds., *Mental Simulation: Evaluations and Applications.* Oxford: Blackwell.

Currie, G. 1997. "The Moral Psychology of Fiction," in S. Davies ed., *Art and Its Messages.* University Park: Penn State Press.

Damasio, A. 1994. *Descartes' Error: Emotion, Reason, and the Human Brain.* New York: Avon Books.

Damasio, A. 1999. *The Feeling of What Happens: Body, Emotion, and the Making of Consciousness.* London: Vintage Books.

Davies, S. 1991. *Definitions of Art.* Ithaca, NY: Cornell University Press.

Davies, S., ed. 1997. *Art and Its Messages.* University Park: Penn State Press.

Davies, S. 2004. "The Cluster Theory of Art," *British Journal of Aesthetics* 44: 297–300.

Davies, S. 2009. "Responding Emotionally to Fictions," *Journal of Aesthetics and Art Criticism,* forthcoming.

Dawkins, R. 2004. *The Ancestor's Tale.* London: Weidenfeld and Nicolson.

Dennett, D. C. 1987. *The Intentional Stance.* Cambridge, MA: MIT Press/Bradford Books.

Dennett, D. C. 1995. *Darwin's Dangerous Idea: Evolution and the Meanings of Life.* London: Penguin Books.

Dickie, G. 1974. *Art and the Aesthetic: An Institutional Analysis.* Ithaca, NY: Cornell University Press.

Durkin, K. 1995. *Computer Games: Their Effects on Young People.* Sydney, NSW: Office of Film and Literature Classification.

Dutton, D. 2000. "But They Don't Have Our Concept of Art," in N. Carroll ed., *Theories of Art Today.* Madison: University of Wisconsin Press.

Dutton, D. 2001. "Aesthetic Universals," in B. Gaut and D. M. Lopes eds., *The Routledge Companion to Aesthetics.* New York: Routledge.

Dutton, D. 2006. "A Naturalist Definition of Art," *Journal of Aesthetics and Art Criticism,* 64: 367–377.

Dutton, D. 2009. *The Art Instinct.* London: Bloomsbury Press.

Eco, U. 2000. *Kant and the Platypus*. London: Vintage.

Ekman, P. 1980. "Biological and Cultural Contributions to Body and Facial Movements in the Expression of the Emotions," in A. O. Rorty ed., *Explaining Emotions*. Los Angeles: University of California Press.

Engell, J. and Jackson Bate, W. eds. 1983. *Biographia Literaria: The Collected Works of Samuel Taylor Coleridge*. Princeton: Princeton University Press.

Feagin, S. L. 1994. "The Pleasure of Tragedy," in A. Neill and A. Ridley eds., *Arguing About Art: Contemporary Philosophical Debates*. London: Routledge.

Feagin, S. L. 1996. *Reading with Feeling*. Ithaca, NY: Cornell University Press.

Frasca, G. 2003. "Ludologists Love Stories Too: Notes form a Debate that Never Took Place," Proceedings of the Digital Games Research Conference, Utrecht.

Freedman, J. L. 2002. *Media Violence and Its Effect on Aggression: Assessing the Scientific Evidence*. Toronto: University of Toronto Press.

Gaut, B. 2000. "Art as a Cluster Concept," in N. Carroll ed., *Theories of Art Today*. Madison: University of Wisconsin Press.

Gaut, B. 2007. *Art, Emotion, and Ethics*. Oxford: Oxford University Press.

Gentile, D. A., Lynch, P. J., Linder, J. R., and Walsh, D. A. 2004. "The Effects of Violent Video Game Habits on Adolescent Hostility, Aggressive Behaviors, and School Performance," *Journal of Adolescence*, 27: 5–22.

Goodman, N. 1972. "Seven Strictures on Similarity," in N. Goodman ed., *Problems and Projects*. Indianapolis: Bobbs-Merrill.

Greenfield, P. M. 1984. *Mind and Media: The Effects of Television, Video Games, and Computers*. Cambridge, MA: Harvard University Press.

Griffiths, M. 1999. "Violent Video Games and Aggression: A Review of the Literature," *Aggression and Violent Behavior*, 4(2): 203–212.

Griffiths, P. 1997. *What Emotions Really Are*. Chicago: University of Chicago Press.

Grossman, D. & DeGaetano, G. 1999. *Stop Teaching Our Kids to Kill: A Call to Action Against TV, Movie, and Video Game Violence*. New York: Crown Publishers.

Heim, M. 1991. "The Metaphysics of Virtual Reality," in S. K. Helsel and J. P. Roth, eds., *Virtual Reality: Theory, Practice, and Promise*. London: Meckler.

Heim, M. 1993. *The Metaphysics of Virtual Reality*. New York: Oxford.

Huizinga, J. 1950. *Homo Ludens: A Study of the Play Element in Culture*. Boston: Beacon Press.

Johnson, S. 2006. *Everything Bad is Good for You*. London: Penguin Books.

Juul, J. 2005. *Half-Real: Video Games Between Real Rules and Fictional Worlds*. Cambridge, MA: MIT Press.

Kant, I. 1790/1951. *Critique of Judgement*, trans. J. H. Barnard. New York: Hafner.

Keil, F. C. 1981. *Concepts, Kinds and Cognitive Development*. Cambridge, MA: MIT Press.

Kelman, N. 2005. *Video Game Art*. New York: Assouline Publishing.

Kenny, A. 1963. *Action, Emotion, and Will*. London: Routledge and Kegan Paul.

Kent, S. L. 2001. *The Ultimate History of Video Games: From Pong to Pokemon and Beyond – The Story Behind the Craze that Touched our Lives and Changed the World*. New York: Prima.

Kerlow, I. V. 2000. *The Art of 3D Computer Animation and Imaging*, 2nd edn. New York: Wiley.

King, B. and Borland, J. 2003. *Dungeons and Dreamers*. Emeryville: McGraw-Hill.

Kivy, P. 1990. *Music Alone: Philosophical Reflections on the Purely Musical Experience*. Ithaca, NY: Cornell University Press.

Kutner L. and Olsen, C. 2008. *Grand Theft Childhood: The Surprising Truth About Video Games and What Parents Can Do*. New York: Simon and Schuster.

Lamarque, P. 1996. *Fictional Points of View*. Ithaca, NY: Cornell University Press.

Le Doux, J. 1998. *The Emotional Brain*. London: Weidenfeld & Nicolson.

Levinson, J. 1979. "Defining Art Historically," *British Journal of Aesthetics*, 19: 232–250.

Levinson, J. 1997. "Emotion in Response to Art: A Survey of the Terrain," in M. Hort and S. Laver eds., *Emotion and the Arts*. Oxford: Oxford University Press.

Levinson, J. ed. 1998. *Aesthetics and Ethics: Essays at the Intersection*. Cambridge: Cambridge University Press.

Livingston, P. 2001. "Narrative," in B. Gaut and D. M. Lopes eds., *The Routledge Companion to Aesthetics*. London: Routledge.

Lopes, D. M. 2001. "The Ontology of Interactive Art," *Journal of Aesthetic Education*, 35(4): 65–81.

Lopes, D. M. 2003. "Digital Art," in L. Floridi ed., *The Blackwell Guide to the Philosophy of Computing and Information*. Oxford: Blackwell.

Microsoft 2007. Press release, October 4. Archived at www.uk.reuters.com/article/technologyNews/idUKN0438777720071005.

Miller, R. W. 1998. "Three Versions of Objectivity: Aesthetic, Moral, and Scientific," in J. Levinson ed., *Aesthetics and Ethics: Essays at the Intersection*. Cambridge: Cambridge University Press.

Moravcsik, J. 1993. "Why Philosophy of Art in a Cross-Cultural Perspective?" *Journal of Aesthetics and Art Criticism*, 51: 425–436.

Murray, J. 1998. *Hamlet on the Holodeck*. Cambridge, MA: MIT Press.

Neill, A. 1994. "Fiction and the Emotions," in A. Neill and A. Ridley eds., *Arguing About Art: Contemporary Philosophical Debates*. London: Routledge.

Newman, J. 2004. *Videogames*. New York: Routledge.

New Zealand Ministry of Internal Affairs 1993. *Films, Videos, and Publications Classification Act*. New Zealand Ministry of Internal Affairs.

Nichols, S. & Stich, S. 2000. "A Cognitive Theory of Pretense," *Cognition*, 74: 115–147.

Nussbaum, M. 1986. *The Fragility of Goodness: Luck and Tragedy in Greek Tragedy and Philosophy*. Cambridge: Cambridge University Press.

Nussbaum, M. 1990. *Love's Knowledge: Essays on Philosophy and Literature*. New York: Oxford University Press.

Pinker, S. 1994. *The Language Instinct*. New York: Harper Collins.

Pinker, S. 1997. *How the Mind Works*. London: Penguin Books.

Plato 1987. *The Republic*, 2nd edn., trans. D. Lee. London: Penguin Books.

Poole, S. 2000. *Trigger Happy: The Inner Life of Videogames*. London: Fourth Estate.

Popper, K. R. 1972. *Objective Knowledge: An Evolutionary Approach*. Oxford: Clarendon Press.

Radford, C. 1975. "How Can We Be Moved by the Fate of Anna Karenina?" *Proceedings of the Aristotelian Society*, Supp. Vol. 49: 67–80.

Robinson, J. 1995. "Startle," *Journal of Philosophy*, 92: 53–74.

Robinson, J. 2007. *Deeper Than Reason: Emotion and Its Role in Literature, Music, and Art.* Oxford: Oxford University Press.

Rozin, P., Haidt, J., and McCauley, C. R. 2000. "Disgust," in M. Lewis and J. M. Haviland-Jones eds., *Handbook of Emotions*, 2nd edn. New York: Guilford Press.

Salen K. and Zimmerman, E. 2004. *Rules of Play: Game Design Fundamentals.* Cambridge, MA: MIT Press.

Scruton, R. 1974. *Art and Imagination.* London: Methuen.

Sibley, F. 1959. "Aesthetic Concepts," *Philosophical Review*, 68: 421–450.

Singer, P. 2007. "Virtual Vices," *Project Syndicate*. Archived at www.project-syndicate.org/commentary/singer26/English.

Smuts, A. 2005a. "Are Video Games Art?" *Contemporary Aesthetics*, 3.

Smuts, A. 2005b. "Video Games and the Philosophy of Art," *Aesthetics Online*. Archived at www.aesthetics-online.org/articles/.

Tavinor, G. 2005a. "Videogames and Interactive Fiction," *Philosophy and Literature*, 29(1): 24–40.

Tavinor, G. 2005b. "Videogames, Fiction, and Emotion," in *Proceedings of the 2nd Australasian Conference on Interactive Entertainment.* Sydney: Creativity and Cognition Studios.

Tavinor, G. 2007. "Toward an Ethics of Videogames," *Proceedings of Futureplay 2007, Toronto.* ACM Digital Library.

Tavinor, G. 2008. "The Definition of Videogames," *Contemporary Aesthetics*, 7.

Thaler, R. H. and Sunstein, C. R. 2008. *Nudge: Improving Decisions About Health, Wealth, and Happiness.* New Haven: Yale University Press.

US Court of Appeal, Sixth Circuit, James vs. Meow Media. Archived at www.caselaw.lp.findlaw.com/cgi-bin/getcase.pl?court=6th&navby=case&no=02a0270p.

Walton, K. 1978. "Fearing Fictions," *Journal of Philosophy*, 75: 5–27.

Walton, K. 1990. *Mimesis as Make-Believe.* Cambridge, MA: Harvard University Press.

Weitz, M. 1956. "The Role of Theory in Aesthetics," *Journal of Aesthetics and Art Criticism*, 15: 27–35.

Wertheim, M. 1999. *The Pearly Gates of Cyberspace.* London: Virago Press.

Wittgenstein, L. 1968. *Philosophical Investigations.* Oxford: Blackwell.

Woolley, B. 1992. *Virtual Worlds.* Oxford: Blackwell.

Wright, W. 2007. Keynote speech to the 2007 South by Southwest Music, Film and Interactive Conference, Austin, Texas. Archived at www.wonderlandblog.com/wonderland/2007/03/sxsw_will_wrigh.html.

Yanal, R. J. 1999. *Paradoxes of Emotion and Fiction.* University Park: Penn State Press.

Young, R. M. 2007. "Story and Discourse: A Bipartite Model of Narrative Generation in Virtual Worlds," *Interaction Studies*, 8(2): 177–208.

Zangwill, N. 2001. *The Metaphysics of Beauty.* Ithaca, NY: Cornell University Press.

INDEX

Note: name order for fictional characters is given as first name then surname

Printed and bound by CPI Group (UK) Ltd, Croydon, CR0 4YY

16/04/2025

14658543-0002